HOW THE RAILWAY WORKS

Meeting Point

HOW THE RAILWAY WORKS

Dan Harvey

Ian Allan
PUBLISHING

First published 2015

ISBN 978 07110 3812 7

Published by Ian Allan Publishing Ltd, Addlestone, Surrey, KT15 2SF

Printed in Bulgaria

Visit the Ian Allan Publishing website at www.ianallanpublishing.com

Picture credits
Unless otherwise stated, all photographs are by the author.

FRONT COVER Glasgow Queen Street

BACK COVER Edinburgh Trams

PREVIOUS SPREAD King's Cross, London

CONTENTS

Introduction

How does the railway work?

The UK rail system is undergoing a transformation. The combination of track and train that we inherited from our Victorian forebears is being reorganised and reinvented to meet modern needs. At the heart of these changes is unprecedented demand, which is leading more people to travel by train than did a hundred years ago when the rail network was much larger.

This book is about how the component parts of today's rail system fit together. It is about different organisations and their relationships with each other. It is about the ongoing quest for a workable system following privatisation in the 1990s. And it is about technology reinventing the way we travel.

Some of the terms used in this book are regularly the subject of heated debate, but for clarity and consistency I have used them as follows:

- Inter-city refers to a main-line train or route such at the West Coast, East Coast or Great Western
- A High Speed Train is a Class 43 as used on the Great Western and East Coast routes
- High-speed rail refers to lines where trains operate at speeds in excess of 125mph
- National rail refers to the railway lines in England, Scotland and Wales that are managed by Network Rail

ABOVE **The Edinburgh tram line opened in 2014. Although construction was beset by difficulties, initial passenger numbers have surpassed expectations.**

There are a few other points to note. The chapters in this book do not refer to the railway in Northern Ireland unless specifically stated. References to the Coalition Government relate to the Conservative/Liberal Democrat coalition in office between 2010 and 2015 and led by Prime Minister David Cameron. References to the Labour Government relate to the 13 years before that when Tony Blair, and later Gordon Brown, was Prime Minister.

While writing this book it has become clear that many of the topics covered merit a volume of their own. I hope the experts in each field will forgive my précis of areas they know far more about than me. It seems unlikely that any explanation of the UK rail system can hope to cover every relevant issue in the detail it deserves, but hopefully *How the Railway Works* will serve as a comprehensive overview that will provide a springboard for those interested in specific areas to continue their research.

Many of the subjects discussed in *How the Railway Works* are 'live' issues and their inclusion in this book carries with it the risk that details will be superseded by events. The railway does not stand still.

DAN HARVEY

LEFT **In Scotland the Government insisted that ScotRail train branding be retained when a new operator took over the franchise.**

RIGHT **A landmark design and plenty of retail – the western concourse at King's Cross epitomises the modern station terminus.**

1 • The central framework

Great Britain's national rail network consists of 15,753 route kilometres open to passenger and freight train services with more than 2,550 stations.[1] There is a small rail system in Northern Ireland and rail systems in Scottish and English cities, London Underground being the largest and best known.

Since privatisation in the mid-1990s, passenger and freight train services on the national rail network have been provided mainly by private sector companies that compete for franchises let by the UK and Scottish Governments.

Under the structure brought about by the Railways Act 1993, the management of rail infrastructure is separate from the operation of trains that run on it. Trains and coaches, often referred to as rolling stock, are owned by different companies and an overarching regulatory body ensures that the correct processes are followed and has the final say in the event of any disputes.

To understand how the railway works it is perhaps worth starting by reminding ourselves what the railway consists of today. It is easy to let media reports and Government announcements presented to paint a particular picture colour our judgement. Taking a step back we can see an industry that, despite myriad challenges, is thriving. However, it is also highly complex.

BELOW Blackfriars station has been extensively rebuilt for the Thameslink Programme. Here, the sub-surface London Underground Circle and District Line has been enclosed in a metal box to ensure debris cannot fall on passing trains. A Thameslink service passes above.

The modern railway

In 2013/14 rail passengers made just under 1.6bn journeys with franchised operators, travelling over 37bn miles.[2] These figures show that the number of train journeys made is the highest since the early 1920s – despite Britain's rail network having been scaled back considerably as a result of the Beeching era cuts, which closed so many lines and stations.

Following a period of decline over several decades, rail journeys in Great Britain have seen large increases since the mid-1990s. The number of journeys has doubled since 1994/95, increased by a quarter in the past five years, and by half in the last ten years.[3]

Most rail journeys start or finish in London and South East England – 62% in 2012/13 – compared with 7% for Scotland and 2% for Wales. Rail use is highest among young working-age adults and lowest among the over-70s and under-17s.[4]

In recent years 8-9% of freight moved in Great Britain has been transported by rail. Freight traffic is measured in net tonne kilometres (NTKm), taking into account the weight of the goods and the distance they travel. In 2013/14 the amount of freight moved by rail was 23bn NTKm. Of the freight moved, 36% was coal, the highest proportion for any commodity, 27% was domestic intermodal freight, and 2% was international freight.

Rail has one of the lowest passenger casualty rates of any mode of transport. For the seventh consecutive year, in 2013/14 there were no passenger or staff casualties in train accidents.[5]

In 2013/14, franchised train operators received £8.2bn in revenue from passengers. Increased rail use has seen a rise in revenue in recent years, doubling in real terms since 1997/98.

Government support to the rail industry was £5.3bn in 2013/14, most of which was the £3.5bn grant paid to Network Rail. Government support rose through much of the 2000s, partly due to increased spending on infrastructure and renewals in the wake of the Hatfield and Potters Bar accidents. This also reflects investment in new infrastructure such as upgrading the West Coast Main Line, building the High Speed 1 route, and spending on Crossrail.

National rail fares increased on average by 102% between January 1997 and 2014, which corresponds to a 23% increase in real terms. This increase compares to a 10% real terms reduction in motoring costs over this period, and a 25% increase in bus and coach fares.

Regulated fares such as off-peak and season tickets increased on average by 5% in real terms over this period, compared to 32% for unregulated Standard Class fares.

Passenger trains run 364 days a year, with no trains on Christmas Day. Few services operate on Boxing Day – although train operators are coming under increasing pressure to lay on services.

The track gauge – the distance between the inner faces of the two running rails – of the national network is 1,435mm (4ft 8½in). This matches most main lines in continental Europe. The railway in Northern Ireland uses the wider 1,600mm (5ft 3in) Irish gauge.

Government control

Responsibility for Britain's railways rests with the Department for Transport (DfT). The DfT is tasked with putting Government rail policy into action and delivering the level of service expected by the electorate. That includes making sure that trains run, that they run on time, operate safely and with due consideration for any security concerns.

When all is going well the Department will supervise investment in the rail system, including major programmes such as High Speed 2, and the process of letting rail franchises. Sometimes events – severe weather, accidents, security concerns – mean that its focus has to adapt accordingly.

The DfT is led by a team of Government ministers, headed by the Secretary of State for Transport, or Transport Secretary. Typically there are three or four more junior transport ministers, usually one with responsibility for rail issues. Government reshuffles mean that the ministerial team can change every year or so.

Within the DfT the Permanent Secretary is the chief civil servant, responsible for delivering Government policy and answering to MPs on the Department's performance.

There is also now a Rail Executive, which is responsible for procuring most passenger rail services in Great Britain. It does this through franchise competitions in which private companies submit bids to run specified services on the network. The Rail Executive designs, awards and manages franchise contracts. This includes ensuring that franchisees meet their contractual obligations and overseeing fares and ticketing policy.

In the past rail franchising was the responsibility of separate Government agencies – the Office for Passenger Rail Franchising (OPRAF) and later the Strategic Rail Authority (SRA) – before disagreement with Government led to the franchising process being taken in-house. The creation of the Rail Executive makes it easier for the DfT to once again hive off its franchising remit. A number of industry experts have voiced concerns that the DfT is not best placed to manage the franchising process, and having a separate organisation would have advantages – for example, offering salaries to attract top talent higher than is acceptable within a Government department and distancing ministers from controversial decisions.

In Scotland planning and delivery of rail policy, strategy and investment is the responsibility of Transport Scotland, the national transport agency for Scotland. Transport Scotland's rail directorate carries out appraisals of capital projects, advises on rail investment decisions, and draws up the specification of railway outputs that the Scottish Government wishes to buy.

The Railways Act 2005 provided greater devolved decision-making, whereby Scottish ministers have the authority to set a strategy for rail in Scotland, which includes the specification and funding of investment in the rail network. Usually one Scottish minister has responsibility for transport, including rail.

Although devolution proposals should see Wales gain powers over the country's rail network, particularly the Welsh rail franchise, currently services in Wales are controlled by the Department for Transport in London. In recent years a range of devolution proposals have been set up, prompted by the 2014 Scottish independence referendum. These are likely to change the way rail services are governed in many parts of the UK.

Network Rail

Network Rail became responsible for the infrastructure – including track, signals, bridges and stations – that makes up the national rail network in 2002. The organisation was set up by the Labour Government of the time to replace the London Stock Exchange-listed company Railtrack, which had, depending on your viewpoint, gone or been forced into administration after running out of money.

Network Rail was set up as a company limited by guarantee. It has no shareholders and pays no dividends. Until recently it had it has appointed members who supposedly have powers to hold the company to account. In reality the organisation depends on the Government for funding and organises its operations to comply with rail policies set in London and Edinburgh.

The structure of the company was influenced by the Labour Government's desire to avoid adding rail liabilities to the national debt. By creating an organisation that was technically in the private sector, the Government was able to keep Network Rail's liabilities off its balance sheet, despite the organisation relying on state handouts. As will be examined later, Network Rail is now a public sector organisation and its structure is under review by Government.

Network Rail's customers are primarily passenger and freight train operators. However, the organisation has a direct interface with the public at the main-line stations it operates. Network Rail performs a range of different roles – from maintaining

ABOVE An Arriva-operated CrossCountry 'Voyager' service stops at Cheltenham station.

track and railway assets to setting timetables, planning for future rail needs, and letting the vast number of contracts required to keep the railway functioning effectively.

Operating the network

Network Rail charges train operators for access to rail infrastructure. The charges are determined by the five-yearly periodic reviews overseen by the Office of Rail and Road (ORR). Every year Network Rail publishes a Network Statement, which sets out the information anyone wanting to run trains on its infrastructure will need to know.

For operational purposes Network Rail has divided Britain into ten sectors, which it calls routes and which broadly align with the services run by different train operating companies. The ten sectors are Anglia, East Midlands, Kent, London North Eastern, London North Western, Scotland, Sussex, Wales, Wessex and Western.

Performance

The public performance measure, or PPM, is the rail industry's standard measure of performance. PPM combines figures for punctuality and reliability into a single performance measure and indicates the percentage of trains that arrive at their station on time. 'On time' in this case means trains arriving at their terminating station within 5 minutes for commuter services and within 10 minutes for long-distance services.

This definition of 'on time' may not match the way passengers use the term but it remains a measure of punctuality commonly used across Europe. However, concern that it may be misleading has led to the development of right-time performance figures that measure the percentage of trains arriving at their terminating station early or within 59 seconds of schedule.

Causes of train delays attributed to Network Rail include infrastructure faults, trespass, weather, vandalism and cable theft. The organisation says that a third of delays are caused by factors over which it has little or no control.

In February 2015 the national public performance measure stood at 90.7%, with

ABOVE **Crossrail has been constructed using eight 1,000-tonne tunnel boring machines built in Germany. This is one of the TBMs used to build the western tunnels.**

the moving annual average (which is calculated using the figures for the past year) standing at 89.7%. For right-time performance the moving annual average figure was 65%.

Timetabling

As infrastructure manager Network Rail is responsible for producing the timetable used across the national rail network. This is updated twice a year, with new timetables coming into force in May and December.

Freight and passenger train operators seeking to run new or amended service patterns put forward their requirements to Network Rail, which then works with train operators to determine how many trains can safely run and at what times. This is published as the working timetable.

This timetable balances demand for trains serving small communities and non-stop fast trains as well as the requirements of businesses that rely on freight. With 22,500 trains running every day, the timetabling process has to take into account many factors:

- Speed limits vary across lengths of track, for example at bends and over points
- Only one train can occupy a given section of track at any time
- Because of the above, any increase in the number of fast trains on a route requires a reduction in the number of trains serving small stations or carrying freight
- Signalling infrastructure varies across the rail network, so the safe distance between trains may change along a route
- There is variation in the minimum time gaps between trains using a platform at a station
- Time is necessary for improvement work and routine maintenance
- Performance issues – if trains are timetabled too closely together there is little flexibility, making it harder to get trains back on time following an incident

ABOVE To build Crossrail, piles for Canary Wharf station were sunk into the North Quay dockbed to form perimeter walls and sand inside was then excavated. In the background contractors have marked the arrival point for a tunnel boring machine.

BELOW Above ground the scale of Crossrail Canary Wharf construction activity within the drained dock can be seen. Behind this, a Docklands Light Railway service passes on a viaduct.

When compiling the working timetable Network Rail has to abide by the Timetable Planning Rules. These factor in many of the considerations above, regulating the standard timings between stations and junctions together with other matters enabling trains to be scheduled into the working timetable for the various parts of the main rail network.

Network Rail also has to consider the Engineering Access Statement. This sets out the location, number, dating and duration of possession access (restrictions of use) that Network Rail requires to deliver inspection, maintenance, renewal and enhance work activities to the infrastructure. An Engineering Access Statement for each timetable period is agreed following consultation with train operators.

A further consideration in timetabling is the track access agreements held by train operating companies. These give a train operator 'firm rights' and mean that it gets priority in the timetabling process.

Because a single change to one route covered by the national rail timetable can impact on different routes and connections with other train services, devising new timetables is something of an art form. Software modelling systems are used to help Network Rail and train operators work out the implications of timetable changes. For example, RailSys is a software package that models different combinations of train services and provides the ability to try different options – if one service does not meet performance criteria, alternatives can be tested – so that gradually a working timetable can be assembled. The results can also be used to identify any additional infrastructure necessary to operate a service – for example, new train passing loops or station platforms.

Following publication of the working timetable, tweaks can be made and train operators can respond to the proposals. A final version of the timetable comes into force about six months following publication of the working timetable, and is then available online

BELOW The historic London Underground system plays a major role in moving people around the capital. This is Earl's Court station in west London.

ABOVE At Farringdon a new Thameslink station entrance has been built opposite the existing London Underground entrance on Cowcross Street. The wall with train departure displays will in future provide access to escalators down to Crossrail platforms.

as the electronic National Rail Timetable (eNRT). Timetables for individual routes are made available to passengers online and in hard copy by the relevant train operators.

Only when the timetable comes into force does it become clear whether the planning and modelling process has worked effectively. As was seen at London Bridge in early 2015, the real-world business of running trains often throws up additional performance issues that require further changes to timetables.

Industry planning

Network Rail is required to plan how to meet future demand for passenger and freight train use, and has embarked on what it calls the Long Term Planning Process. Previously it used the Route Utilisation Strategy (RUS) programme to develop detailed reports looking at the interventions likely to be needed in the future for different rail routes. With the benefit of hindsight, some of the RUS conclusions appear influenced by the politics of the day and the amount of money available. More radical solutions are now being considered, partly driven by the significant increases seen in rail use in recent years.

The Long Term Planning Process attempts to take into account the views of the rail industry, funders, specifiers and customers in planning how to develop the rail network. It consists of market studies, cross-boundary analysis and route studies – all of which aim to predict future demand for the railway and come up with an appropriate response. Draft market and route studies are followed by a 90-day consultation and, subject to any representations to the Office of Rail and Road, a final version is published 60 days later.

Maintaining, renewing and developing the network

Network Rail is responsible for the general day-to-day upkeep of the railway, such as looking after tracks, signals and power supplies. This includes more than 20,000 miles of track, 40,000 bridges and tunnels and 6,300 level crossings.

Having inherited from Railtrack a backlog of maintenance and renewals to deal with, following the deferral of maintenance during the 1990s, Network Rail is struggling to keep on top of this vast workload. This is compounded by the need to provide capacity for the additional train services that have been introduced since privatisation, and to fit work around timetabled services.

Most engineering activity takes place at night and at weekends to minimise disruption to passengers and allow lines to be closed. For larger-scale works Network Rail has to decide whether to sequence activity over a number of weekends or schedule a shutdown that, while inconveniencing passengers, will tend to be more efficient (less time being needed to bring engineers on and off site, switch off/on power supplies, etc). Major works are often scheduled for shutdowns in the summer, Easter or at Christmas, and provide the opportunity to commission new systems and structures – although they also carry the risk of a high-profile overrun if the railway is not ready by the time commuters return to work.

Line closures must be planned and agreed with passenger and freight train operators many months ahead and, with individual works usually part of a more complex programme, any changes to scheduling may impact on other projects. This makes rescheduling engineering works difficult.

Part of the regular maintenance work required is tamping, the process of packing down the ballast on which sit the sleepers, under the metal rails. When track has been heavily used or has been relaid, gaps in the ballast need to be filled so that the sleepers do not move as trains pass, allowing traffic to run smoothly and reducing noise and vibration. Tamping machines (as big as a train) are used to do this, but the work is slow and noisy.

From pretend private to public sector

Attempts to keep Network Rail debt off the Government books have been recognised as an artificial constraint and the Coalition Government accepted that reclassification of the company was inevitable. A notable change occurred on 1 September 2014 when, under arcane European accounting rules, Network Rail was reclassified as a public sector body.

The Office for National Statistics wants Network Rail to comply with European criteria. This involves the European System of Accounts 2010 (ESA10) market test, which, unlike the previous market test, considers net interest charges when determining whether an organisation is a public corporation or part of central government. ESA10 therefore reaches a different conclusion from ESA95, the effect of which transfers Network Rail's £30bn net debt to the Government's balance sheet, increasing public sector net debt by around 2% of GDP and public sector net borrowing by 0.2% of GDP.

According to the Office for National Statistics (ONS): 'Because of government's risk exposure in guaranteeing Network Rail's debt, ONS has concluded that, under ESA10 rules, Network Rail is a government controlled body and, as such, is within the public sector... Consequently, since the financial indemnity which guarantees Network Rail's debt is provided by central government, Network Rail is a central government controlled, non-market body classified as part of the Central Government sector.'

Not only does this change transfer Network Rail from the private to the public sector at a stroke, but the change also applies retrospectively all the way back to April 2004.

So how significant is the change to the workings of the railway? Transport Secretary Patrick McLoughlin told Parliament that the ONS decision did not affect planned improvements and investment in the railways, including Network Rail's £38bn settlement for Control Period 5. He said that plans for High Speed 2 and the rail franchising programme set out in March 2013 remained unchanged.

However, the reclassification has served as a trigger for far-reaching changes at Network Rail. As a Government body, ministers have acquired greater freedom to exert control over it – for example, in limiting executive bonuses or requiring parts of the company to be sold off. In 2015 the Transport Secretary exerted his new power - gained following reclassification - to appoint a Network Rail Special Director who is effectively the government's eyes and ears within the organisation. The Freedom of Information Act 2000 now applies to Network Rail, giving the public the right to request, and be given, information that was previously off limits.

In a statement Network Rail said that, at least initially, the company will continue to raise debt to fund its ongoing investment programme while longer-term funding options are considered. There is a possibility that financing costs may fall as a result of the reclassification.

ABOVE A First Great Western High Speed Train heads towards Exeter on the beautiful but vulnerable stretch of coastal railway near Dawlish.
Roger Fieldhouse

At the time of writing the Government in Westminster had set the stage for a major overhaul of Network Rail. In June 2015 the Transport Secretary announced three reviews of the organisation including one by High Speed 1 Chief Executive Nicola Shaw who was appointed to advise ministers how they should approach the future shape and financing of Network Rail. Her findings were to be presented jointly to the Department for Transport and the Treasury.

In July 2015 the Chancellor of the Exchequer's Budget stated that the government will change the way it channels public money through the rail industry, directing it through train operating companies so that Network Rail focuses firmly on the needs of train operators and, through them, passengers. This looks set to give train operating companies additional power.

These developments indicate that further changes are to come in the way the railway is organised. The Shaw report is likely to open up all sorts of possibilities for the way the infrastructure currently under Network Rail control is managed.

Stations

Network Rail owns most of the 2,550-plus stations on the national rail network, but most are maintained and operated on a day-to-day basis by the train operating companies responsible for running services on routes that serve those particular stations. Measures are being adopted to simplify the interface between Network Rail and train operators to encourage train firms to invest in stations and improve facilities.

Eighteen of Britain's biggest and busiest stations are managed by Network Rail. These tend to be stations served by multiple train operators and where there is a requirement for extensive maintenance and ongoing capital investment. In London, Network Rail manages Cannon Street, Charing Cross, Euston, King's Cross, Liverpool Street, London Bridge, Paddington, St Pancras International (under a contract with HS1 Ltd), Victoria and Waterloo. Across Britain it manages Birmingham New Street, Bristol Temple Meads, Edinburgh Waverley, Glasgow Central, Leeds, Liverpool Lime Street, Manchester Piccadilly and Reading.

Station usage statistics are collected by the Office of Rail and Road based on data produced for the MOIRA rail planning tool, which use figures derived from LENNON, the rail industry's ticketing and revenue system. During 2013-14 the total journeys made at the ten busiest stations accounted for 509 million journeys during the year (see Table 1).

In the mid-1990s stations on the national network were classified into six categories based on a combination of passenger usage and annual income from ticket sales. This system can be used to set consistent minimum station standards and as a basis for maintenance and investment planning. The lower the station category, the more stations in that category there are (see Table 2).

Table 1: Top 10 busiest stations, 2013-14

Rank	Station	Total entries and exits (m)
1	London Waterloo	98.4
2	London Victoria	91.4
3	London Liverpool Street	63.0
4	London Bridge	56.4
5	London Euston	41.9
6	London Charing Cross	40.2
7	London Paddington	35.1
8	Birmingham New Street	34.7
9	London King's Cross	29.8
10	Leeds	27.7

Source: Steer Davies Gleave, Station Usage 2013-14

As well as Britain's national rail stations, there are just over 50 stations in Northern Ireland (22 of which are staffed[6]), on city networks, including London Underground and the Glasgow Subway, and stations on heritage and independent lines. Light rail systems may have stations (for example, Docklands Light Railway), or stops (tram lines).

Track access charges

Track access charges are paid by train operators to Network Rail for running rail services on the network. The level at which they are set allows Network Rail to recover costs incurred due to use of the rail infrastructure, but not to charge more than its allowed revenue requirement. Charges are determined by the Office of Rail and Road every five years as part of the periodic review process.

In May 2014 the Rail Delivery Group (RDG) announced a detailed cross-industry review of track access charges. The review, which is being

ABOVE Pictured at St Pancras International, Hitachi Class 395 'Javelin' trains provide the UK's first domestic high-speed rail service.

Table 2: Station categories

Category	Category name	No of stations
A	National Hub	28
B	Regional Hub	67
C	Important Feeder	248
D	Medium Staffed	298
E	Small Staffed	679
F	Small Unstaffed	1,200
Total		**2,520**

Source: Network Rail: RUS Stations, August 2011

carried out in conjunction with the Government, devolved administrations and the Office of Rail and Road, will enable the rail industry to take a fresh look at how train operators are charged to run trains on track infrastructure. The RDG believes that there is scope to reduce red tape and improve value for money.

The intention is for a review team led by economic and finance adviser FTI Consulting to bring together owners of Britain's passenger train and freight operating companies with Network Rail and work with other industry parties, including local transport executives and passenger groups. The project is supported by engineering and services contractor Amey, law firm Dentons and engineering specialist TRL.

The RDG says that the review is being launched following the Brown review of the rail franchising programme, published in January 2013. It recommended that a full review of the track access charging regime be carried out ahead of the rail industry's next five-year funding period, Control Period 6, which starts in 2019. The full Review of Charges work programme is expected to be complete by early 2016.

Regulation

The Office of Rail and Road (ORR) is the regulatory body that has the final say in many aspects of how Britain's rail network functions. It is the independent safety and economic regulator for the railways.

Formerly known as the Office of Rail Regulation (and before that the Office of the Rail Regulator), the Office of Rail and Road was born after the Government handed to the ORR responsibility for monitoring and enforcing the performance and efficiency of Highways England, which replaced the Highways Agency on 1 April 2015. These changes were specified in the 2015 Infrastructure Act.

In practice the ORR's role in relation to railways is overarching and far-reaching. It monitors health and safety on all networks and takes enforcement action where necessary. It allows the privatised rail system to function by putting in place regulatory frameworks and acting as arbiter in the event of any dispute. It has the final say on who can run trains and how much they must pay. It steers investment by deciding if governments have provided sufficient resources to meet their stated goals and whether Network Rail's plans for spending that money are appropriate.

The Railways Act 1993 requires operators of railway assets to be licensed. Different licences are required for different types of operations – networks, trains, stations and light maintenance depots. These licences, including the Network Rail licence, are issued and enforced by the Rail Regulator.

Beyond making sure that the privatised rail system is safe and can operate on a day-to-day basis, the ORR has other responsibilities and aims that are harder to quantify. It wants to make Network Rail more efficient. It wants to ensure value for Network Rail's customers, such as train operators. It wants to provide passengers with better services.

While the Regulator does not have a role in regulating the train and freight operating companies, its decisions regarding Network Rail have a direct effect on train services. The Regulator can fine Network Rail for breaches in its network licence, which it has done on a number of occasions since 2002. Indeed, the ORR makes much of its role in holding Network Rail to account.

But what happens when Network Rail misses key targets shows that any threats made by the Regulator can ring hollow. A fine may be demanded and paid, but life carries on as before. What is more, any money taken away from Network Rail is ultimately money that it will not have available to improve the railway for passengers. Recognising this, the Government has allocated money it received from Network Rail fines to rail projects such as rolling out wi-fi internet access on board trains.

As well as overseeing Network Rail-owned infrastructure, the ORR's remit extends to the London Underground, light rail systems, heritage railways and High Speed 1, and it is set to gain powers in relation to the Channel Tunnel. The Government has also given the ORR responsibility for overseeing investment in the strategic road network, increasing the ORR's powers further.

As an independent body, the ORR is not bound to agree with Government. Tom Winsor, the former head of the Office of the Rail Regulator, which eventually became the ORR, clashed with ministers over railway reforms and is credited with forcing the Treasury to make available additional money to ensure that the railway could continue operating effectively. More recently, the ORR's relationship with Government has appeared more amicable.

Rail Delivery Group

In 2010 the Labour Government appointed Sir Roy McNulty, former Chairman of the Civil Aviation Authority, to undertake a study examining value for money in the rail industry. Sir Roy published his final report in May 2011, which concluded that the UK rail industry should be looking to achieve efficiency savings of approximately 30% by 2019 and proposed recommendations that, together, could deliver cost savings of between £700m and £1bn per annum by 2019.

Sir Roy found that there were ten principal barriers to efficiency in the rail industry, including fragmentation of rail industry structures and interfaces; the way in which

major players in the industry have operated; roles of government and industry; nature and effectiveness of incentives; legal and contractual frameworks; and relationships and culture within the industry.

One of his recommendations was for the industry to set up a new cross-industry body that could take responsibility for coordinating workstreams that rely on the input and cooperation of different companies and organisations. In 2011 the Rail Delivery Group (RDG) was born.

The RDG is made up of senior representatives of the passenger and freight train operators and Network Rail, who meet monthly to form a 'rail industry' view on a range of issues. This includes deciding on infrastructure investment priorities, which can be fed into the initial industry plans that set out funding choices for the five-year control periods.

After initially being set up as a voluntary organisation, in 2013 the RDG became a company limited by guarantee, and participation by industry members became mandatory through clauses added to Network Rail and train operating company licences. Later in the year the RDG assumed responsibility for policy formulation and communications on behalf of train operators – a role previously handled by the Association of Train Operating Companies (ATOC).

When Sir Roy McNulty recommended setting up a delivery group he warned that it must not become a talking shop. RDG workstreams include contractual and regulatory reform, Europe, strategic planning, franchising, station strategy, freight, rolling stock, sustainability, planning, people, health and safety, information

ABOVE How it used to be: St Pancras station was saved from demolition following a campaign involving Sir John Betjeman, and the 1970s addition to King's Cross has since been torn down to reveal Lewis Cubitt's train shed and create a new public square.

and ticketing, transparency, technology and operations, and asset, programme and supply chain management. The publicly available meeting summaries provide an indication of discussions relating to these and other issues – although it is not always evident what action has resulted. What is clear is that the RDG actively promotes the recent achievements of the railway and makes sure that train operating companies are presented as central to this success.

ATOC, which was set up after privatisation in 1993, continues to exist as an organisation funded by train operators with responsibility for running National Rail Enquiries, the Rail Settlement Plan, Rail Staff Travel and trade association work including operations, engineering and major projects teams.

Standing up for the passenger

Passenger rights and responsibilities when travelling by train in the UK are set out in the National Rail Conditions of Carriage. This is an agreement with national rail train operating companies into which passengers enter when they buy a ticket. It gives the passenger the right to make the journey, or journeys, between the stations or the zones shown on the ticket purchased. It also sets out the passenger's rights and any restrictions to those rights. The National Rail Conditions of Carriage is available at ticket offices and online.

Should passengers experience delays, cancellations or poor service on the railway for reasons within the control of a train operating company or Network Rail, they are entitled to compensation in accordance with the arrangements set out in each train operating company's Passenger's Charter. The amount of compensation offered varies between train operators, but if you are delayed by more than an hour you are likely to receive, as a minimum, compensation in the form of travel vouchers.

Claims need to be made within 28 days of completing a journey and should be accompanied by the ticket purchased. Most operators offer an online claims process, saving passengers the trouble of having to submit a postal claim.

The National Rail Conditions of Carriage allows companies to avoid paying refunds where circumstances are outside their control – for example, in the case of vandalism, exceptionally severe weather and when the police or emergency services close a line. However, the Delay Repay scheme, which has been rolled out by most operators, means that passengers can claim compensation for any delay of 30 minutes or more even if it was not the fault of the operator.

Under Directive 1371/2007 the European Union has attempted to strengthen the rights of rail passengers and set out minimum quality standards that have to be guaranteed to all passengers on all lines. This has been fully implemented for international rail services but not all provisions apply for domestic services in the UK.

Transport Focus

In Britain rail passengers' interests are represented by Transport Focus, an independent watchdog that aims to get the best deal for rail travellers. Formerly Passenger Focus, the organisation morphed into Transport Focus on 30 March 2015 after the Government decided it should represent road users as well as passengers, and stipulated the change in the Infrastructure Act 2015. Passenger Focus replaced the previous Rail Passengers Council and regional Rail Passengers Committees in July 2005. It later gained responsibility for representing bus as well as train passengers.

Transport Focus is structured as an executive non-departmental public body, sponsored by the Department for Transport, with up to 14 board members. The Scottish Government, Welsh Government and the Greater London Authority each appoint a member to the board.

In terms of rail, Transport Focus has a number of roles. It works with the Government, Network Rail and train operators to try and ensure that passengers' needs are taken into account in policy and investment decisions. Often the mechanism for achieving

ABOVE The western Crossrail tunnel portal at Royal Oak is seen during construction. The tunnels contained huge ventilation tubes, conveyor belts to remove clay excavated by the tunnel boring machines, and a narrow gauge railway to take staff and supplies to and from the TBMs miles under London.

this is by responding to the many consultations run by the DfT, ORR and other bodies.

Transport Focus also monitors railway service levels, paying particular attention to disruption, fares and ticketing, the quality of service provision, and investment, and flags up any concerns that arise. It undertakes research and collects information on the railway, the National Rail Passenger Survey being its highest-profile workstream. This involves consulting more than 50,000 passengers a year to build a network-wide picture of passengers' level of satisfaction with rail travel. Passenger opinions of train services are collected twice a year from a representative sample of journeys.

Transport Focus can also help passengers by following up complaints. For passengers unhappy with the service they have experienced, the first step is to contact the appropriate train operating company in writing and give details of the journey. If they are not satisfied with the response they receive, they can then contact Transport Focus, which can consider the best way to take the matter further. This is known as an appeal complaint and the watchdog cannot become involved unless the individuals have been in touch with the company concerned first. If they have, the watchdog will make representations to mediate with the train company on behalf of the passengers. It will also assess whether it feels that the complaint was handled fairly and appropriately, taking into account the rail industry's statutory obligations and guidelines.

Scrutiny

In Westminster a range of mechanisms exist in Parliament to probe Government decisions and scrutinise the actions of the Department for Transport and the rail industry.

Oral Questions take place in the House of Commons for an hour, Monday to Thursday, and follow a departmental rota. When it is the turn of transport, the Secretary of State for Transport and the DfT ministerial team answer a range of written and spoken questions. While they are obliged to supply accurate information, the clarity of answers can vary considerably.

Westminster Hall debates offer an opportunity for MPs to secure discussion of a rail-related topic. The debates conclude with a contribution from a rail minister, who responds to points brought up in the discussion.

Legislation brought before the Commons and the Lords often has rail-related provisions that may be debated in both houses. On occasions legislation is drawn up specifically for the railway – for example, for Crossrail and High Speed 2. Members of Parliament vote on a bill and if a majority is secured the bill receives Royal Assent and becomes law.

The National Audit Office (NAO) scrutinises public spending on behalf of Government and holds Government departments and bodies to account in an attempt to safeguard the interests of taxpayers. The NAO is independent of Government and regularly publishes reports on rail issues.

Parliamentary committees

Select committees in both the House of Commons and the House of Lords check and report on areas ranging from the work of Government departments to economic affairs. In the Commons departmental committees have a minimum of 11 Members of Parliament, who are selected from the three largest political parties and who decide upon lines of inquiry, then collect written and oral evidence. Findings are reported to the Commons, printed, and published on the Parliament website.

The Transport Committee is charged by the House of Commons with scrutiny of the Department for Transport and its associated public bodies – such as the ORR and HS2 Ltd. Areas for inquiry are chosen by the committee; depending on the subject, external deadlines, and the amount of oral evidence the committee decides to take, an inquiry may last for several months and give rise to a report to the House; other inquiries may simply consist of a single day's oral evidence, which the committee may publish without issuing a report. The committee sometimes commissions research to support an inquiry. In recent years the number of Transport Committee recommendations accepted by Government has increased from a quarter to more than a third.[7]

Another select committee that considers rail issues is the Commons' Public Accounts Committee. Past inquiries have included Crossrail and lessons from major rail infrastructure programmes.

The Select Committee on the High Speed Rail (London-West Midlands) Bill was appointed by the House of Commons on 29 April 2014 after the Second Reading of the bill on 28 April 2014. It takes evidence from the individuals and organisations affected by the High Speed 2 scheme, giving them an opportunity to object to the bill's specific provisions and seek an amendment.

European influence

Britain's status as an island nation has in the past allowed it to sidestep the tide of rail policy-making emanating from Europe. But that has changed and European directives on vehicle accessibility, technical standards and interoperability now significantly affect the railway in Britain. As with most things Europe, this can bring benefits but also bureaucracy.

ABOVE At Bristol Temple Meads local, regional and inter-city trains operated by First Great Western can be seen side by side.

The European Union has an ambitious strategy for rail that is designed to create a single, efficient and competitive market for rail throughout Europe. This includes opening up domestic rail markets to foreign companies, promoting competition and harmonising technical and safety standards. Providing an EU-wide framework for rail legislation poses challenges for member states but, having had a privatised set-up since the early 1990s, Britain has much more experience of competition issues than its neighbours, so in many ways is well placed to accommodate the changes.

EU rail reforms are being put into place through a series of legislative 'packages' that represent steps towards a common legal framework for infrastructure management and operations.

The First Railway Package was adopted by the European Commission in 2001 and implemented in the UK in November 2005. It is designed to open up the international rail freight market and establish a general framework for the development of European railways. This includes clarifying the relationships between the state, infrastructure manager (i.e. Network Rail) and train operators.

The Second Railway Package was adopted by the EC in 2004 and implemented in the UK in 2006. It includes safety and interoperability directives and makes provision for the European Railway Agency to coordinate groups of technical experts seeking common solutions on safety and interoperability. It also states that national and international freight train services should be able to use the entire European network from 1 January 2007.

The Third Railway Package was adopted by the EC in 2007 to open up international passenger services to competition within the EU by 2010. A directive on how train operators should be charged for the use of infrastructure was implemented in 2009. Another directive, designed to standardise passenger rights with regard to insurance, ticketing and accessibility, was implemented in 2009 for international passenger services, but has not been implemented in full for UK domestic services.

In 2010 the EC set out plans to amend and consolidate the First Railway Package. This was intended to clarify rules for the funding

ABOVE London Overground has transformed local rail routes with high-frequency services and modern, air-conditioned rolling stock. Here a Bombardier-built Class 378 'Capitalstar' waits at West Croydon.

and management of infrastructure and ensure that access to rail-related facilities such as depots is available to train operators. The changes were finalised in 2012 and were due to be implemented in UK law during 2015.

Finally, the Fourth Railway Package was unveiled by the EC in 2013 as the last step towards a legal framework for a single European rail area. It has several separate legislative measures covering infrastructure governance and funding, competitive tendering of public service obligation contracts, technical authorisation, safety certification, and the role of the European Rail Agency (ERA).

Based in France, the ERA is an agency of the European Union and was set up to support the development of an integrated railway across Europe where services are not restricted by national borders and safety is paramount. The agency acts as the system authority for the European Rail Traffic Management System and helps draft and refine the Technical Specifications for Interoperability (TSI).

TSI

Technical specifications for interoperability set out how railway systems and components should work in order to be compatible with the requirements of railways across Europe and comply with applicable laws and other regulations.

The Department for Transport describes a TSI as a common, harmonised, technical standard needed to satisfy the essential requirements of interoperability, which includes safety, reliability and availability, health, environmental protection and technical compatibility.

TSIs may contain specific requirements relating to either 'structural' subsystems (such as infrastructure, rolling stock, energy, and control/command and signalling) or 'functional' subsystems (such as maintenance, traffic operation and management and telematics applications for passengers and freight services). In addition, there is a 'transverse' category indicating that the TSI is concerned with bridging the gap between structural and operational subsystems – for example, there are transverse TSIs relating to persons with reduced mobility, and safety in railway tunnels.

TSIs are drafted and amended by the European Railway Agency under a mandate from the European Commission. Organisations responsible for managing any rail project must ensure that the essential requirements of safety, reliability and availability, health, environmental protection and technical compatibility are met.

Towards the Fourth Railway Package

Many of the EC rail reforms to date have dovetailed with the policies of successive UK Governments, which have supported liberalisation of the EU rail market. After all, in Britain the rail sector is one of the most open in Europe, and it has long been the case that UK companies have wanted to be able to enter European markets with the ease with which French, Dutch and German operators have established a presence in the UK.

However, as the recurring theme of rail privatisation in this book will show, the separation of track and train – as laid down by the First Package – is not welcomed by everyone and there are plenty of people who would like to see the UK move back towards a system where the state runs the railways and trains on a more integrated basis.

The main concern of UK Government surrounding the Fourth Railway Package pertains to the prescribed role of an independent infrastructure manager. With Network Rail currently fulfilling this role, would there be a need for it to undergo a complex and unnecessary reorganisation? Implementation could also affect the ORR, potentially handing its responsibility for granting track access agreements to a centralised European body.

For the Commission's plans to ask the European Rail Agency to identify common safety-critical tasks and develop a training model and system of EU certification, the Government is more supportive. On interoperability, the UK is concerned about the proposal to change the authorisation process for trackside signalling and vehicles, transferring powers from national safety authorities to the ERA, in particular those relating to notified national safety and technical rules. Similarly, for safety, the Government has raised concerns about responsibility for issuing safety certificates being switched from national safety authorities to the ERA.

Trans-European Transport Network

The Trans-European Transport Network (TEN-T) Programme was established by the European Commission to support the construction and upgrade of transport infrastructure across the European Union. TEN-T has been allocated specific funds to deliver important transport infrastructure projects in line with the Commission's goal of encouraging competitiveness, job creation and links between member states.

The TEN-T network comprises road, rail, air and water transport routes in Europe, and was created with a view to coordinating improvements to primary roads, railways, inland waterways, airports, seaports, inland ports and traffic management systems, providing integrated and intermodal long-distance, high-speed routes.

It has two layers: a core network, which covers strategically important EU transport routes, and a comprehensive network, which includes main, regional routes. Funding for all TEN-T projects is delivered through the Connecting Europe Facility, which is part of the EU's Structural and Cohesion fund. Examples of UK rail projects that have secured TEN-T grants include the North West electrification, the Ely freight loops, the Crossrail/West Coast Main Line link, and the Belfast Victoria station intermodal transport hub scheme.

2 • Passenger services

Arguably the defining feature of Britain's post-privatisation railway is the franchising system under which train operating companies bid for the right to run train services.

As franchising authority, the Department for Transport is responsible for the design and procurement of new and replacement rail franchises across the national rail network. The DfT will advertise a franchise opportunity, then typically three or four bidders will be invited to tender for a contract that will be based on a specification drawn up by the DfT after some level of consultation with the parties that will be affected by the franchise, often referred to as stakeholders. The winning bidder becomes responsible for operating trains on the franchise routes and, depending on the franchise structure, will either pay the Government a premium or receive a subsidy to deliver the specified service level.

Franchising

Ever since rail privatisation, different governments have wrestled with the question of what is the optimum length for a franchise. Train operators are keen to be left alone to get on with the job of running trains and argue that 15-20-year contracts encourage investment by offering a sufficient timescale to generate a return on investment. But throughout a franchise term Government is under pressure to respond to passengers and taxpayers who demand service improvements and value for money. It therefore needs the opportunity to intervene and sometimes reset franchises.

A couple of long franchises survive from awards before franchise terms were reined in. Chiltern Railways in particular is an unusual example of a franchise, given that it is a 20-year agreement with the full term linked to the successful delivery of at least three major enhancement schemes. Subsequent franchise awards have been much shorter, driven by Government desire for control, uncertainty about the future, and enhancement schemes distorting the profile of a franchise, making calculating a reasonable level of premium/subsidy years into the future almost impossible.

The Coalition Government supported a move back towards longer franchises but, for reasons that will be discussed below, was in most cases forced to settle for short-term interim arrangements. The exception is the Essex Thameside franchise, which began in 2014 and is due to run for 15 years until 2029.

Putting together a bid

Bidders for a rail franchise will usually set up a company that will operate the franchise if successful. The bidder will be required to provide some form of security including a season ticket bond and a performance bond, which represents its minimum liability should the franchise experience financial difficulties.

The bidding process is complex as the companies involved must show that they can meet a wide range of requirements in order to be eligible to run the franchise. Bidders may be allowed to use a confidential 'data room' where they have access to commercial information about the franchise's performance that can then be used as a basis for putting together an informed bid.

For those bidders that satisfy the competition requirements, the DfT will use financial models to help decide which it feels is best placed to be awarded the contract. The DfT keeps potential operators up to date with its franchise schedule through open days and similar supplier events. When it is ready to begin procurement, a notice will be placed in the Official Journal of the European Union and bidders will subsequently be invited to tender. A preferred bidder will be appointed, then a

ABOVE **London Marylebone, once slated for closure and conversion to a bus station, is now a thriving terminus for trains operated by Chiltern Railways.**

contract signed in advance of the franchise start date.

For national rail franchises the appointed train operating company usually takes revenue risk – that is, it estimates the number of people likely to use the train services included in the franchise and then makes a bid to the DfT setting out the premium (how much money it will pay) or subsidy (how much it will need to receive) in order to provide the level of service required by the Government. This is spread over the lifetime of the franchise and is sometimes referred to as a payment profile.

Franchise finances

Given the many variables that affect how many people travel by train, there are risks for both Government and operator in agreeing a payment profile. For example, if the economy dips, the number of commuters is likely to decrease and throw the operator's financial projections into turmoil. Conversely, if the economy improves, the operator may see a wider profit margin than was envisaged on contract signature. This will be welcomed by the train operating company's shareholders, but may be embarrassing for a Government trying to show taxpayers that it has negotiated a good deal.

Since the first franchises were let, a variety of circumstances at both extremes have emerged. Some train operators have run out of money while others have done rather well from their involvement with the railway. In an attempt to address the risk and make provision for the unforeseen, various mechanisms have been developed. These include 'cap and collar' whereby a train operator's profits are capped if the franchise exceeds expectations, but it receives additional subsidy if revenue projections are lower than expected. The problem with this is that it can reduce the incentive for a train operator to maximise returns. Recent contracts have preferred a profit-share mechanism where taxpayers as well as the franchisee benefit during the good times.

In some instances the DfT has agreed to let management contracts whereby a franchise is run at cost and the Department pays a small percentage fee to the operator. This has been used where a short-term arrangement is required or if there are extenuating circumstances – such as major engineering work – where the Government decides that it does not want the train operator to be preoccupied with maximising revenue above all else.

A similar approach is to let a concession where the authority tendering the contract retains revenue risk. The contractor passes on the fare receipts it collects and is paid an agreed fee. This model is used by Transport for London for the London Overground and Crossrail, but the DfT has been cautious about using concessions for national rail services.

When it all goes wrong

Private companies can and have been given responsibility for running trains. But if they are unable to do so for any reason it ultimately falls on the Government to step in. Not running a train service is deemed politically unacceptable, so contingency measures are needed. These are fulfilled by the operator of last resort – a team of people appointed by the DfT who are constantly on standby to take over the running of a franchise if the operator is unable to continue.

In addition to this background contingency presence, the operator of last resort has on occasions had to scale up and become a fully fledged train operator, taking over from Connex in 2003 to operate the Southeastern franchise and, more recently, to run services on the East Coast Main Line.

In July 2009 the DfT established Directly Operated Railways, a state-owned company that fulfils the Secretary of State's requirements under Section 30 of the Railways Act to secure the continued provision of passenger railway services should an existing franchise not be able to complete its full term.

The East Coast experience

In 2009, following a downturn in the economy, National Express Group decided it could not afford to make the premium payments to Government it had agreed when the East Coast franchise had been signed in 2007. With the Government unwilling to renegotiate the terms of the franchise, National Express capped spending on it, which then became limited to the terms of the franchise bonds. When the money ran out, state-owned Directly Operated Railways stepped in to run services under the East Coast brand. East Coast ran trains until March 2015, when the franchise was returned to the private sector. The Coalition Government awarded the franchise to Virgin East Coast (a joint venture in which Stagecoach had a 90% stake and Virgin 10%).

East Coast has become a totem for those who feel that the current franchising system is not fit for purpose and believe that train operations should in part or in whole be returned to the public sector. State-owned East Coast proved a reliable custodian of the railway, ending the uncertainty during National Express's tenure of the route and, before it, that of GNER – the Sea Containers-owned franchise that was well regarded but collapsed after submitting a bid for the franchise based on premiums that (as with National Express) proved unrealistic.

On top of this, East Coast paid a premium to Government, returning more than £1bn to the Treasury during its time running the franchise. Critics of the franchising system – including the Labour Party and trade unions – suggest that under other franchises similar returns are being absorbed by private train operators and in some cases are ending up with governments in France, Germany and the Netherlands, which are the ultimate owners of a number of Britain's rail franchisees. If profits from Britain's railways can go to foreign governments, why can't they go to our Treasury?

Others suggest that a like-for-like comparison of franchise premiums and subsidies creates a distorted picture. The Rail Delivery Group claims that differences are due to many factors. For example, in 2012-13 West Coast train operator Virgin paid £302m to lease trains on average nine years old while

ABOVE **When revenue targets failed to meet projections, state-owned Directly Operated Railways took over from National Express to run trains on the East Coast Main Line. The franchise was later returned to the private sector.**

East Coast paid £53m for trains on average three times older. This disparity inevitably affects the money a franchise holder has left to return to Government.

The situation will likely change in future following the DfT's signing of a contract with Agility Trains to supply two new fleets of Intercity Express Programme Trains. The cost of these will be recouped through payments by the future East Coast franchisee over 27½ years and is expected to seriously eat into any profits generated by the franchise.

Whether state-run East Coast represented good value or not, the Government's decision to return the franchise to the private sector two months before a General Election – prioritising this competition while putting the West Coast competition on hold – fuelled accusations that the coalition had been pursuing an ideologically driven agenda.

The West Coast experience

In August 2012 the Department for Transport named First Group as winner of the new West Coast franchise. As franchise competitions go this was dynamite – the award would unseat the Virgin/Stagecoach partnership, which, as Virgin Trains, had run the West Coast routes since 1997 and brought the Class 390 'Pendolino' fleet into service. Theresa Villiers, rail minister at the time, described the new West Coast deal as the first of the new longer franchises to be let by the coalition. First Group had committed to pay the Government £5.5bn during a 13-year franchise term with payments weighted towards the end of the franchise term.

Three weeks later Virgin Trains, one of three other bidders for the West Coast franchise, announced that it had begun court proceedings following the Government's decision to award the franchise to First. It claimed the procurement process had ignored the DfT's own assessment that Virgin's bid (which had offered to pay premiums of £4.8bn) was more deliverable and a lower risk. 'We question whether First Group's bid has been correctly risk-adjusted by the Department given all of its supposed incremental value is delivered after 2022,' the company said in a statement. 'The current process is geared to selecting the highest-risk bid and needs to be independently audited to prevent a repeat of former franchise failures.'

In October 2012 Secretary of State for Transport Patrick McLoughlin announced the cancellation of the West Coast franchising competition following the discovery of what he called 'significant technical flaws' in the way bids were evaluated. DfT Permanent Secretary Philip Rutnum added: 'The errors exposed by our investigation are deeply concerning. They show a lack of good process and a lack of proper quality assurance.'

The collapse of the West Coast procurement left the Government liable for the bidders' costs and other expenses totalling more than £54m.[8] It also resulted in a period of soul-searching with the Government commissioning a review to examine the cause of the crisis from Centrica Chief Executive Sam Laidlaw, and a review of the way forward from former Eurostar boss Richard Brown. Brown declared the franchising system essentially sound but advocated a package of measures designed to improve the evaluation of bids and avoid a future crisis.

Even before the West Coast collapse the DfT was struggling to keep to the schedule required to put new franchise arrangements in place before existing contracts expired. With the West Coast situation forcing it to put the refranchising process on hold, any hope of letting contracts in time was lost and the Department had to come up with temporary arrangements.

There have been many twists and turns in the rail franchising story that followed the privatisation of Britain's railways. The West Coast crisis shone a light on the railway's public-private relationship: it showed that in commercial dealings the Government must follow its own processes to the letter or risk paying a hefty price. It also made clear that for all the talk of partnership working, train operators retain a fundamentally hard-nosed approach to commercial negotiations and will put their shareholders' interests before anything else.

Virgin Trains' decision to challenge the franchise award to First paid off. With the West Coast competition abandoned, the DfT was left with little option but to agree a deal with the incumbent operator. When the franchising programme restarted the Department made sure that re-letting the West Coast was well down the list of franchise competitions, and in June 2014 it announced that Virgin Trains would continue operating the West Coast franchise until at least March 2017.

Making DfT fit for purpose

As master and coordinator of the franchising system, the Department for Transport's role is crucial. Rail privatisation and the experiences of the East and West Coast main lines have forced the Government to transform the way it handles rail issues. A malleable British Rail has been replaced with commercially astute private companies that ultimately answer to their shareholders.

Put simply, when it comes to negotiating the financial terms for a franchise, the party with the best negotiators is likely to come out on top. For a franchise that spans several years, that can have significant repercussions for Government and taxpayers. One of the many challenges facing the DfT is to recruit the best people in a market where the private sector can usually pay more.

In an effort to make management of franchises more robust after the West Coast experience, in 2014 the DfT set up a Rail Executive in an attempt to create a unit that is suitably resourced with the experienced staff needed to handle the challenges of letting and managing rail franchises. With state-owned companies such as Crossrail Ltd and HS2 Ltd able to pursue a more commercial approach – including offering higher salaries – than a Government department, there are advantages to being able to spin off franchising into a dedicated unit.

It remains to be seen how far this will go; in the past franchising has been handled by stand-alone organisations such as the Office of Passenger Rail Franchising and the Strategic Rail Authority. The creation of the Rail Executive lays the foundations for a similar future approach. Previous arrangements have ended when ministers felt the need for direct control over how funding is spent, bringing the management of rail franchising back into the Department.

A new franchising programme

The suspension of the DfT's franchising programme following the collapse of the West Coast competition left the Department unable to let a raft of planned long-term franchises before existing contracts expired. Franchises usually specify a short optional extension, subject to agreement with the DfT and the franchisee, but once this is used up a new contract must be agreed.

European Union procurement rules prohibit the Government from simply extending a contract at its convenience until a new deal is agreed. Therefore, to put in place interim arrangements the DfT came up with a strategy of agreeing short extensions followed by direct award contracts, typically of a few years duration, which would buy time to let the preferred long-term contracts. This would fit within EU rules and, as most incumbent train operators would benefit from direct awards, challenges from within the industry seemed unlikely.

In some cases multiple direct awards have been agreed with a train operator. First Group has operated core Great Western routes since 1998, taking on the current franchise area in 2006. In 2011 it chose not to take up an option in its contract for a three-year extension, a decision that allowed it to avoid premium payments to the Government that were weighted towards the end of an extended franchise term. In January 2013, following the collapse of the West Coast franchise procurement, the Transport Secretary scrapped the competition to let a new Great Western franchise. The Government later agreed a direct award with First to run Great Western until September 2015. Then in March 2015 it announced a second direct award that will keep First as operator until at least April 2019 – a deal partly predicated on the need to have an experienced operator in place while major upgrade projects (electrification, Intercity Express Programme, Crossrail) are delivered on the route. The result is that First, despite forgoing the right to continue to operate the franchise, has actually remained train operator on the route for longer without having to make the payments specified in the 2006 franchise agreement.

Whatever your view on this, the DfT has managed to restore order to the franchising programme and many in the rail industry have hailed the new programme, including the direct awards as stepping stones to longer-term arrangements, as a pragmatic approach. While payment profiles still carry a lot of weight, the consideration of other factors,

Table 3: DfT-let franchise estimated start dates

Franchise	Start date
Essex Thameside	2014
East Coast	2015
Northern	2016
TransPennine	2016
Greater Anglia	2016
West Coast	2017
London Midland	2017
East Midlands	2017
Southeastern	2018
Wales and Borders	2019
Great Western	2019
South West	2017
Cross Country	2019
Thameslink, Southern, Great Northern	2021
Chiltern	2021

Source: DfT Rail Executive

ABOVE **London Overground is run as a concession let by Transport for London, which retains revenue from fares. A joint venture of Deutsche Bahn and MTR held the contract to run services until 2016.**

such as the quality of train service offered by a bid, have been evident in recent contract awards. The revamped schedule attempts to spread the workload for those involved in judging bids, as well as the train operators putting them together, by making sure that there are no more than three franchise competitions in any one year.

While this has ensured that experienced, competent train operators, including First and Virgin, remain in place to keep train services and investment programmes going, the situation can also be viewed as one where private companies earn a return on non-competed contracts that are agreed without market-testing.

Under the Coalition Government, two non-direct-award rail franchises were let – the previously discussed East Coast franchise and that for Essex Thameside, operated by National Express under the C2C brand. According to the DfT's rail franchise schedule, the following medium-to-long-term franchises will start as indicated in Table 3.

Train operators

So who are the companies that operate trains in Britain? Among the line-up are the four big London-listed public limited companies (plcs) – First Group, Go-Ahead, National Express and Stagecoach – which have grown out of bus and coach businesses. Arriva used to make it a big five but is now owned by Germany's Deutsche

Bahn (DB). DB, together with Abellio and SNCF/Keolis, represent an emerging trend in the UK rail sector – that of state-owned companies from abroad playing an integral role in the operation of Britain's privatised railway.

Abellio

Previously known as NedRailways, Abellio is the international arm of Dutch state-owned Nederlandse Spoorwegen. As well as running various bus operations in Britain, Abellio operates the Merseyrail franchise in partnership with Serco and had a similar arrangement for the old Northern franchise.

The company achieved a major success in the UK rail sector by winning the contract to run the ScotRail franchise, which began in 2015. Prior to that it was awarded a contract to operate trains in Greater Anglia until late 2016. Abellio has helped bring Dutch transport ideas to the UK, delivering significant improvements to facilities for cyclists at key stations.

Deutsche Bahn

Germany's state-owned rail operator reduced the number of big UK transport plcs from five to four when it acquired Arriva in 2010. Largely as a result of the deal, DB's interests extend across the UK rail sector with involvement in myriad regions and initiatives.

At a stroke the takeover made DB operator of local and regional trains in Wales and CrossCountry inter-city services. The organisation runs the London Overground in partnership with MTR and operates the Tyne & Wear Metro. DB owns open access train operator Grand Central and operates the Royal Train.

DB is also a potential rival to Eurostar – although planned international services have failed to materialise as envisaged when the operator ran an ICE train to St Pancras in 2010.

First Group

After moving into the rail market during privatisation, First Bus was renamed First Group in 1997 and is now one of the four big London-listed transport plcs. As well as having rail and bus divisions in the UK, it runs

BELOW After turning down an optional extension to its Great Western franchise, First Group has been handed new contracts that will see its tenure extend until at least 2019 while major infrastructure schemes are delivered.

Greyhound – the only national operator of scheduled inter-city coach transportation services in the US and Canada – as well as bus services across North America. The company is based in Aberdeen.

First Group was until recently the UK's largest rail operator, transporting around a quarter of all train passengers. But the Government's franchising programme means that First's rail operations are now at a critical juncture: the company has lost the Thameslink and ScotRail franchises, although a Great Western direct award guarantees revenue from rail for years to come. First also operates Croydon Tramlink and the Heathrow Connect service; the latter is due to be subsumed by the new Crossrail concession.

Go-Ahead

Another of the four big London-listed transport plcs, Go-Ahead is a major player in the UK rail market. The company operates passenger services through GoVia, a joint venture which is 65% owned by Go-Ahead and 35% by Keolis.

ABOVE A local First Great Western service stops at Slough. The Class 165 'Thames Turbo' diesel units will be redeployed following electrification of the route and the arrival of new electric multiple units.

GoVia is currently responsible for three franchises – London Midland, Southeastern and the sprawling Thameslink, Southeastern, Great Northern franchise. London Midland provides commuter services out of London Euston and Birmingham while Southeastern operates train services in Kent, including the UK's first high-speed domestic rail service, which was launched in December 2009 and provided the 'Javelin' shuttle during the 2012 Olympic and Paralympic Games.

In September 2014 GoVia became responsible for running the Thameslink, Southern and Great Northern franchise, the largest rail franchise in terms of passenger numbers, trains, revenue and staff. Because of the major disruption to train services expected during the rebuilding of London Bridge station, scheduled to conclude during 2019, the franchise has been let as a management contract, with GoVia due to pass ticket revenues directly on to the Government.

Go-Ahead is also one of Britain's main bus operators. In 2014 the company said it operated 4,400 buses and had a 7% share of the UK bus market outside London where it is one of the biggest operators.

Keolis

Until relatively recently Keolis has had an understated presence in the UK rail market. Operating as the smaller partner in franchise ventures with Go-Ahead (GoVia) and First Group (TransPennine Express), the role of the company has not been obvious to outsiders.

In recent years Keolis has taken a more ambitious approach to UK rail, indicating that it is prepared to run franchises on its own or as the main partner. The company achieved a coup in July 2014 when it wrestled the Docklands Light Railway franchise from Serco after putting forward a 70/30 bid with Amey (which will handle the maintenance side of the operation). Keolis is due to operate the DLR until at least April 2021.

Keolis is 70% owned by French state-owned rail and train operator SNCF and, with Abellio and Deutsche Bahn, has contributed to the paradox of state-run overseas organisations being able to run trains in Britain when British state-owned train operators have not been allowed (except as a temporary measure). Canadian pension fund Caisse de depot et placement du Québec owns the remaining 30% of Keolis shares.

MTR

Hong Kong-listed MTR is part-owned by the Chinese Government and is best known for

BELOW GoVia (GTR) is responsible for introducing new Siemens-built Class 700 trains into service on Thameslink routes. The Thameslink Programme will add new through-London services and increase train frequencies. *Siemens*

running the Hong Kong metro. It also operates light rail and Airport Express services in the city.

In November 2007 MTR gained a foothold in the UK when it was chosen as part of the London Overground Rail Operations Limited (LOROL) joint venture to run London Overground services. In July 2014 the company – this time on its own – secured the contract to operate Crossrail services for at least eight years from 31 May 2015.

MTR's growing presence in the UK builds on previous forays overseas. The company is the lead shareholder in the operation of the Melbourne train system in Australia, runs the Stockholm Metro concession in Sweden, and has an international consulting business. In China it operates the Beijing Metro Lines 4 and 14 and the Daxing Line extension, Shenzhen Metro Longhua Line and Hangzhou Metro Line 1.

National Express

London-listed National Express ran more rail franchises in Britain than any other company in 1997. But more recently it looked as if the group could end up without a rail presence.

In November 2009 the National Express-run East Coast franchise was taken over by state-owned Directly Operated Railways (DOR). National Express Group, which had been facing financial difficulties, decided it was no longer economic to operate the franchise and chose to cap the amount of money it would make available to the franchise. With the Labour Government of the day refusing to renegotiate the terms of the franchise, it had to call in DOR, the operator of last resort.

National Express received opprobrium for walking away from the East Coast deal it had agreed in 2007 but, as the UK lurched into recession, it can be argued that the company faced circumstances it could not have foreseen. The saga has prompted scrutiny of the validity of high premium bids for franchises – given that National Express proved that it could avoid paying them – and the level of security franchisees provide in the form of bonds, which serve as non-refundable deposits.

Although the Transport Secretary at the time, Andrew Adonis, initially warned that National Express could be stripped of its other two rail franchises, this never came to pass and the company has gradually returned to favour in the eyes of the Government. Although the firm lost its East Anglia franchise to Abellio, in 2014 the Department for Transport awarded it a new 15-year deal for the Essex Thameside (C2C) franchise, safeguarding its presence in UK rail until 2029.

Having rehabilitated itself, National Express, which also operates the Midland Metro tram system, has resumed bidding for other franchises and, although it has yet to add to its presence in Britain, the company has won contracts to operate a range of train services in Germany.

RATP

Best known as operator of the Paris Metro, RATP Group established subsidiary RATP Dev in 2002 to expand overseas. The company's UK rail presence is limited to operating and maintaining Manchester Metrolink, the UK's largest tram network. But the speed with which RATP Dev has added UK bus companies to its portfolio is indicative of its ambition for acquiring new ventures. RATP Dev also has interests in Italy, Switzerland, Algeria, Morocco, South Africa, USA, Brazil, India, China and South Korea, and is one to watch.

RATP Group describes itself as a state-funded public corporation and is led by a chairman appointed by the President of France.

Serco

British outsourcing company Serco has fingers in many pies – from running detention centres, maintaining ballistic missile early warning systems and operating London's cycle hire scheme. As operator of the Docklands Light Railway since 1997 the company became a rail stalwart, but this came to an abrupt end when it lost out to Keolis in the competition for the new DLR contract, which began in December 2014.

Serco partnered with Abellio to operate the Northern franchise (expected to end in 2016) and Merseyrail (which is due to end in 2028). Despite losing the DLR, Serco has signalled its desire to be involved in the next generation of rail franchises through winning the Caledonian Sleeper contract, which began in 2015. It has promised a step change in the quality of rolling stock and passenger facilities, building on its experience of running luxury sleeper trains in Australia.

Stagecoach

Another of the four London-listed plcs and the second to be based in Scotland, Stagecoach was founded in Perth in 1980 by current chairman Brian Souter, his sister Ann Gloag and her former husband Robin.

The company has similarities with First Group – both have UK rail and bus businesses and both have extensive bus operations overseas. Brian Souter was previously the company's high-profile chief executive and has not been shy in expressing his views on the rail industry. This campaigning stance has been continued by his successor Martin Griffiths, who has criticised proposals for bringing train operations under state control.

ABOVE At Reading a South West Trains 'Desiro' unit awaits its next journey to London Waterloo.

Stagecoach has had a relatively stable rail portfolio based on South West Trains and Virgin Rail Group, in which it has a 49% stake. The company secured the East Midlands Trains franchise in 2007 and operates the Sheffield Supertram network.

Virgin

Arguably the train operator most recognised by the public, Virgin Rail Group has been 49% owned by Stagecoach since 1998 and runs the West Coast franchise. The company lost the CrossCountry contract to Arriva in 2007 but has a 10% stake in the Virgin East Coast franchise that began in 2015 (Stagecoach holds the remaining equity).

Virgin Rail Group has played a pivotal role in defining the privatised rail industry in Britain, introducing tilting 'Pendolinos' on the West Coast Main Line and negotiating an agreement to run 140mph train services, which had to be abandoned with far-reaching cost implications for the Government. More recently, its decision to contest the Government's award of a new West Coast contract to First Group triggered the major overhaul of the rail franchising process described above.

Open access

One of the arguments for rail privatisation in the 1990s was that it would encourage competition on the rail network. Entrepreneurial train operators could target under-served destinations or existing markets where there was potential for growth or improved service.

Open access is the mechanism created to achieve this. Prospective operators submit bids to the Office of Rail and Road for train paths and, if the ORR approves, they get to run train services in addition to those of the franchised operator on a particular route.

In practice this presents a number of difficulties. With many key rail routes operating at or close to capacity, identifying paths for a new, additional rail service is rarely straight-forward and tends to involve prospective operators having to lobby Network Rail to undertake work that will release new capacity. Franchised train operators tend to be unenthusiastic about having an upstart operator using their route because of the implications for their service performance and revenue. They are therefore likely to formally object when a track access application is submitted.

These factors mean that prospective open access operators often devise weird and wonderful routes to use rail corridors where there is space for a new service. Trains may not call at key stations to provide reassurance that they will not extract revenue from franchised train operators.

This risk of revenue extraction is a key reason why successive Governments have been less than enthusiastic about open access. Carefully calculated franchise payment profiles risk being upset by a new operator being allowed to run services, leaving Government with a hole in the rail budget. Clearly having 'maverick' operators that are not subject to control by Government or the franchising system is an inconvenience to ministers and much of the rail industry.

Perhaps a more legitimate concern has been that open access operators do not pay their way. Payment for track access agreements reflects just that, and means that open access operators do not have to pay premiums to Government, a feature of many franchise agreements. Therefore open access operators are perceived as having an unfair advantage and not contributing to the cost of maintaining the railway. The ORR has recognised this issue and in June 2013 proposed a package of open access reforms including higher track access charges. However, in October 2013 it decided not to implement any of the options, noting that there was 'little support for the options from open access operators and some issues of concern to funders'.[9]

At the time of writing two open access operators provide services to and from London King's Cross station: Grand Central (with two routes linking Sunderland and Bradford Interchange) and Hull Trains. The operators are now majority owned by Deutsche Bahn and First Group respectively. Alliance Rail Holdings, which includes members of the original Grand Central team, hopes to run new open access services from London Euston as well as King's Cross. In March 2015 First Group lodged plans with the ORR to run a new open access train service linking London King's Cross with Edinburgh and calling at Stevenage, Newcastle and Morpeth stations.

Heathrow Express is often referred to as an open access operator in that it exists outside the rail franchising system. The operating company is wholly owned by Heathrow Airport and the service exists because of historic investment in rail links to the airport. This means that there is an established case for its existence and perpetuity, which does not apply to the East Coast open access operators. The operator wants to run the new Western Rail Access to Heathrow service, which is scheduled to start in the early 2020s.

With open access operators running only a small number of train services and routes, the effect of open access on the UK railway can be said to be limited. However, open access proposals, applications and services have had an impact on the standards of service expected from franchised train operators and have led to pressure for new direct train services to towns and cities including Blackpool, Lincoln, Shrewsbury and Wrexham.

In June 2013 the ORR noted: 'Despite the very limited role that competition currently plays, there is evidence that it drives passenger benefits including lower fares increases, higher growth in passenger numbers, direct services to new destinations, and various service quality benefits.'[10]

Other operators

One unforeseen consequence of the Beeching era line and station closures in the 1950s and '60s was that railway enthusiasts would step in to acquire many of the assets deemed surplus to requirements by the Government of the day.

Today there are more than 100 heritage railways – routes that are not part of the national rail network – which together are worth £250m to the UK economy each year.[11] A report by the All Party Parliamentary Group on Heritage Rail concluded that apart from the economic benefits, heritage railways also provide employment for more than 3,700 staff nationally and are supported by 18,500 loyal volunteers.

Heritage rail services are generally subject to a 25mph speed limit. They operate without subsidy and rely heavily, if not exclusively, on volunteers to do everything from cleaning toilets to running trains. This is different from the community (often rural) railways of the national rail network, which depend on subsidy from Government and use paid staff and train drivers.

Typically heritage railways run between 200 and 250 days a year as a visitor attraction rather than a transport provider, but in some cases the difference between 'heritage' and 'normal' railways is starting to blur. While many heritage railways are the domain of enthusiasts and provide an opportunity to experience a nostalgic reminder of the days of steam trains, they are also increasingly providing practical modern-day public transport services that connect to and feed the national rail system.

Recent extensions to heritage railways show just what can be achieved (as well as reminding us of the remarkable patience and dedication of those supporting the historic lines). For example, in 2013 the Bluebell Railway in Sussex was extended to East Grinstead, allowing Thameslink/Southern passengers arriving at the national rail terminus to change for a connection to Sheffield Park. In 2014 a second platform was reinstated at Whitby station, which is shared by national rail and the North Yorkshire Moors Railway; this new infrastructure allowed an increase in the number of NYMR trains serving Whitby. From 2016 the Swanage Railway is due to run regular services to and from Wareham, allowing customers of South West Trains to catch a connecting train to the Purbeck coast. The importance of railways to Britain's economy has been recognised by Government grants to support projects such as these.

According to Chris Austin at Railfuture[12], at least 45 heritage lines have the potential to be linked with the national network, directly or via an interchange station. However, for this to

ABOVE Charter services including steam trains can be seen from time to time on the national network. The 'Torbay Express' runs on selected dates during the summer. *Roger Fieldhouse*

happen there needs to be a business case and funding, and, most importantly, the volunteers that have safeguarded the heritage railway must be persuaded of the need to link up.

Charters

Specialist companies have developed to organise charter train trips using old and not so old rolling stock and to run railtours to scenic destinations around Britain. For example, Riviera Trains provides rolling stock for railtour customers including Bath Travel/Cruise Saver Travel, Bath Spa Express, Branch Line Society, Cheshire Cat Tours, Pathfinder Tours, Retro Railtours, Steam Dreams, Torbay Express, Train Chartering Co and UK Railtours.

Modern rolling stock is sometimes hired out by charter companies to franchised and open access train operating companies to meet high demand for travel – such as that experienced during the London 2012 Olympic and Paralympic Games.

Royal Train

The first Royal Train journey took place on 13 June 1842 and the tradition of the Royal Train has survived into the 21st century – although perhaps it may not last much longer.

Dedicated carriages are retained for today's Royal Train, which enables members of the Royal Family to travel overnight and at times when the weather is too bad to fly, and to work and hold meetings during lengthy journeys. During the past decade the train has been used for between 10 and 20 journeys a year.

The exact number and combination of carriages forming the Royal Train is determined by factors such as which member of the Royal Family is travelling and the time and duration of the journey. DB Schenker Class 67 locomotives are usually used to haul the Royal Train and, when not required, are used for charter train services and on other occasional passenger services.

The current Queen's and Duke's Saloons came into service in 1977 when they were extensively used during the Silver Jubilee Royal tours. They had begun life in 1972 as prototypes for the standard InterCity Mark 3 passenger carriage and were later fitted out for their royal role at Wolverton, where work on the Royal Train is normally done.

Network Rail manages the Royal Train and owns the rolling stock. Day-to-day operations are carried out by Deutsche Bahn's DB Schenker rail logistics arm. Journeys on the train are organised so as not to interfere with scheduled services.

The cost to the Royal household of travelling by Royal Train is substantial, and pressure to provide value for money to the taxpayer has led to the Royal Train being used less often. Members of the Royal Family, including the Queen, sometimes use scheduled train services, which are cheaper and provide public relations opportunities. Sovereign Grant figures show that the total cost of rail travel (including annual rolling stock lease payments of £200,000) decreased from £900,000 in 2013 to £700,000 in 2014.[13]

With the Royal Train carriages approaching 50 years old, the question of whether the train should be replaced has arisen in Parliament. But given the train's limited use it seems unlikely that the substantial cost of replacing this anachronism will be authorised.

3 • Freight

Freight train volumes declined in the second half of the 20th century as the enthusiasm for moving goods by rail waned. Now railway freight in Britain is making a comeback and the decline in the need for moving dirty materials such as coal is increasingly being offset by intermodal opportunities for firms to bypass crowded roads and reap efficiencies from super-size containers and investment in deep-sea port facilities.

Consideration of changes to business supply chains and advances in the rail industry reveal that there remains plenty of potential for rail freight to play an increasingly relevant part in freight distribution, taking advantage of the economies of longer and heavier trains, more electric haulage and integration with other parts of the supply chain.

The marketplace

The railway currently accounts for 11% of the UK's inland surface freight and is expected to double the volume of goods it moves (measured in net tonne kilometres) by 2043. Freight operators run trains across the length and breadth of the UK – moving china clay from Cornwall, delivering supermarket goods to Inverness, transporting oil from Milford Haven and shipping containers from the southern ports to locations across the UK. Rail freight carries everything from high-end whiskies, to fuel for power stations, to luxury cars for export.

Rail freight transports goods worth £30bn a year, moving one in four of the containers entering the UK and half of the fuel used in electricity generation. It can shift freight more quickly, safely and reliably than lorries as well as transporting goods in bulk. According to the Rail Delivery Group, rail freight generates more than £1.5bn a year in economic benefits for UK companies through improved productivity, reduced congestion and wider environmental benefits.

Five freight operators dominate the market:

- DB Schenker Rail UK – The largest rail haulier in Britain employs more than 3,000 people. A subsidiary of Germany's Deutsche Bahn, DB Schenker has headquarters in Doncaster. Prior to 2009 the company was known as English, Welsh & Scottish Railway (EWS).
- Colas Rail – Owned by French conglomerate Bouygues, Colas offers a range of freight services and runs maintenance trains for Network Rail.
- Direct Rail Services – DRS is a wholly owned subsidiary of the Nuclear Decommissioning Authority, making it the only publicly owned rail freight company. It was established in 1995 and its main business is transporting spent fuel from nuclear power stations to Sellafield in Cumbria for processing. DRS has extended its activities in other areas and has more than 350 staff. From May 2015 DRS locomotives and coaches provided some of passenger operator Northern Rail's services between Carlisle and Barrow-in-Furness.
- Freightliner – The largest intermodal operator, much of Freightliner's business is moving containers from ports to rail freight terminals inland. The company employs 2,500 staff. In March 2015 the business was bought by US railroad company Genesee & Wyoming.
- GB Railfreight – A subsidiary of Europorte, part of Eurotunnel, GBRf says it has a team of 600 people operating more than 1,000 train loads a week for customers including E.ON, Network Rail, EDF Energy, UK Coal, Merrill Lynch, Tarmac and Drax.

The major rail freight companies directly employ more than 5,000 people and have a combined annual turnover of more than £850m. The businesses of these and smaller rail freight operators hinge on trying to ensure that the cost of inland distribution by rail freight is competitively priced compared to road. These firms are open access operators that have reserved slots in the timetable, which they use only when they need to do so. Rail freight companies currently pay access charges on an incremental basis: they do not contribute to the substantial core costs of the rail network.

As with passenger services, the DfT and Transport Scotland define the respective high-level strategy and taxpayer funding for the rail freight industry. In addition to promoting improvements to railway performance, the Office of Rail and Road approves the level and structure of charges that freight operators pay Network Rail in order to run services.

Rail freight companies do not have many of the financial protections afforded to passenger operators in franchise agreements. They are fully exposed to changes in the charging regime and assume the risks associated with rolling stock and other infrastructure investments.

ABOVE Freight train operators provide fuel for many of Britain's power stations. Here DB Schenker locomotive No 66118 stands at Eggborough Power Station after arriving from Immingham. *Courtesy of Paul Simon Wood, DB Schenker Rail UK driver*

Since privatisation rail freight revenue has grown by £260m, or 44%. Two-thirds of this revenue comes from the industry's traditional markets where rail is typically the best suited mode of transport; for example, coal for power generation and other single customer bulk commodities.

In recent years coal has been the dominant commodity, accounting for 32% of all the goods moved by rail. This is forecast to change significantly as environmental legislation is expected to result in an 80% fall in the volume of coal transported by 2023. But Network Rail's 2013 Freight Market Study suggests that this decline in coal moved will be more than offset by the forecast growth of the intermodal and biomass markets by 2023. Domestic intermodal – the moving of goods by rail for part of their journey within the UK – is set to grow, as is the growth in transporting goods

Table 4: Rail freight forecasts to 2019 and 2030 (billion tonne km)				
	2006	2019	2030	Average annual growth 2006-30
Solid fuels	8	6	5	-2%
Construction	4	4	5	1%
Metals and ore	3	3	3	0%
Ports: intermodal	4	10	17	6%
Domestic: intermodal	1	6	12	11%
Other	3	3	3	0%
Total	22	32	45	3%
Source: Network Rail/DfT Strategic Rail Freight Interchange Policy Guidance				

unloaded from ports – partly helped by major developments at Felixstowe and the new London Gateway.

The ability of freight operators to move goods quickly, safely, reliably and in bulk makes the railway ideal for all sorts of uses. As well as coal, trains transport biomass and spent nuclear fuel. Rail freight carries finished Minis, Land Rovers and Jaguars from factories in the Midlands and the North West to ports for export all over the world. Major construction projects such as Heathrow Terminal 5 and the Olympic Park have benefited from the reliability and capability of rail freight. Freight trains have helped shift excavated material from Crossrail tunnelling, and London receives 40% of its raw construction materials by rail freight. The equivalent of 55,000 heavy goods vehicles worth of domestic rubbish is transported out of Britain's major cities by rail each year.

Looking after the interests of this part of the rail industry is the Rail Freight Group, a company limited by guarantee. Originally formed in 1991 to represent the views of those involved with the rail freight industry, any revenue it collects (annual membership costs £1,495 as of September 2014) is put back into providing services to members.

Loading and unloading locations

There are several hundred existing freight sites in Britain with connections to the national rail network. Types of site include private sidings, facilities owned by freight operating companies, Network Rail sites, and land bank sites held by Network Rail for potential future freight use. To establish a connection to the national rail network from a new freight site, an agreement must be put in place between Network Rail and the freight operating company or 'adjacent facility owner'. There is a charge payable for connection.

Network Rail lists more than 60 strategic freight sites, but the size and capability of these vary and many are not in the right location to function as part of a modern supply chain. Facilities include intermodal-only rail freight interchanges, rail-linked warehousing freight interchanges, and bulk material terminals – which handle products such as coal, aggregates, cement and cars. Bulk terminals are almost always owned and operated by a single company handling a particular type of product.

Recent trends have seen a decline in the amount of bulk material transported by rail and a move towards intermodal use whereby consumer goods are conveyed by rail for part of their journey before being transferred to road for the final leg.

However, over the years the location of rail freight interchanges has not changed much in terms of geographic spread, and for those in urban locations there is often little or no opportunity to expand. As a result of the physical constraints and lack of available warehousing, some rail freight locations have closed.

The Government-endorsed solution to

ABOVE DB Schenker Rail UK is the largest freight haulier in Britain and employs more than 3,000 people. This is one of the operator's trains pictured at Rotherham Steel Terminal. *Courtesy of Michael Pattrick, DB Schenker Rail UK driver*

meeting modern needs and to allow more freight to be transported by rail is to develop strategic rail freight interchanges (SRFIs). An SRFI is a large multi-purpose rail freight interchange and distribution centre linked into both the rail and trunk road system. It has rail-connected warehousing and container handling facilities and may also include manufacturing and processing activities.

The aim of an SRFI is to optimise the use of rail as part of a freight journey by maximising the distance goods can travel by train, then making it easy to move them as required to reach their final destination. SRFIs are a key element in reducing the cost to users of moving freight by rail and are therefore important in making it easy to transfer freight from road to rail.

To work effectively, SRFIs need to be located close to the business markets they will serve – major urban centres, or groups of centres – and linked to key supply chain routes. The need for effective connections for both rail and road means that the number of locations suitable for an SRFI will be limited.

Existing operational SRFIs and other intermodal rail freight interchanges are situated predominantly in the Midlands and the North of England. In London and the South East, away from the deep-sea ports, most intermodal rail freight interchanges and rail-connected warehousing are on a small scale and/or poorly located in relation to the main urban areas where the demand for goods lies.

To date only one SRFI has been granted planning consent in the whole of the South East. This is partly because SRFIs often attract opposition from local communities, as planning battles in the East Midlands and Hertfordshire have shown.

That may be partly because, as defined in the Planning Act 2008, an SRFI is a larger-than-typical rail freight interchange in excess of 60 hectares. As a minimum, an SRFI should be able to accommodate four trains per day and, where possible, be capable of increasing the number of trains handled. SRFIs should ideally have the capability to handle 775-metre trains with appropriately configured on-site infrastructure and layout. This should seek to minimise the need for on-site rail shunting and provide for a configuration that, again ideally,

will allow main-line access for trains from either direction.

Whether welcomed or not by nearby residents, rail freight forecasts indicate the need for an expanded network of large SRFIs across the regions to accommodate the anticipated long-term growth in rail freight. These also indicate that new rail freight interchanges, especially in areas poorly served by such facilities at present, are likely to attract substantial business, generally new to rail.

ABOVE Energy and fuel suppliers rely on freight train operators. GB Railfreight's customers include E.ON, Greenergy, EDF, UK Coal and Drax. *GB Railfreight*

Size matters

The ability to move a railway vehicle and its load on a particular part of the national network depends on the height and width profile, known as the loading gauge, of the route concerned. A train must comply with the route loading gauge to ensure that it does not scrape or collide with structures, particularly bridges and tunnels but also station platforms, canopies and overhead or lineside equipment.

In Britain the loading gauge of routes varies, reflecting historical demand for different types of trains and the construction policy of the original railway companies. Loading gauge profiles for freight vehicles are identified by a 'W' prefix and a number. As the route number rises so, broadly speaking, does the size of the vehicle that can pass. A W6 freight train or wagon will be able to operate over most of the national rail network.

For rail freight to turn a profit, big trains are better. One of the key demands of the rail freight industry has been for gauge enhancement to allow greater access to the network for the increasingly prevalent 'high cube' 9ft 6in W10 containers, which are fast becoming a global standard, being transported by ships and unloaded at ports. With this in mind Network Rail has been funded by Government to carry out extensive gauge enhancements to strategic freight routes so that freight operators can run trains with larger loads.

The route from the West Coast Main Line to Southampton has been upgraded and a series of projects on the Nuneaton-Felixstowe route (including new rail connections at Nuneaton and Ipswich) have been completed, with more planned during Control Period 5. The DfT says that a strategic rail freight interchange should be located on a route with a gauge clearance of at least W8, or one that is capable of enhancement to a suitable gauge. However, the rail industry is already looking beyond W8 and W10 at how it can accommodate W11 and W12 trains to ensure compatibility with deep-sea transported containers.

Investment in freight

The Rail Delivery Group says that rail freight operators have invested more than £2bn in new locomotives, wagons and other capital equipment since the 1990s. To date 70% of investment has been targeted at enhancing capacity and capability; for example longer, heavier trains. The remainder of the investment has been focused on improving freight performance on the network, for example by making rolling stock more reliable. Operator plans for Control Period 5 see investment equally split between enhancing capacity and improving performance on the network.

Network Rail (via the Strategic Freight Network), Government (through the Transport Innovation Fund) and other funding sources spent more than £500m to improve freight capacity and performance during Control Period 4. A further £200m has been allocated for the development of the Strategic Freight Network in England and Wales in Control Period 5, and £30m has been committed to the Scottish Strategic Rail Freight Investment Fund.

These investments cover a range of capacity, capability and performance enhancements that benefit rail freight. They include improving gauge clearance to allow deep-sea containers to be transported along main lines and via diversionary routes, and allowing longer freight trains to operate by extending loops, enhancing signalling and adding additional chords (curves connecting different routes).

As well as the money spent by rail freight operators and Government, many infra-structure providers that rely on the rail network have themselves made investments to improve

BELOW GB Railfreight is a subsidiary of Europorte, part of Eurotunnel, and transports more than 1,000 train loads a week. *GB Railfreight*

the performance and capability of rail freight. Ports, power stations and distribution centres have all made significant investments in infrastructure. In the past seven years more than £250m has been spent by Britain's ports on rail-connected facilities to handle container and bulk traffic (at Felixstowe, Southampton, London Gateway, Hull and Immingham) with further investment anticipated.

The future for rail freight

Rail freight exists to provide a cost-effective and sustainable transport service for its customers. Its future will be determined by market trends that are affecting businesses generally and their supply chains in particular. These factors can be contradictory – for example, globalisation alongside consumers' increasing awareness of sustainability issues.

In his role as a vice-president of the Chartered Institute of Logistics and Transport, Jim Steer outlined the following market trends affecting users of rail freight:

- Globalisation: increased trade as a percentage of GDP has been a continuous trend for many years and is set to continue.
- Centralisation: businesses continue to seek economies of scale by centralising production and distribution.
- Rising commodity costs: an increasing population and global prosperity inevitably put pressure on the prices of commodities including coal, oil, steel and other metals.
- Rising costs of road transport: fuel and congestion costs and possible road pricing may make sending goods by road less attractive.
- Sustainability: whether driven by Government, consumers, or businesses themselves, there are signs that supply chains are changing to improve sustainability.
- E-Logistics: the rise of the internet means more home shopping and home deliveries of goods.
- Supply chain changes: the past two decades have seen a concerted move towards centralised supply chains. While this may continue, market changes will see a wider variety of supply chain solutions being adopted; for example, some businesses may locate their hubs at ports rather than in the Midlands.

The rail freight sector is well placed to respond to these changes given that rail is less sensitive than road to changes in the price of oil. On average, a gallon of diesel will move a tonne of goods 246 miles on rail but only 88 miles by road.[14] Rail is also effective at moving a high volume of goods to and from ports, while trends in the rail freight sector and wider supply chain are leading businesses to invest in rail hubs surrounded by large distribution centres. With Network Rail and freight operators working to provide support for longer and heavier trains, it will increasingly by possible for rail freight to generate efficiencies and compete against road transport. Rail also has the edge on sustainability, not only in terms of greenhouse gases, but also because of its relative safety and impact on communities.

While there is plenty to suggest that rail freight can continue to play a key role in transporting goods, the sector also needs to respond to a range of challenges if it is to prosper and provide an effective distribution mechanism for suppliers.

Despite investment in the past decade, there continues to be a lack of rail-connected distribution facilities. Most retail and manufacturing centres are a long way from a rail head. Until the planning system makes it easier to build intermodal terminals, efforts to get more freight on to the railway are likely to be thwarted.

Other challenges include network capacity limitations, prompted by the surge in passenger use of the railway as well as an increase in the number of freight trains that operate. Therefore, freight operators are supportive of potentially transformational investments such as the European Rail Traffic Management System and High Speed 2, which have the potential to release more freight paths.

Track access charges

Operators are also looking for access charge stability. Given that these account for a significant proportion of their businesses' costs, a stable structure for determining freight access charges is vital to give operators the confidence to make the long-term investments in trains and other assets that will enable freight services to run.

In 2013 the ORR announced a new package of charges for freight operators to access the rail network, which is to be phased into use from 2016.[15] It says that the changes, including price caps for transporting different materials, will better reflect industry costs and give businesses certainty to plan for the future.

In setting the new access charges, the Regulator noted that rail freight trains create costs of £280-£400m each year through factors such as the wear and tear on tracks. Under the previous charging regime, freight companies typically covered only around 21-28% of these costs, with passengers and taxpayers making up the shortfall.

If the rail freight industry can grasp and respond to the challenges it faces, there are plenty of opportunities to build on progress to date. For example, it is clear that the volume of rail freight being transported through the Channel Tunnel is well below the potential of the infrastructure: the tunnel was forecast to carry 35 trains per day in each direction, but the reality is barely 10% of this. If pricing mechanisms and the complexities of operating trains across multiple domestic railways can be addressed, more freight services will run.

While some traditional road hauliers such as Stobart, Malcolm and Russells have taken seriously the opportunities offered by rail freight, others either ignore the possibilities or expect rail freight to replicate road freight services. To maximise the benefits of rail freight, businesses may need to restructure their supply chains, but in the long term this could give them a competitive advantage.

ABOVE Major developments at ports, including London Gateway and Felixstowe, are creating additional demand for moving goods by rail.
GB Railfreight

4 • Funding and investment

Most of the money required to operate, maintain and enhance Britain's national rail network comes from train fares paid by passengers and central government grants. Funding is allocated in five-year blocks, known as control periods, with CP5 running from 1 April 2014 to 31 March 2019. Changes to fares – usually increases – typically take effect on the first day of the calendar year.

Finding the money to meet the perpetual requirements for routine maintenance, improvements, upgrades and pet projects demanded by those within the rail industry, passengers and elected representatives is a constant challenge. The question 'where does the money come from' dominates most aspects of how the railway works and has resulted in a never-ending quest to find ingenious ways to top up the railway budget.

So while most of the money comes from fares and central government rail budgets, there are many other potential sources of funding. Within the railway funding envelope it has become established practice for Network Rail to borrow against its assets to release additional money to spend, and industry bosses are encouraged to develop commercial opportunities that could reduce the call on the public purse. Outside, there are local government funding streams to tap and opportunities to line up private finance.

How much does the railway cost?

Between 1 April 2012 and 31 March 2013 the cost of running Britain's railways was £12.3bn. This represents a real terms increase of 2.1% on 2011-12 and a rise of 0.1% compared to 2011. However, when increases in passenger numbers are taken into account the cost of running the railways in 2012-13 was up 0.2% on the year before and down 6.2% on 2010-11.

During 2012-13 the rail industry had income of £12.9bn. This breaks down as £7.7bn (60%) from fares and £4bn (31%) in net Government funding, with the remaining £1.2bn (9%) attributed to other income received by Network Rail and train operators – for example, rents from retail premises and car park charges.

Who pays for it?

Both the Coalition and Labour Governments attempted, with some success, to move away from a 50/50 taxpayer/farepayer funding model and require users of the railway to pick up a greater share of costs. The ORR says that passengers' contribution to industry costs has increased over the past three years (up to 59.2% from 57.4% the year before and 55.6% in 2010-11).[16] The Holy Grail for those in government is to eliminate the state subsidy, and these figures suggest that the trend is in the right direction even if the ultimate goal remains some way off.

In 2012-13 total income from passenger fares was 3.6% higher than in the previous year because of the rise in the number of passenger journeys on the network. Government funding decreased by 4.2% compared with 2011-12, and was down 9.1% on 2010-11.

The core Government spending on the railway splits into the Network Grant – money given to Network Rail – and franchise subsidies payable to train operators. In 2012-13 the Network Grant was £4bn and Government made franchise payments of £1.9bn. However, some franchises pay premiums to the Government and in 2012-13 a total of £1.9bn was returned, cancelling out the franchise subsidies.

During the year train operators received £8.4bn, £7.7bn of this from passenger fares.

ABOVE London Underground's '72' Bakerloo Line rolling stock is due to be replaced by the New Tube for London programme – but not until the late 2020s. In the meantime body shells have been welded and reinforced to ensure the carriages remain safe for passengers.

The train operators passed on £2bn of this to Network Rail in payments for track access and other charges. Train firms paid £1.5bn for rolling stock charges, £2.3bn to staff and £2.5bn for other costs – a total of £8.3bn.

Network Rail ended up with £6.6bn during the year – a Network Grant of £4bn, track access charges payable by train operators amounting to £2bn, and other income of £0.6bn. The organisation spent £6bn of this – £2.7bn went on operating costs, £1.8bn for depreciation and £1.5bn for financing costs.

There are significant variations between England, Scotland and Wales in the level of Government funding for the railway. As a proportion of total income England had the lowest level of Government funding, 27% of the total England industry income, compared to 54% for Scotland and 56% for Wales. Government funding varied from £2.19 per passenger journey in England to £7.60 per passenger journey in Scotland and £9.33 per passenger journey in Wales.

Private sector contribution

Private investment in the railway industry – expenditure not by Network Rail or Government on fixed assets – is dominated by spend on rolling stock.

According to the ORR, £423m was invested in the railways by private companies during 2013-14.[17] This is 10% lower than the previous year and, in real terms, a fall of 12.7% when rebased to 2013-14 prices. The highest level of investment seen during recent years was £743m in 2006-07, which at today's prices is equivalent to £939m.

During 2013-14 more than £323m was spent on rolling stock, accounting for 76.2% of private investment, which could include payments by leasing companies for new rolling stock that will be leased to train operators.

In 2013-14 no private investment was made in track and signalling, which includes new routes and new electrification, reflecting the fact that Network Rail spend is not included in this data. Private investment in stations, including retail outlet buildings, during 2013-14 was £28.6m, accounting for

6.8% of total private investment. This investment level is consistent with the previous four years.

During 2013-14 other investment, which includes all other spending associated with the rail business, such as non-rail vehicles and IT costs, was just over £72m, accounting for 17% of total private investment. This represented the lowest level of other investment since 2009-10.

Setting a budget

As mentioned above, funding for the railway – specifically how much money Network Rail is allowed to spend – is allocated in five-year control periods. This is one of the cornerstones of the privatised system and is generally viewed as one of the more successful because once five-year budgets are set they are difficult to unpick by Government. In contrast, British Rail often had to operate within the constraints of short-term funding settlements and budgets subject to the whims of ministers and the ever-changing political landscape.

The process for determining the five-year control period budget is overseen by the Office of Rail and Road, which carries out what is known as a periodic review. This gets under way in earnest when the UK and Scottish Governments each publish a High Level Output Specification (HLOS) – detailing what they want the railway to deliver during the control period – and Statements of Funds Available (SoFA) – setting out how much money they are willing to spend on the railway.

Following this Network Rail publishes a strategic plan explaining how it intends to deliver the outputs required by each Government, and the ORR produces a Draft Determination detailing how much money it thinks Network Rail needs to carry out this work. It can require the Governments to provide more funding or scale back their ambitions for the railway if it feels the output specification is incompatible with the money made available. The Regulator may also call on Network Rail to add or remove investments from its plan as it sees fit.

There is then usually a period of 'horse trading' during which Network Rail argues that it needs more money to achieve the outputs required of it. The ORR will typically accept some but not all of these points, then publish a Final Determination offering a slightly more generous settlement.

All parties are obliged to provide the information above within clearly defined timescales so that the Final Determination can be issued two years before the control period is due to begin. In the past the Final Determination has marked the point at which the budget for the next five years is largely fixed and everyone – rail industry, stakeholders and the public – then knows what to expect.

Control Period 5

Funding for the current control period – CP5 – was set out by the ORR's Final Determination in October 2013. This concluded the Regulator's periodic review (in this case PR13), the process to work out how much money Network Rail should be allowed to spend in different areas between 1 April 2014 and 31 March 2019.

Table 5: Network Rail spending overview

	CP4 (adjusted) £bn	CP5 Final Determination £bn
Operating expenditure	13.756	13.367
Renewals	12.686	12.107
Enhancements	11.294	12.818
Total expenditure	**37.735**	**38.293**

Source: ORR PR13 Final Determination, page 30

ABOVE The Digby Wyatt train shed at Bristol Temple Meads contains a car park and pedestrian route. However, funding has been agreed to reinstate platforms in order to provide additional station capacity.

The total expenditure stipulated by the ORR for CP5 was £38.293bn. As Table 5 shows, the budget allocated splits roughly into three parts: £13.4m has been set aside for operating the railway, including routine maintenance; £12.1m has been allocated for renewals (like-for-like replacement of life-expired track and other infrastructure); and £12.8m for enhancement projects. These figures are not dissimilar to the amount of money that was spent during Control Period 4 (2009-14).

Statements from Coalition (and subsequently Conservative) Government ministers and the Department for Transport have regularly referred to 'the £38 billion investment being delivered by government/Network Rail between 2014 and 2019'. Talk of 'investment' is perhaps misleading given that two thirds of this money is being used simply to keep the existing rail network going. In terms of creating a bigger and better railway, the ORR sanctioned investment is £12.8bn.

For Control Period 5 the ORR introduced an enhancements cost adjustment mechanism (ECAM). The logic behind this stems from £7bn of the £12bn worth of schemes backed by Government for delivery in CP5 not having been developed to a sufficient degree where there was confidence in costings around the time of the Final Determination. Therefore the ORR agreed an overall funding envelope, but offered Network Rail flexibility as to budget allocations for individual projects.

According to the ORR: 'As outputs and scope become more clearly defined we expected that costs could rise for some projects and fall for others and should the overall amount exceed the levels originally assumed in the final determination then governments would decide the way forwards; as it would affect how much funding Network Rail will receive in CP6 (from 1 April 2019 to 31 March 2024) from the network grant and access charges.'[18]

ECAM is accompanied by an ongoing process of monitoring and ORR reviews of project costings. Despite the argument for funding flexibility, the reality is that with so many schemes at so many different stages of development, the information available is piecemeal. This is not helped by the sensitivities accompanying CP5 project cost overruns which have seen the ORR, Network Rail and DfT shy away from making up to date information public. Therefore keeping track of Network Rail's progress is more difficult than it was during Control Period 4.

In June 2015, just over a year into the CP5 programme, Transport Secretary Patrick McLoughlin told Parliament that key aspects of Network Rail's investment programme were costing more and taking longer than planned. As a result, work on two major electrification schemes was paused and a revised railway upgrade programme was due to be published in autumn 2015.

Regulatory asset base

The regulatory (or regulated) asset base (RAB) is often referred to as Network Rail's credit card. It provides a mechanism for funding renewals and enhancements now and paying for them later. The theory is that by delivering this work the value of the rail network increases and this can retrospectively be used to help pay for the investment.

At each five-year periodic review the Office of Rail and Road determines a percentage annual rate of return and multiplies it by the value of the RAB at the end of the previous control period. The resulting total is added to Network Rail's income during the new control period. This money can then be used to pay the interest on the RAB borrowing.

Although this mechanism has allowed Network Rail to continue to borrow large sums of money, the capital investment has not been paid down. Instead, the organisation has a burgeoning debt mountain and it remains unclear how – or if – this money will ever be repaid. Continuing the credit card analogy, Network Rail can be likened to a card holder who pays little more than the minimum payment required to service the RAB debt.

BELOW Once there were four tracks and soon there will be again: at Lawrence Hill station new tracks are to be laid to increase capacity between Bristol Parkway and Temple Meads.

ABOVE The disused 'Varsity line' between Bicester and Bletchley is to be reopened as a twin-track, electrified passenger railway as part of the East West Rail Link scheme.

Since the RAB was established under Railtrack in 2000, debt has increased from around £3bn to £33bn in 2013/14.[19] Over the years it has been used for a range of purposes, including mopping up the overspend in maintenance that was required after the 2000 Hatfield disaster. In recent years Governments have looked to it to finance additional investment in the rail network – such as for the Edinburgh-Glasgow Improvement Programme – which would otherwise exceed permitted budgets.

The Office of Rail and Road limits how much can be borrowed against the RAB annually and requires Network Rail to each year pay amortisation – a relatively small payment to reduce the debt, which is roughly one-thirtieth of the total RAB value. In theory the increase in value of the RAB each year makes additional borrowing sustainable. Network Rail says that the gearing measure of regulatory asset base to regulatory net debt of 65% remains comfortably within the 75% limit set by the ORR.[20]

Despite this, the amount of borrowing against the company's assets continues to rise, prompting some commentators to question whether this is sustainable and to suggest that a future Government will have to write off some or all of the debt. With Network Rail now a Government body and subject to stricter Treasury financial controls, what some might argue has been a cavalier approach to borrowing seems unlikely to continue.

A variation on using the RAB to pay for projects is the ORR's Investment Framework process. While a framework-funded enhancement is still paid for up front by borrowing against the RAB, the cost is recouped through train operators paying a facility charge, typically over a 30-year period. This allows the capital cost of a scheme to be paid back and the charge can be added to a franchise holder's fixed track access charge, allowing it to be transferred to a new franchisee when the current agreement expires.

This gets round the recurring problem of franchise holders wanting long-term certainty before committing to investment. A train operator whose franchise is due to expire in a couple of years is unlikely to underwrite an enhancement scheme, but may be prepared to pay a facility charge for two years if the liability for the remaining cost will pass to the next franchisee. The DfT agrees for the facility charge to span multiple franchise periods (if required). In effect, the train operator and its successor(s) have a mortgage with Network Rail until the facility charge term ends.

The Investment Framework use of the RAB has not been widely adopted but it is being used by Chiltern Railways to deliver the Evergreen 3 scheme to create a new rail route between London Marylebone and Oxford.[21]

BELOW Network Rail has invested in high output machinery, which can automatically lay ballast, sleepers and rails, to speed up track renewals and increase productivity during overnight possessions.

Railway as revenue earner

Government grants and income from fares are essential to keep the railway going. But as the custodian of infrastructure and associated property assets valued at a hefty £49.8bn[22], Network Rail is in a position to earn revenue from some of its assets that can make a contribution to railway running costs. Unsurprisingly, the Government is keen for Network Rail to pursue any reasonable opportunities that can minimise the call on the public purse.

There are many different sources of income for Network Rail. These include a nationwide estate of more than 3,000 advertising hoardings, while the rebuilt Blackfriars station includes a photovoltaic roof, one of the largest in the world, which generates power to reduce the station's energy bill.

Network Rail and Transport for London have substantial property holdings and attempt to manage these in ways that will bring in income that can be reinvested in the railway. Often this is through small-scale

ABOVE Cramped King's Cross Thameslink station was shut in 2007 and replaced a short distance up the line by cavernous St Pancras Thameslink. The Class 319 train seen here is due to be cascaded as new rolling stock is delivered.

arrangements such as letting out railway arches as offices or workshop space.

In 2008 Network Rail and construction firm Kier entered into a joint venture known as Solum Regeneration with the aim of completing major redevelopments of under-utilised station sites that could make them worth more and generate other income. The focus is on commercial property rather than transport improvements – although station enhancements can be included in individual schemes. Projects have been completed at Epsom and Walthamstow Central with approvals secured to build a multi-storey car park at Haywards Heath. In 2015 Capital & Counties Properties acquired Kier's share of Solum Regeneration although Kier remains involved with property redevelopments on and around railway station sites.

Retail

In recent years increasing importance has been attached to the role retail can play within a transport environment. St Pancras International, reopened to serve High Speed 1 in 2007, is regularly cited as an example of a destination station – somewhere people will go to shop and eat, not just to travel from.

Letting out retail units to sell food or other goods at stations is seen by Network Rail as a major opportunity to boost its 'other' income. Like-for-like station retail sales were up 7.8% year on year in February 2014, outperforming the high street, and Network Rail has made no secret of its desire to increase this revenue stream.

The February 2014 retail trading figures reported that Network Rail had more than 500,000 square feet of retail space at 520 units across 16 of the stations it owned and operated (before taking on Reading and Bristol Temple Meads), with annual footfall of more than a billion people.

But how can it balance the revenue-earning potential of opening more retail units with the need to provide space to accommodate a growing number of passengers? One

ABOVE Mezzanine levels provide space for more shops – generating rental revenue for the railway. This is the balcony at King's Cross, and similar structures have been built at Waterloo and Euston.

innovative approach was to construct a balcony running the length of the station concourse at London Waterloo with new escalator connections that allowed space on the first floor of the station to be opened up as shops in 2012. Retail kiosks in the middle of the concourse were then removed to improve passenger flows. A similar approach has been adopted at London Euston.

Network Rail is also planning major station upgrades to provide a significant increase in the number of shops and restaurants. The King's Cross western ticket hall is a prime example of this and helped to generate a 26% year-on-year increase in retail sales.

Train operators, which generally manage smaller stations, also have an opportunity to generate income from car park charges, letting out space at stations and providing vending machines. Merseyrail has rolled out a series of Mtogo outlets, which combine a station ticket office with a convenience store and are modelled on parent company Ned Rail's experience of Holland's Albert Heijn retail chain – with its emphasis on chilled food. In 2014 there were Mtogo stores at Hamilton Square, Hooton, Lime Street Underground, Liverpool Central, Maghull, Moorfields, Moorfields Old Hall Street, Southport and Liverpool Waterloo.

In December 2013 Network Rail announced plans to provide parcel collection facilities at stations. While the internet makes it easy to buy online, many commuters struggle to find time to be at home for when packages are delivered. The Doddle chain – a joint venture with entrepreneur Lloyd Dorfman – offers a solution, and the aim is to capitalise on the huge number of people passing through stations.

Parcel collection services are emerging as a new revenue opportunity for station owners. London Underground is experimenting with a range of initiatives including parcel collection lockers at stations and partnerships with Amazon, Tesco and Waitrose. With most

Underground station ticket offices due to shut by the end of 2015, there will increasingly be vacant space at stations that can be converted to retail, and any income reinvested in the transport network.

Overseas work to fund the railway back home?

One of the unforeseen consequences of rail privatisation has been to open up Britain's rail market to state-owned organisations outside the UK. As discussed in Chapter 2, Abellio, Deutsche Bahn and Keolis/SNCF all play a major role in running trains in Britain despite ultimately having headquarters and profit centres in the Netherlands, Germany and France respectively.

Post British Rail there is no direct equivalent in the UK to explore market opportunities abroad. But Network Rail, the nearest fit to the state-owned rail giants on the continent, has in recent years set up a stand-alone consulting arm positioned to pitch for business overseas.

Network Rail Consulting was launched in 2012 to follow up opportunities to use its home-grown rail expertise in the USA, India, Australia, New Zealand, Brazil, northern Europe and the Middle and Far East. Its first major contract win was in 2013 when Transport for New South Wales appointed the infrastructure firm to act as independent safety assessor for the design and delivery of the £4.8bn North West Rail Link in Sydney. In 2015 it secured its largest contract to date working with Serco and Freightliner Group to support the Saudi Railway Company's North South Railway, one of the largest rail projects in the world.

Network Rail has repeatedly played down the potential of the consulting business to earn big money, tending instead to focus on how it can share expertise and act as an ambassador for Britain's railways. However, there is clearly an opportunity – depending on how successful the consulting team is in winning work – to generate income that can be invested back in Britain.

BELOW Network Rail has set up a chain of parcel collection stores under the Doddle brand as one of its many initiatives to develop additional revenue streams for the railway.

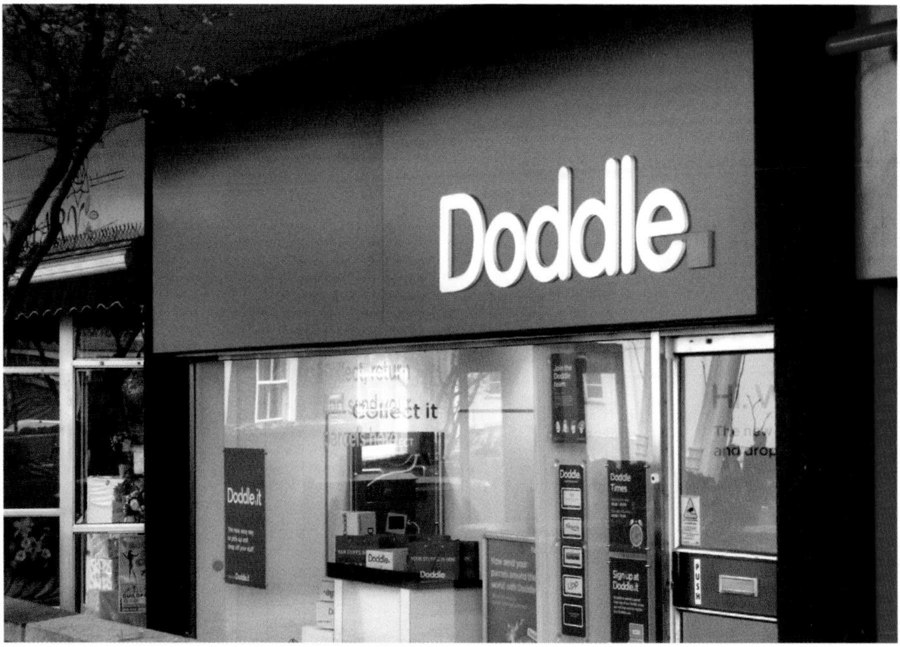

Beyond the railway

Beyond Network Rail and the Regulator-determined funding settlements are opportunities to attract additional money for rail from a range of public and private sources.

Local transport funding

Outside dedicated Government funding for rail, one of the biggest opportunities for securing additional public money is through the process by which grants are awarded for major transport schemes – typically those costing more than £5m. Rail has to compete with roads, buses and cycling for funding, but any successful bids allow improvements to the railway on top of what the ORR settlement allows. Often grants are agreed on the condition that some sort of private funding contribution is provided.

Prior to the 2010 General Election these 'local transport majors' were nominated through the Regional Funding Allocation process. Subsequently the Coalition Government overhauled devolved decision-making, dismantling the regional apparatus in favour of a system of city regions and mega business districts known as local enterprise partnerships. However, RFA rail schemes developed under the Labour Government (such as the Croxley rail link and enhanced Nuneaton-Coventry service) are only now being built and, until these projects are completed, the defunct system continues to exert influence.

The Local Growth Fund system created by the Coalition Government covers major transport schemes for implementation between 2015 and 2021. According to ministers it devolves decisions on which major transport schemes to prioritise, and allows businesses, represented through local enterprise partnerships, to influence the shortlist of schemes.

The money available is split into two tranches with a 'formula' element to be shared out between local transport bodies according to the size and population of the area they represent. There is then a 'competitive' element of the Local Growth Fund: bids are invited with decisions ultimately taken by central government, arguably negating the significance of the devolution move.

Whatever the devolution credentials, 'growth deals' have made significant extra funding available for rail. Allocations announced in 2014 included money for Midland Metro light rail extensions, new trams for Manchester, work to improve or provide 20 railway stations, electrification of the railway to Hull, resignalling of the Cornish main line, and reopening of the Halton Curve in Cheshire.

Assorted funding pots

There are many different funds established by Government that, on occasions, provide further cash for rail projects. Pots are often created as part of Government initiatives and hence come and go between administrations and often have an unashamedly political purpose.

Examples of this in practice include, under the Coalition Government, additional resources for the railway from funding pots to deliver the Todmorden Curve (Regional Growth Fund) and to link the Swanage Railway to the national network at Wareham (Coastal Communities Fund). The Labour Government's Community Infrastructure Fund paid for Aylesbury Vale Parkway station.

Public Private Partnerships

Opportunities to secure funding to improve the railway without increasing fares or taxes are always attractive to Government, and private finance can potentially offer a means of achieving this. At its simplest level a company might decide to contribute to the cost of a project because it has benefits for its business. The Coalition Government hopes that the local enterprise partnership (LEP) structure, which gives business leverage in transport planning decisions, will provide an incentive for firms to contribute financially. Others have their doubts – the House of Commons Transport Committee's inquiry into local transport funding found no evidence that there are significant sources of additional funding easily available to LEPs.[23]

ABOVE **A handful of stations are usually added to the national rail network each year. This is Newcourt, on the Exmouth branch line, which opened in 2015 to serve a new housing estate.** *Roger Fieldhouse*

There are also a number of more formal Public Private Partnership (PPP) models that have been used or adapted for rail purposes. These are characterised by joint working and risk sharing between the public and private sectors, and they can include relatively simple outsourcing-type partnerships – where services are provided on short- or medium-term contracts – or longer-run private finance partnerships such as the Private Finance Initiative (PFI).

An ambitious PPP model was chosen by the Labour Government to deliver major investment in the London Underground network. This was forced through despite opposition from London's Mayor at the time, Ken Livingstone. The PPP proved massively complex and resulted in a situation where the public-sector-operated Underground was unable to compel three private consortia to act in the ways it felt would be of most benefit to passengers. The consortia also struggled to meet their investment and maintenance obligations and eventually ran out of money. The final consortium was returned to the public sector in 2010, giving the Mayor (Livingstone was succeeded by Conservative Boris Johnson) full control over the investment programme. It is a curious paradox that Labour initiated the part-privatisation of the Underground network while under Tory control it has been renationalised.

Private Finance Initiative

For large stand-alone projects, the Private Finance Initiative (PFI) was a feature of Labour's term in office. It worked by getting private companies to raise the money needed for a capital project, which would be paid back with fees, typically over 30 years, from the public purse. The advantage was that major schemes could go ahead where there was no money to pay for them up front.

On the minus side, PFIs raised concerns that taxpayers were committed to servicing a long-term debt that could prove unaffordable or might compromise other local budgets. Concerns have also been raised about the charges and the fact that a project could end up

CASE STUDY – NOTTINGHAM EXPRESS TRANSIT

To deliver a light rail system in Nottingham, the the Arrow consortium (which included Nottingham City Transport and tram-builder Bombardier) had to find the necessary funds while the state undertook to reimburse 70% of its initial investment over a period of 27 years. It was also agreed that Arrow would cover any extra costs in case of problems during the works. To recuperate the remaining 30% the private partner was granted management of the line on the basis of a contract guaranteeing quality of service. If the conditions were not fulfilled the state's monthly contributions would decrease. This previously untried formula took a long time to work out – more than seven years from the project's launch to the implementation of phase one.[24]

When plans to build two NET lines were developed a new deal was drawn up. It was agreed that the line one concession would be absorbed into a new 23 year concession covering the old and new lines. The competition to let the concession saw Arrow lose out to Tramlink Nottingham, a consortium of Alstom, Keolis, Trent Barton-owner Wellglade and Vinci Construction, with financial backing from Meridiam Infrastructure and Infravia Fund.[25]

costing much more than if paid for up front by the state. According to the Treasury in 2012, 'the Private Finance Initiative (PFI), the form of PPP used most frequently in the United Kingdom, has become tarnished by its waste, inflexibility and lack of transparency.'[26]

Reforming PFI

The acknowledgement of PFI's weaknesses coupled with acceptance that it remains a useful financing mechanism have prompted attempts to come up with an improved model. The Coalition Government championed PF2, a series of reforms to the PFI that offer greater flexibility, transparency and tighter management of risks by the public sector to avoid the high charges levied when the private sector ends up pricing for all eventualities.

A similar approach has been taken in Scotland where the SNP-led Government has hailed the merits of a Non-Profit Distributing (NPD) model as an alternative to PFI. The NPD approach aims to eliminate uncapped equity returns and limit these returns to a reasonable rate set through competition. NPD is therefore a 'not for profit' model – contractors and lenders are expected to earn a normal market rate of return.

In terms of rail, PF2 and NPD have yet to make a major impact. The Scottish Government attempted to have the Borders Railway scheme built using NPD, but in 2011 abandoned this approach in favour of getting Network Rail to deliver the reopening project using conventional rail industry funding mechanisms.[27]

Developer contributions

It has become an established principle that property developers should make a contribution to the cost of any infrastructure improvements that are needed to make their project viable. For example, a developer building a shopping centre will typically agree to pay for local transport improvements, which could include upgrades to rail services, in order to secure planning permission.

A widely used mechanism to achieve this is a Section 106 agreement (S106) – that's Section 106 of the Town and Country Planning Act 1990. These agreements focus on site-specific mitigation of the impact of development.

There has been considerable debate about the best way of securing funding contributions for new infrastructure and how much it is appropriate for property developers to pay. The 2008 Planning Act introduced the Community Infrastructure Levy (CIL), which is now being used to help fund rail projects, notably Crossrail. The CIL has not replaced S106 agreements and has been developed to address the broader impacts of development.

The interrelation between CIL and S106 can be difficult to grasp. The Planning Advisory Service states that 'there should be no circumstances where a developer is paying CIL and S106 for the same infrastructure in relation to the same development' but adds 'the balance between the use of S106 and CIL will be different

ABOVE Network Rail is paid to maintain and renew the national network. Here a worker can be seen cutting through a rail at Long Marston.

depending on the nature of the area and the type of development being undertaken.'[28]

CIL charging regimes are gradually being adopted across England, and as a funding mechanism for rail it remains at an early stage. The one exception is Crossrail, which has a funding package predicated on £300m of S106 contributions plus £300m of CIL contributions. In November 2013 Transport for London revealed that it expects to make up a shortfall in Crossrail S106 contributions with a surplus of CIL payments[29], a move indicating that these two funding mechanisms remain interchangeable to some extent.

Europe

Grants from the European Union are regularly cited as funding sources for rail schemes. The basic premise is that member states (including the UK) pay into Europe, which then pays out with the emphasis on supporting initiatives in areas where there is seen to be a need to support regeneration.

The European Regional Development Fund (ERDF) Programme is one such fund established by the European Commission to help local areas stimulate their economic development by investing in projects that will support local businesses and create jobs.

In the UK the Department for Communities & Local Government (DCLG) acts as managing authority for this funding, which is organised by separate UK regions. The managing authority is the body designated by the European Union member state to ensure that EU structural fund programmes are implemented and that their activity conforms to EC regulations. The DCLG provides the framework for how ERDF programmes should be delivered, reporting to ministers and the European Commission. The Deansgate-Castlefield, Exchange Square and Manchester

Victoria elements of Manchester Metrolink's Second City Crossing are one example of a programme part-financed by the ERDF.

Grants for rail are also regularly awarded from the Trans European Transport Network Fund. This money is available to enhance designated long-distance TEN-T routes and can benefit both passenger and freight services. Recent awards have included money for electrification schemes in the North West and passing loops near Ely in Cambridgeshire.

Money in the form of long-term loans is available from the European Investment Bank (EIB), the European Union's bank, which is owned by and represents the interests of EU member states. The EIB is based in Luxembourg.

Over the past ten years the European Investment Bank has provided more than £6.8bn to support investment in transport infrastructure across the UK. This has included long-term loans for new Crossrail, Thameslink, Intercity Express Programme and Eurostar trains, upgrading the Docklands Light Railway and the London Overground network. New city tram networks in Manchester and Nottingham as well as the High Speed 1 line have also benefited from European Investment Bank financing.

Financing new trains

Most trains in service on the national rail network are owned by three rolling stock leasing companies (RoSCos) – Angel, Eversholt and Porterbrook. In the early years of rail privatisation the standard approach was for train operators to lead the procurement for new rolling stock; they would team up with the RoSCos, which, with clear demand for a new fleet, would be happy to arrange finance and other practicalities. Perhaps the most emblematic example of this is the West Coast 'Pendolino' fleet, commissioned by Virgin and which quickly became a symbol of the privatised railway.

In recent years train operators have had less opportunity to bring new fleets into service. Although the DfT maintains that it is for the private sector to take the lead when it comes to buying trains, there has been little evidence of this in recent years. The allocation of rolling stock has become entwined with franchise agreements (including several short-term, interim contracts) and the programme to electrify lines, the business case for which has been calculated partly on being able to redeploy trains around the network. Therefore the DfT has often been quite specific about what trains should be used where.

Despite passenger numbers surging and a requirement for new trains emerging across the country, RoSCos have been reluctant to order new trains without a clear indication that the Government will sanction the fleet for passenger service (by allowing a franchisee to commit to the higher leasing costs that would be payable for the new trains). This refusal to order speculatively combined with a shortage of trains has led to some innovative approaches to get extra units into passenger service: in December 2011 Porterbrook, South West Trains and the DfT announced a deal to merge former Gatwick Express 'Juniper' trains with SWT 'Junipers' to create ten-car trains suitable for commuter services.

Therefore the decision on whether to fund new trains largely comes down to the UK or Scottish Governments and will usually be tied in to a long-term franchise.

To complicate matters further, the DfT recognised a need for two major train procurements linked to investment programmes and decided that it was best placed to manage arrangements. A new fleet of Thameslink trains is required to make the most of the Thameslink Programme, which will provide more north-south train paths through London and offer longer services and new direct journey opportunities by the end of 2018. There was also an impending need to replace the High Speed Trains in use on many inter-city routes which, although recognised as some of the best trains in the UK, have been in service since the 1970s and early 1980s.

Each of these comprise multi-billion-pound

ABOVE Reading station has been transformed in recent years with close to £1bn being spent to provide a new concourse above the railway, five new platforms and new entrances. A new viaduct has been built as part of the efforts to untangle the railway approaches to the station and avoid trains delaying each other.

investments. Rather than shell out up front, the DfT required train builders to provide financing arrangements that would allow these major investments to be paid for over many years. The clear advantage was that the new trains could be ordered without having to find billions of pounds.

However, agreeing the complex financing arrangements – involving many banks and other partners – has proved time-consuming. A private finance deal led by Siemens to build the Thameslink trains was agreed in June 2013 two years after the company was named as preferred bidder. A second, more conventional order was subsequently placed to make new trains available for Thameslink routes in advance of the Siemens sets being delivered. The Government dropped a similar financing plan for Crossrail trains amid fears that it too could be beset by hard-to-control financing delays, something that would prove embarrassing if there were no trains available to use on completed Crossrail infrastructure.

With the Intercity Express Programme, the Government has agreed a 27½-year deal to finance, design, manufacture and maintain 866 new carriages with Agility Trains, a consortium led by train-builder Hitachi. The cost of this will be recouped through lease payments by train operators totalling £5.7bn during the life of the contracts. Therefore while the introduction of new trains has been secured, the operators of the new East Coast and Great Western franchises will not only be obliged to use these sets but also pay the premiums negotiated by Government.

Once longer rail franchises have been let, the DfT is clear that it wants responsibility for buying trains to return to the public sector. Until then the Government is likely to continue to take the lead when it comes to deciding whether or not the railway needs new trains.

5 • Devolved power

Northern Ireland

The railway in Northern Ireland operates independently of the national rail system serving England, Scotland and Wales. It consists of 333 route kilometres of track, nearly two-thirds of which is single track. The maximum permitted speed is 90mph and there are no electrified routes. Most of the network is controlled by two- or three-aspect signalling, with four-aspect used on the Dargan Bridge and semaphores on some sections of track.

Northern Ireland Railways (NIR) is not self-contained. 'Enterprise' services run by Iarnród Éireann (Irish Rail) link Belfast and Dublin providing a cross-border link. There are just over 50 stations, many little more than rural halts. Approximately one third of stations are staffed.

Train services in the province today largely follow the routes left after implementation of the 1963 Benson Report, a study undertaken on the recommendation of the more widely known Dr Richard Beeching, which resulted in similar rationalisation of the rail network to that implemented on the mainland. Six routes survive in Northern Ireland: Cross Border, Newry, Bangor, Larne, Londonderry (Northern) and the short Portrush branch.

While the scale of the rail network in Northern Ireland is much smaller than in Britain – and is used by far fewer passengers – the province has witnessed a similar upturn in the number or people choosing to travel by train, with 12.9 million using the network in 2013. This can partly be attributed to an increase in the number of car parking spaces provided at stations. Passenger numbers have doubled in little more than a decade and Northern Ireland's railway is increasingly a travel mode of choice.

In Northern Ireland the railway is used by passenger trains only. No freight has been carried on the network since 2003.

Ownership and operations

Unlike the semi-privatised structure in Britain, the Northern Ireland rail system is state-owned – Northern Ireland Railways owns and operates the network. It is part of Translink, the main provider of public transport in Northern Ireland, and in turn owned by the Northern Ireland Transport Holding Company.

The EU has granted Isolated Rail Network status, which exempts Northern Ireland from otherwise mandatory compliance with requirements aimed at standardising infrastructure connections across mainland Europe.

Class 3000 (C3K) CAF trains operate mainly on the Bangor, Portadown and Londonderry Lines. Class 4000 trains were introduced on the Larne Line and Portrush branch line between 2011 and 2013. Trains are wheelchair accessible and services operate Monday to Saturday with a reduced frequency on Sundays.

Northern Ireland's Department for Regional Development provides a capital grant for Northern Ireland Railways to operate rail services. The funding helps maintain and develop the rail infrastructure and rolling stock.

The system runs at a loss. Investment is monitored by the Northern Ireland Government's Public Transport Services Division, which checks that projects demonstrate value for taxpayers' money and that expenditure falls within budgetary limits. Between 2004/05 and 2013/14, the Department for Regional Development funded more than £400m of capital works on the railway in Northern Ireland.

Rolling stock

The coaches and locomotives for the cross-border 'Enterprise' service are jointly provided by NIR and Irish Rail. Each company owns two seven-car sets. The 'Enterprise' trains are now more than 17 years old and a refurbishment programme is under way. An overhaul of the

ABOVE In Northern Ireland trains are operated by public sector organisation Translink. Spending is allocated by the Department for Regional Development. *Translink*

mechanical system and interiors of the rolling stock was completed in 2009.

'Enterprise' rolling stock has a design life of around 30 years and European funding is likely to be sought to progress plans to electrify the Belfast-Dublin line so that when replacement trains are ordered they can be electric multiple units

Since 2002 Northern Ireland Railways has taken delivery of 23 Class 3000 (C3K) and 20 Class 4000 (C4K) trains built by CAF in Spain. NIR is considering a 'New Trains Three' project, which would add up to 60 extra carriages to the fleet at a cost of around £100m. This could allow train capacities to be extended to up to six-car configurations.

The next 20 years

In May 2014 the Northern Ireland Government published a Railway Investment Prioritisation Strategy, an upbeat 20-year plan for maintaining, modernising and even expanding the network, which was informed by a public consultation during 2013.

This consultation noted that in 2011/12 there were 11.4 million passenger journeys by rail in Northern Ireland and this was forecast to increase to 14.5 million by 2035. However, since then 2013/14 figures revealed that passenger journeys had already reached 13.2 million. The strategy document notes that, 'Should the upturn in the growth rate since 2011/12 continue beyond 2015/16, instead of easing to the more moderate level forecast in the consultation paper, the long-term passenger forecasts for the network will need revision.'

The strategy splits possible investment projects into three priority areas. Priority one would focus on maintaining and improving the existing network and trains, priority two would remove bottlenecks to service improvements, and priority three would enhance/extend the network.

The latter two categories are presented as improving the European TEN-T network; EU funding is viewed as one potential source of funding for projects. The line from Belfast to Cork is designated as part of the European core network and the lines from Belfast to Londonderry and Belfast to Larne were confirmed as part of the European comprehensive network.

NORTHERN IRELAND RAILWAY INVESTMENT PRIORITISATION STRATEGY PROJECTS

Priority one
Completion of the Coleraine to Londonderry track relay
Track relays between Coleraine and Antrim and at Lurgan station
A rolling programme of track rehabilitation and signalling upgrades
Refurbishment of 'Enterprise' rolling stock
Refurbishment of Class 3000 and 4000 trains
Refurbishment of stations and halts including Adelaide, Ballymena, Londonderry and Lurgan
Purchase of up to 60 extra carriages
A programme of new park and ride facilities
Development of new halts, particularly where linked to park and ride facilities
Passenger information and ticketing projects

Priority two
Third track from Adelaide to Great Victoria Street to serve the new Belfast Transport Hub
Dualling of Dargan Viaduct and Donegall Quay Halt
Third line from Lagan Junction to Central Station

Priority three
Enhancement of the Northern Line between Bleach Green and Antrim
Feasibility studies into longer-term extensions of the network on the following routes:
- along the A6 corridor between Antrim and Castledawson roundabout
- along the M1/A4 or A3/A29 corridors towards Dungannon/Armagh
- to serve Belfast International Airport

According to the Northern Ireland Government, projects set out in the Railway Investment Prioritisation Strategy would significantly increase the capacity of the rail network, lay the foundations for its future electrification and facilitate the first significant expansion in that network for more than 50 years. However, funding remains a challenge – if the £44m annual funding provided in recent years is maintained, £880m would be available over 20 years. However, £620m would be needed just to maintain existing track and trains.

Scotland

The 2,800km of track (and approximately 350 stations) that make up Scotland's railway include some of the most remote lines in the UK, while lines in Strathclyde form the busiest commuter network outside London. Around a quarter of the railway in Scotland is electrified.

The Railways Act 2005 devolved to Scottish ministers the authority to set a strategy for rail in Scotland, which includes the specification and funding of investment in the rail network.

Under the Act Scottish ministers have a statutory requirement to submit a High Level Output Statement (HLOS) and Statement of Funds Available (SoFA) to the Office of Rail and Road for consideration and approval. These work in the same way as the HLOS and SoFA that the Department for Transport is required to provide for the rest of the national rail network in England and Wales.

In December 2008 Scottish ministers published the Strategic Transport Projects Review (STPR), the first nationwide, multi-modal, evidence-based appraisal process undertaken in Scotland. The document recommends 29 investment priorities for delivery over a 20-year period including the Edinburgh Glasgow Improvement Programme (EGIP) and the Aberdeen to Inverness Rail Improvements project, both of which are included in the Scottish HLOS that was published on 21 June 2012. The HLOS sets out a programme to invest more than £3bn in Scotland's railway to enable Network Rail to operate, maintain and enhance the rail infrastructure in Control Period 5 from 2014 to 2019.

In Scotland planning and delivery of rail policy, strategy and investment is the responsibility of Transport Scotland's rail directorate. Transport Scotland, a Scottish Government agency, carries out appraisals of capital projects, advises on rail investment decisions, and draws up the specification of the railway outputs that the Scottish Government wishes to buy.

Scottish franchises

Transport Scotland also manages the ScotRail franchise. This operates most passenger trains

ABOVE Scottish Government agency Transport Scotland is responsible for letting and managing the ScotRail franchise, one of the devolved administration's biggest contracts by value. Here a Class 170 can be seen at Stirling station.

in Scotland with the exception of long-distance, cross-border services. ScotRail is one of the largest contracts for which the Scottish Government is responsible and the current contract has an estimated value of £6bn.

From August 2004 to March 2015 the franchise was operated by First Group through the company First ScotRail Ltd. Passenger numbers rose by 30% during the course of the franchise. Prior to that the franchisee was National Express. On 1 April 2015 Abellio took over the operation of the franchise after Transport Scotland awarded it a seven-year contract with an option to extend until 2025. A number of major changes to the franchise are due to take effect during Abellio's stewardship, including the introduction of a new fleet of electric trains between Edinburgh and Glasgow and the opening of the Borders Railway, the longest new (or reopened) domestic railway in the UK for more than 100 years.

On 22 September 2008 a new ScotRail brand was launched and the Scottish Government insisted that this should be maintained, despite the change from First to Abellio. This is intended to avoid the costs of rebranding trains and stations that usually occurs when franchises change hands.

Caledonian Sleeper services operate six nights a week along the West Coast Main Line between London Euston and destinations in Scotland. The current Lowland Sleeper comprises services to/from Glasgow and Edinburgh, while the Highland Sleeper consists of services to/from Aberdeen, Inverness and Fort William.

Since April 2015 there have been two Scottish rail franchises. With the start of the new 2015 ScotRail contract the Caledonian Sleeper service has been separated and included in a new stand-alone franchise. In June 2014 Transport Scotland awarded Serco Caledonian Sleepers Limited a 15-year contract to operate the new franchise. Serco

SCOTTISH RTPs

Shetland Transport Partnership (ZetTrans)
Highlands and Islands Transport Partnership (HITRANS)
North-East of Scotland Transport Partnership (NESTRANS)
Tayside and Central Scotland Transport Partnership (TACTRAN)
South-East of Scotland Transport Partnership (SESTRAN)
Strathclyde Partnership for Transport (SPT)
South-West of Scotland Transport Partnership (Swestrans)

has committed to buying new carriages from CAF – due to enter service in 2018 – as part of a £100m programme jointly funded by the UK and Scottish Governments to increase the standard of accommodation offered by the sleeper. This will see pod-style flatbeds provided for the first time on UK train services.

Regional transport partnerships

Scotland has seven regional transport partnerships (RTPs). Their role is to strengthen the planning and delivery of regional transport developments including rail initiatives. Each RTP has a regional transport strategy that is supported by a delivery plan where it sets out when and how projects and proposals can be delivered.

RTPs are independent corporate bodies, as defined in the Transport (Scotland) Act 2005. They act as joint boards, bringing councils together to perform local government functions collectively and strategically over a larger area. All local authorities in Scotland are members of regional transport partnerships.

The largest RTP is Strathclyde Partnership for Transport (SPT), which runs the Glasgow Subway and is responsible for delivering a £300m upgrade of the underground rail system, including a new fleet of trains.

Prior to 2006 reforms, SPT stood for Strathclyde Passenger Transport, a passenger transport executive similar to those in England. The organisation was involved in developing the ill-fated Glasgow Airport Rail Link scheme, and its carmine and cream livery was used on Glasgow trains and station signs. SPT is no longer involved in the everyday operation of the rail network and its branding is being phased out of use.

Glasgow Subway

Tracing its origins back to 1896, the Glasgow Subway is a 10.5km (6.5-mile) circular underground railway that carries around 13 million passengers a year. Sometimes known as the 'Clockwork Orange', trains travel in both directions on adjacent lines – the Outer Circle and Inner Circle. Services operate every 4 minutes during peak periods. The Subway is the only heavy rail underground metro system in the UK outside London and features an unusually narrow track gauge of 1,219mm (4 feet).

The Scottish Government is funding the largest modernisation of the system for more than 30 years, and key elements of the Subway – including trains, signalling and control systems – are being replaced and upgraded. Because Subway tunnels are smaller than other underground rail systems, bespoke driverless trains are being designed that can operate within the Subway's unique environment. Screen gates will be installed at platform level to improve safety. In recent years Subway stations have been overhauled, new escalators installed and smart ticketing introduced.

The future

While the Scottish independence referendum in 2014 did not result in Scotland seceding from the United Kingdom, it appears to have led to an acknowledgement among all the major political parties that greater devolution from Westminster should be pursued with some urgency. This could mean greater transport powers for Scotland; although it currently has control of rail investment, the UK Government vetoed plans by Scottish ministers to consider a publicly owned organisation to run Scotland's railway because this would have contradicted Coalition policy. It is in areas such as this that there has been resentment over London's intervention in Scottish affairs and change could follow. The Scottish Government may also use the devolution agenda to secure a commitment to extend High Speed 2.

Since the independence referendum the UK and Scottish Governments have committed to delivering a £1bn-plus City Deal for Glasgow that, during a 20-year period, could result in a range of rail improvements, including the resurrection of plans for a rail link to Glasgow Airport.

Wales

Unlike Scotland, where responsibility for letting and managing the Scottish rail franchises is a devolved matter, the Department for Transport remains in charge of the Welsh rail franchise.

Currently operated by Deutsche Bahn subsidiary Arriva, the Welsh rail franchise runs most local and regional services in Wales. Other train operators provide longer-distance services that cross the border into North and South Wales.

Although the Welsh Government is not a franchising authority, the Railways Act 2005 gives Welsh ministers a role in specifying train services that operate in Wales. As a co-signatory to the Wales-only franchise, the Welsh Government is responsible for determining the priorities for local and regional services and setting fares.

In reality Welsh Assembly Members have far less influence over rail services than their counterparts in Scotland. Although there is nothing to stop the Welsh Government allocating additional funds to the railway to upgrade stations and provide other improvements (which it has done on many occasions), train services in Wales continue to be underpinned by the franchise contract with Arriva signed in 2003.

Due to expire in autumn 2018, the current franchise was predicated on a 'no-growth' scenario, an assumption that has caused problems as passenger numbers have increased in line with the rest of the UK. No new trains were specified in the contract and Arriva's fleet remains largely the same as that it inherited at the start of the franchise.

In recent years the Welsh Government has paid for a number of rail initiatives including an express service between Holyhead and Cardiff to make it possible to commute between North and South Wales. Wales has also delivered two of the UK's most recent rail reopening schemes, pioneered by local authorities. The Vale of Glamorgan line opened to passengers in 2005, with the Ebbw Vale line following in 2008. Passenger numbers have exceeded expectations and since opening a short extension and two new stations have been added with further upgrade schemes being developed.

Larger-scale rail investment is coming to Wales following the decision by the UK Government to extend electrification of the Great Western Main Line all the way to Swansea, which will allow new electric trains to enter service as part of the Intercity Express Programme. Electrification of the Welsh Valley lines was included in the High Level Output Specification, published in July 2012. Since then there has been a dispute between the UK and Welsh Governments over who agreed to pay for what. However, in November 2014 Coalition Prime Minister David Cameron announced that the UK Government would fund delivery of the Cardiff-Bridgend section of the main-line electrification scheme to Swansea – costing £105m – and contribute £125m towards the costs of the wider Valley lines electrification. The Welsh Government would take over sponsorship and delivery of the Valley lines project, including buying a new fleet of electric trains.

The new Wales rail franchise is likely to be significantly different to the one it replaces. In June 2015 Minister for Economy, Science and Transport Edwina Hart told the Welsh Assembly that a not-for-dividend company was being set up by the Welsh Government to operate the rail franchise on its behalf after

ABOVE A pre-Thameslink Programme picture of London Blackfriars station before it was rebuilt, becoming the first station to span the River Thames. The Class 319 trains seen here have since been cascaded to newly electrified routes in the North of England.

2018. The company would be run on a model similar to that used by Transport for London and was likely to take revenue risk for fares.

Hart said The Welsh Government Transport Company would significantly reduce the amount of profit being taken out of the rail system by train operators, leaving more money to run the service. She also indicated that the operator would play a key role in the delivery of the planned south Wales Metro rail/light rail/bus network.

Metropolitan arrangements

Keeping abreast of transport governance arrangements in some of England's biggest cities has become a full-time job in recent years due to a series of reforms and the emergence of new organisations.

Perhaps a good starting point is the Barbara Castle-led reforms of the 1968 Transport Act, which led to the emergence of Passenger Transport Authorities (PTAs) and Executives (PTEs) in Greater Manchester, Merseyside, South Yorkshire, Tyne & Wear, West Midlands and West Yorkshire. The PTAs, with members from local authorities, set transport policy, which would then be implemented by the PTEs.

So far as rail is concerned, the Railways Act 1993 made PTEs co-signatories to the franchises that covered their areas. The Railways Act 2005 set out a new role for the PTEs in England in relation to rail, following concerns that they were not directly exposed to the consequences of their decisions on fares and service levels. Executives could specify service improvements (if they identified funding) but also service decrements to allow any savings to be spent on other modes of transport in their areas. The Act also removed the PTEs from being direct parties to franchise agreements.

In July 2006 the DfT published guidance on the new role of the PTEs in the rail franchising process: they would be involved in the long-term planning of the rail network and would have a statutory right to be consulted on and have a role in proposing amendments to rail franchises in their areas.

Balancing the desire for local control with the need for workable rail planning and investment has been a recurring theme of recent years. Under the Coalition Government PTAs were scrapped and their role taken up by new combined authorities. These include representatives of local authorities and local enterprise partnerships that have a remit to plan for economic development in their area. They may have a transport committee, which will fulfil some of the functions of the former PTA. The intention is to manage transport as part of a wider coordinated package to support the local economy.

Passenger Transport Executives have survived to implement Combined Authority policies, although the PTE moniker is being phased out and organisations are being restructured. PTEs, or delivery bodies, go under a range of names – Centro (West Midlands), Merseytravel (Merseyside), Metro (West Yorkshire), Nexus (Tyne & Wear), South Yorkshire Passenger Transport Executive, and Transport for Greater Manchester. Where light rail systems exist, the PTEs own infrastructure, oversee operations and plan future developments. In the West Midlands Centro is the name used for the combined policy-setting transport authority and delivery arm.

In terms of heavy rail, PTEs may lobby for and develop enhancement schemes and will be consulted by the DfT on franchise specifications and other rail developments. However, key decisions, such as letting franchise contracts remain the responsibility of the DfT. The exception is Merseytravel, which procures and manages the Merseyrail franchise. The largely self-contained, third-rail electrified network that exists in Merseyside lends itself to a stand-alone arrangement. Under the Merseyrail Electrics Network Order

BELOW At Liverpool Lime Street a Class 185 TransPennine Express service waits at platform 9. Local policy-makers believe that many more new trains are required in the North of England to deliver the 'northern powerhouse' vision set out by politicians.

2002, Merseyrail is exempt from the requirements of the Railways Act 1993, allowing Merseytravel to let a concession to run train services. Merseytravel is leading the procurement for new Merseyrail rolling stock.

Other developments, including the referendum on Scottish independence, have affected the way city rail policy is determined. These include the rise to prominence of local enterprise partnerships, which include many metropolitan areas and provide a platform for the views of businesses as well as local authorities. The Coalition Government granted certain areas new powers and freedoms through City Deals, custom packages that in some cases commit money for investment and promise cooperation to deliver local rail aspirations or devolve powers.

A further consideration is the existence of elected mayors in some cities. While Bristol does not have a PTE, it has a mayor who has supported plans for local rail improvements. Liverpool also has a mayor, and while other cities have rejected proposals for mayors in the past, Coalition and Conservative Government Chancellor of the Exchequer George Osborne has promised that those cities who agree to a directly elected mayor (starting with Manchester) will be handed substantial extra powers. The City Deal for Manchester, announced by Government in 2014, included a pledge from ministers to provide funds for the Metrolink extension to Trafford alongside a commitment from Manchester authorities to give the city a directly elected mayor.

While the mayors in Bristol and Liverpool have limited powers over rail compared to London, having a figurehead to champion a cause can be seen to have had an effect on government policy and investment deals.

Devolving rail powers

Transport authorities in the North of England were encouraged by the Coalition Government to form a new organisation that could oversee procurement of the region's rail franchise (or franchises). This led to the announcement in January 2014 of Rail North, a body representing 33 transport authorities.

While the creation of Rail North laid the foundations for stronger involvement by local authorities in determining the train services that run in the North of England, it stopped short of handing over the decision-making powers that Government had suggested could be devolved and which had been lobbied for by authorities across the North.

Instead, the Department for Transport led the process of letting new TransPennine and Northern franchises, which are due to begin in 2016, and only when the deals are done are new powers set to be devolved to Rail North. It was intended that Rail North '…should take on substantive franchise management responsibilities at the point at which the new franchise contracts come into force.'[30]

Once the new franchises were let, the DfT agreed that the partnership's executive team 'should have substantial delegated responsibility to take the lead in day-to-day franchise management and development of rail outputs.' The executive team would be overseen by a board made up of officials representing Rail North and the DfT.

However, by March 2015 Rail North was already looking obsolete. The Coalition Government's announcement of a multi-billion-pound investment in rail services across the North of England as part of a 'northern powerhouse', loosely scheduled to begin in 2019, was accompanied by the creation of Transport for the North. This is a new transport agency representing authorities across the North of England, which has been given charge of coordinating the proposed investment programme. Governance of Transport for the North, including its relationship with Rail North, was due to be agreed in Autumn 2015.

Meanwhile, plans have also been developed for control of rail services in the West Midlands to be devolved from London – although powers have not been handed over quite as had been expected. In March 2014 Transport Secretary Patrick McLoughlin wrote to Roger Lawrence,

ABOVE Manchester Piccadilly is one of the North's busiest stations. The city wants to be given powers to specify and manage local rail services, building on the Greater Manchester City Deal agreed by central government.

Leader of Wolverhampton City Council and Chair of the West Midlands Joint Committee and Shadow Integrated Transport Authority, saying that the DfT considered that a phased approach to handing over responsibility to a devolved body was preferable to the West Midlands body taking full responsibility from day one.

This prompted a disappointed reply: 'The proposition and business case have been developed at significant cost, and, having worked with your officials on the detail, we were very disappointed to learn that whilst you remain supportive of devolution, that an incremental approach is now preferred. This means devolution to the West Midlands is likely to be post-2017.'[31]

Community rail

Community rail partnerships (CRPs) exist for many rural and local railway lines. They typically comprise the train operating company, local councils and other community organisations, and the Department for Transport says that across Britain around 4,000 volunteers put in more than 1.2 million hours of [unpaid] work for community rail projects.[32]

More than 50 community rail partnerships are represented by the Association of Community Rail Partnerships. CRP activities include lobbying for better bus links to stations, planting and maintaining station gardens, developing walking and cycling routes, finding community uses for disused station buildings, and organising special events that encourage use of the railway. Train operating companies and councils often provide small grants to support their work.

The first CRPs in England were established in the early 1990s, with the first Scottish CRP being established in 2014. During the past decade the Department for Transport has successively designated rural and lightly used railways as community rail lines or services. In 2014 there were 36 lines or services with community rail designation.

ABOVE Unlike other big cities in England, Bristol does not have its own transport authority. But it does have an elected mayor who is supporting efforts to introduce the MetroWest package of new and enhanced local rail services.

The DfT says that designation is intended to improve the financial performance, value for money and social value of these railways to help ensure their long-term future.[33] It claims that separate designation provides the freedom and flexibility to try out new approaches to achieving these aims, and also provides access to small-scale additional funding.

While community rail designation is rarely controversial, it is not clear whether it has provided tangible benefits on top of those generated by already established community rail partnerships. Successfully making a financial business case for infrastructure improvements is one of the more difficult challenges for supporters of rural lines, yet the East Suffolk Lines Community Rail Partnership helped bring about construction of a passing loop at Beccles prior to the East Suffolk lines being designated as community rail services in 2014.

However, many community rail routes have thrived in recent years and designation is designed to support their future development while containing operating costs. Hopefully this will prevent them being singled out as unaffordable in years to come.

ABOVE The notorious 'Pacer' (Class 140-144): originally intended as a short-term solution, the rail-bus design was part-developed by British Leyland. New train orders should see them eventually disappear from the North of England.

6 • London

Outside government and Network Rail, Transport for London (TfL) arguably has the greatest influence over how railways work in Britain. Given that London's population is nudging past eight and a half million and is expected to reach ten million in the 2030s, the capital's rail services have an impact on a vast number of people. To provide transport services for so many people requires one of the biggest rail budgets in the UK, and this gives Transport for London the financial muscle to support the roll-out of new technology or ways of working that subsequently influence rail investment elsewhere.

The Mayor and Transport for London

Established in 2000, TfL has responsibility for the London Underground, Crossrail, a growing network of overground rail services, and the Tramlink and Docklands Light Railway systems (examined in Chapter 12). TfL owns most of the infrastructure and manages renewals and upgrades. It is also responsible for running trains and either operating its own services or letting operating concessions to private companies.

Although the London Underground, DLR and Tramlink are self-contained TfL rail systems, there remains a tension between TfL and national rail services within the capital that TfL sees as vital to meeting the transport needs of London but that fall outside its control. Alongside the day-to-day management of London's rail network, TfL is waging a long-running campaign to persuade Government that it should devolve rail powers to London. In 2007 TfL was given control of the old Silverlink Metro routes, which were transformed into London Overground services. West Anglia routes became part of London Overground in May 2015, although a bid for control of rail services in South East London has so far been rejected. The TfL rail empire will also expand with the phased opening of Crossrail, due to be fully operational as an overground/underground railway in 2020. But the argument for further transfer of rail powers is likely to persist.

TfL structure

TfL is a statutory body created by the Greater London Authority (GLA) Act 1999. This Act gives the Mayor of London a general duty to develop and apply policies to promote and encourage safe, integrated, efficient and economic transport facilities and services to, from and within London.

Government has devolved significant powers over London transport to the elected Mayor, who ultimately sets transport policy for the capital. Transport for London, as one of the agencies answerable to the Mayor, then has to put the policy into practice.

TfL's activities are overseen by a board that is currently chaired by the Mayor. London's Transport Commissioner – the most senior TfL officer at the top of a pyramid of 25,000 employees – reports to the board. Schedule 10 of the GLA Act sets out how the Board may establish committees and how it may delegate certain functions to those committees or senior officers within TfL. Committees include Audit and Assurance; Finance and Policy; Rail and Underground; Remuneration; Safety, Accessibility and Sustainability; and Surface Transport.

Transport for London actually consists of more than 20 linked companies with many subsidiaries reporting to an organisation called Transport Trading Ltd. Business activity is organised into three units – Surface Transport (including buses and cycling), Crossrail, and Rail and Underground. As well as Underground, Overground, DLR and Tramlink, this unit is also responsible for the Emirates Air Line cable car that links the Greenwich Peninsula with the Royal Victoria Dock. Section 175 of the Greater London Authority Act

1999, as amended, outlines TfL's responsibilities regarding rail services in London. TfL took over many of the functions of London Regional Transport and gained responsibility for the Underground in 2003.

Funding

TfL's total income for 2014/15 is expected to be £10.9bn. The organisation receives funding from five main sources – fares, grants, borrowing, Crossrail funding, and other income. It has to balance the need to deliver the services passengers want with the Government's requirement for efficiency savings. By developing commercial income streams TfL hopes to make its public funding go further.

Fares are the single largest source of TfL income, making up 40%, with decisions to raise fares taken each year by the Mayor. Fare increases have been maintained at the Retail Price Index rate in 2014 and 2015 – a real-terms fares freeze. The TfL Business Plan assumes that fares will increase at the rate of RPI plus 1% each year from 2016 to 2021.

Grants from central and local government account for 25% of TfL income. The Department for Transport general grant is used to cover operating costs while the DfT investment grant is used solely for capital improvements to relieve congestion, improve reliability on key routes and provide a good fit with UK transport policies. Through Business Rates Retention TfL receives a proportion of local business rates that are paid via the Greater London Authority. The GLA also provides money towards the Northern Line's Battersea extension – money it gets from incremental business rates generated and retained within a new enterprise zone as well as developers' contributions, raised by Wandsworth and Lambeth boroughs. Finally, there is money from the GLA precept, which is funded from local council tax receipts.

Crossrail income, at 15%, unsurprisingly supports the Crossrail project, which is managed by Crossrail Ltd, a wholly owned TfL subsidiary. TfL contributes towards the cost of Crossrail but also receives money for this

TfL income 2014/15 (£10.9 billion)

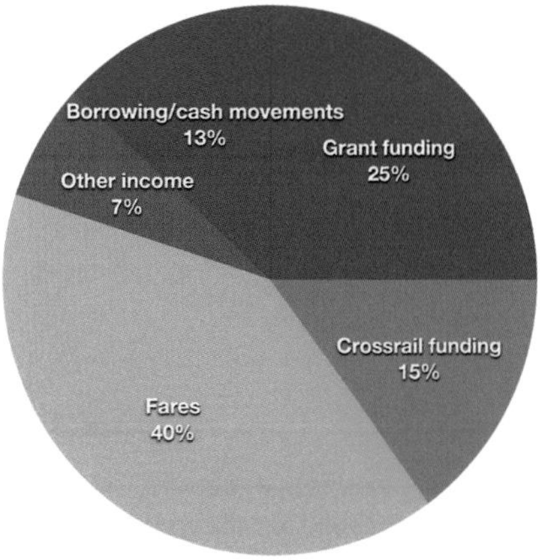

ABOVE Most of Transport for London's income comes from fares and grants from central government. *TfL*

purpose from the DfT, GLA, through the Community Infrastructure Levy and developers' contributions, and from surplus land and property development income (which is expected towards the end of the project).

Borrowing and cash movements make up 13% of income, arising from various financial mechanisms including bonds, commercial paper, loans for specific projects from the European Investment Bank and the Public Works Loan Board. Borrowing limits are set out in TfL's funding agreement with central government.

Other income, at 7%, includes money collected from the Congestion Charge, advertising, sponsorship, property rental and property sales and development. TfL is involved with major property schemes including the redevelopment of Earl's Court and the conversion of London Underground's historic 55 Broadway offices to residential accommodation.

London Assembly

With a hefty budget, a vast sphere of influence and the authority to act on behalf of the Mayor, Transport for London is an undeniably powerful institution. It falls to the London Assembly to try and hold the Mayor and TfL to account for rail and other transport policy.

The London Assembly is an elected watchdog for the capital made up of 25 Assembly Members whose role is to examine how effective are the Mayor's policies, decisions and activities. There are a number of opportunities to do this.

The Assembly's Transport Committee scrutinises all aspects of the capital's transport system in order to press for improvements for Londoners. Its remit includes main-line rail, the Underground, buses, trams, taxis and minicabs, walking, cycling, roads, and issues such as congestion, transport safety and transport sustainability. The committee pays particular attention to how the Mayor's Transport Strategy is being implemented and looks closely at the work of Transport for London and other transport operators.

Assembly Members regularly question the Mayor and senior officials such as the Transport Commissioner at public meetings, as part of their role to hold the Mayor and other bodies to account. Ten times a year the Assembly questions the Mayor in public at Mayor's Question Time sessions. Questions can be submitted to Assembly Members by members of the public, and any questions not answered at the meeting are given written answers. The Assembly also convenes regular plenary meetings to hold to account bodies such as Transport for London.

Each year the London Assembly carries out a detailed examination of the Mayor's spending plans at a series of public meetings. The Assembly then has the right to amend the Mayor's final budget (which in turn shapes TfL's budget) by a two-thirds majority at a meeting in the new year.

TravelWatch

London TravelWatch represents the interests of transport users in and around the capital. Established in July 2000 it is officially known as the London Transport Users Committee.

TravelWatch is sponsored and funded by the London Assembly and is independent of train operators. The Assembly appoints board members who are supported by staff who carry out day-to-day work such as following up complaints about transport in London that have not been satisfactorily resolved by the transport provider.

The passenger watchdog promotes integrated transport policies and presses for better public transport, with higher standards of quality, performance and accessibility, liaising with transport operators, providers, regulators and local authorities as appropriate.

In 2011 London Assembly members proposed abolishing TravelWatch and taking its responsibility for monitoring TfL services in-house while passing oversight of national rail services to Passenger Focus. However, an amendment to the Localism Bill, which would have put this into practice, was rejected.[34]

Independent Investment Programme Advisory Group

The Independent Investment Programme Advisory Group (IIPAG) provides independent assurance and expert advice to the Mayor of London concerning TfL's investment programme. This includes all maintenance, renewal, upgrades and major projects, but not operational issues or the activities of Crossrail Ltd. The IIPAG considers issues of economy, efficiency and value for money in preparing its advice. It focuses on how projects are managed and TfL's approach to complex technical issues.

The Underground

The London Underground can trace its history back to when the world's first underground railway, the Metropolitan Railway, opened between Paddington and Farringdon, serving six intermediate stations. In 2013 celebrations were held – including special steam train services – to mark 150 years of operation.

However, despite its illustrious history and claims to railway firsts, the reality is that Transport for London has inherited a system of tunnels and stations that were not designed for the number of trains and passengers that now use them. There is an urgent requirement to modernise and expand

ABOVE At Farringdon station the Moorgate branch seen here on the left has been closed to allow platforms to be extended to accommodate longer 12-carriage trains. The tunnel on the right takes trains south to City Thameslink station.

BELOW Oxford Circus is one of London Underground's busiest stations, served by the Bakerloo and Central lines.

ABOVE The London Underground sub-surface railway and national rail Thameslink route run side by side at Farringdon. Trains for both railways have subsequently been replaced.

BELOW New S Stock on the Metropolitan Line at Farringdon station. The Bombardier-built trains have open-carriage connections and air-conditioning.

the system, but achieving this depends on overcoming massive engineering challenges, finding large amounts of money, and identifying ways to limit the disruption to passengers while work is undertaken. Today the network has 270 stations and 11 lines serving central London and the capital's northern suburbs:

- **Bakerloo:** Relatively speaking this is one of the lesser-used Tube lines. TfL is developing plans for a southern extension that could run to Hayes via Old Kent Road and Lewisham.
- **Central:** Opened in 1900, the 'Tuppeny Tube' became the second Underground line to use automatic train operation when new technology was introduced in the 1990s.
- **Circle:** This branding was introduced just before 1950 to make sense of former Metropolitan and District railway routes. In 2009 the perpetual loop was abandoned in favour of an end-to-end service between Hammersmith and Edgware Road, which makes it easier to operate trains regularly and for services to recover from any disruption.
- **District:** Several connected routes from the west join up to run through central and east London to Upminster. The short branch to Kensington Olympia has been demoted to special events only. Overground trains regularly serve this station.
- **East London:** Rail services through Brunel's Thames Tunnel became part of the Tube network in 1933. The East London Line closed in 2007 and reopened as part of the London Overground network in 2010.
- **Hammersmith & City:** Formed out of parts of the Metropolitan and District routes, the H&C was designated a Tube line in 1988. Since Circle Line services were restructured in 2009, the H&C no longer has any stations that are not shared with other lines.
- **Jubilee:** Originally known as the Fleet Line, the Jubilee opened in 1979 to Charing Cross. The Jubilee Line extension to Stratford via Canary Wharf opened in 1999, just in time to serve the newly built Millennium Dome, now the O2.
- **Metropolitan:** This serves the housing developments, which became known as 'Metroland', built to the north-west of the capital after the First World War.
- **Northern:** This opened in 1937 and was created from two separate railways, the City & South London Railway and the Charing Cross, Euston & Hampstead Railway. An extension from Kennington to Battersea is scheduled to open in 2020.
- **Piccadilly:** Famed for its examples of 1930s art deco station architecture, this line has been expanded west to Heathrow with the Terminal 5 extension opening in 2008.
- **Victoria:** Opened between 1968 and 1971, this is the capital's most recently opened all-new Underground line, but the design has been criticised for not including provision for growth in passenger numbers, which creates difficulties for TfL today. Equipped with Automatic Train Operation, the Victoria was the first automatic passenger railway in the world.
- **Waterloo & City:** Often referred to as 'The Drain', this two-stop route links Waterloo and Bank. It was transferred from British Rail to LU in 1994.

How it works

The London Underground (LU) network can be split into deep-level 'Tube' lines and the sub-surface lines, which came before and were built using the less sophisticated 'cut-and-cover' technique. These sub-surface routes – the Metropolitan, Circle, Hammersmith & City and District – are often referred to by TfL as the Sub-Surface Railway (SSR).

As the name suggests, most of the London Underground consists of underground railway. However, many routes also operate on the surface and some use or run parallel with Network Rail infrastructure and serve stations (such as Queen's Park) run by a train operating company or concession holder. Train operators also use LU infrastructure, notably Chiltern Railways, which runs trains along the Metropolitan route between Amersham and Harrow-on-the-Hill.

ABOVE London Underground has more than 400 escalators, many of them built to bespoke designs, which must be regularly maintained to keep them in working order.

Underground trains operate on a four-rail system, consisting of two running rails and two electrified conductor rails. The positive conductor rail is located on the outside of the running rails, generally on the opposite side from the platform in stations; the negative conductor rail is located centrally between the running rails. The conductor rails provide 630 volts direct current to power the train.

Each line is operated from a control centre where line information specialists and signallers are based. The role of the line controller includes keeping trains running to the timetable and restoring service patterns following any disruption. Line information specialists provide service information and updates to stations and other parts of the network as well as monitoring the performance of the line. Signallers work with line controllers to regulate and route trains.

On the national rail network train operating companies run trains, but on the Underground drivers are employed by LU. In contrast to most of the UK, this is a true example of a public-sector-run railway. Attempts to part-privatise the system in the 1990s resulted in three complex public private partnership (PPP) agreements that proved expensive, litigious and an impediment to the wide-ranging upgrade programme, and ultimately collapsed with TfL/LU taking on the responsibilities of the PPP consortia. At the time of writing London Underground is controlled by a Conservative Mayor, but maintenance, upgrades and train operations are run by public-sector TfL, which lets contracts to private-sector firms as required.

New Tube for London

The New Tube for London, formerly known as the Deep Tube Programme, is a multi-billion-pound initiative to develop a new fleet of trains and associated systems for the London Underground Piccadilly, Bakerloo, Central and Waterloo & City lines.

Driven by a need to replace aged assets and provide additional capacity, the programme attempts to learn from the mistakes of the PPP by looking at what these Underground lines need to operate most effectively. Rather than put a rolling stock contract out to market, LU is attempting (with the help of suppliers) to address some of the difficult engineering challenges of the deep lines, such as ventilation and track maintenance, and work out how air-conditioning can be fitted to trains and lightweight rolling stock introduced. It is also trying to develop a design that is suitable for all deep Tube routes.

The benefits will initially be seen on the Piccadilly Line, which by the early 2020s will get new trains to replace 1973 rolling stock. Other lines will follow, but the Bakerloo Line's 1972 stock is expected to remain in service until the late 2020s at the earliest. Train bogies are likely to be shared between carriages, reducing the number of wheelsets in order to cut the amount of heat generated as trains pass through tunnels. Automation of trains is a key feature of the New Tube for London programme, with LU working towards eventual driverless operation.

Towards driverless trains

Many Underground lines already operate more than one train every 2 minutes in each direction during peak hours. Constructing parallel lines to increase capacity has so far been deemed too difficult and expensive. Instead, TfL is proposing increases to the already intense service levels. This is only possible by further automation of the system.

The International Association of Public Transport defines four grades of automation (GoA). These are specified according to which basic functions of train operation are the responsibility of staff and which are the responsibility of the system itself, as outlined in Table 6.

The technology required to automate metro systems such as the London Underground consists of the following systems:

Automatic Train Protection (ATP) – the system and all equipment responsible for basic safety; it avoids collisions, red signal overrunning and exceeding speed limits by applying brakes automatically. A line equipped with ATP corresponds (at least) to a GoA1.

Automatic Train Operation (ATO) – ensures partial or complete automatic train piloting and driverless functionalities. The ATO system performs all the functions of the driver, except for door closing. The driver only needs to close the doors and, if the way is clear, the train will automatically proceed to the next station. Many newer systems are completely computer-controlled.

Automatic Train Control (ATC) – performs automatically normal signaller operations such as route setting and train regulation. The ATO and the ATC systems work together to maintain a train within a defined tolerance of

Table 6: The four grades of automation

Grade of automation	Type	Setting train in motion	Stopping train	Door closure	Operation in event of disruption
1	ATP with driver	Driver	Driver	Driver	Driver
2	ATP and ATO with driver	Automatic	Automatic	Driver	Driver
3	Driverless	Automatic	Automatic	Train attendant	Train attendant
4	Unattended train operation	Automatic	Automatic	Automatic	Automatic

its timetable. The combined system will marginally adjust operating parameters – such as the ratio of power to coast when moving and station dwell time – in order to bring the train back to the timetable slot defined for it.

ABOVE Most of the North London Line now forms part of the London Overground network. New trains and higher-frequency services have resulted in passengers flocking to what had been a neglected part of the capital's rail infrastructure.

At GoA4, ATC systems work within an overall signalling system with interlocking, automatic train supervision, track vacancy detection and communication functions.

London Underground lines already use automatic train operation. The Victoria, Central, Jubilee and Northern lines are GoA2 systems. The Docklands Light Railway, which is driverless except in the event of disruption, when a train operator can take control, is GoA3. The sub-surface lines are due to operate with GoA2 by 2022.

As part of the New Tube for London programme, London Underground intends to convert the Piccadilly Line to GoA2 by 2026 and the Bakerloo Line to GoA2 by 2035.[35]

Further signalling upgrades as part of the programme could result in driverless, unattended train operation on the Underground. LU is planning to introduce GoA4 on the Piccadilly (2029), Central (2032) and Bakerloo (2045). TfL says that full automation will reduce operating costs and optimise service operation, supporting peak service frequencies of up to 36 trains per hour in each direction.

Implementing these systems will require major changes to staffing on the Underground, with train drivers no longer required for some lines. Trade unions have opposed the proposals and LU will need to carefully navigate this sensitive area. Should it succeed in introducing GoA4 systems, it would make the Underground less vulnerable to industrial action by drivers.

Platform edge doors, currently used at Jubilee Line extension stations and due to be installed at Crossrail stations, are likely to be required for GoA4 systems.

London Overground

The London Overground was born in 2007 when the Mayor of London and TfL succeeded in their bid to take over the management of lines that had previously been operated as part of the National Express-owned Silverlink franchise.

The East London Line project expanded the network to create an orbital rail route all the way around London. As of 31 May 2015, when West Anglia routes became part of the London Overground, the network consisted of 111 stations and the total route length was 167km (104 miles).

TfL inherited the North London, West London and Watford Junction-Euston lines, which use a combination of third rail and overhead electrification. It was also handed the diesel-train-operated Gospel Oak to Barking line, the one non-electrified passenger railway within TfL's rail networks.

These routes had been neglected over a prolonged period and TfL immediately sought to address this by providing Underground standards of service. This included staffing all stations, introducing 62 new trains, refurbishing stations and providing support for Oyster smartcard ticketing.

London Overground trains and stations are operated (until 2016 at least) by London Overground Rail Operations Ltd (LOROL), a joint venture between MTR and Deutsche Bahn, under a concession agreement let by TfL. Unlike most of the train operating franchises let by the Government, TfL takes revenue risk for London Overground services. Therefore LOROL effectively has a management contract with incentives to hit agreed performance targets rather than its income being dependent on how much money the train operation makes.

East London Line extension

In 2007 the London Underground East London Line linking Shoreditch and Whitechapel to New Cross and New Cross Gate closed. Following a £1bn upgrade it reopened in 2010 as part of the Overground network. The project provided a connection to the national rail network to allow trains to run south to

BELOW The London Underground East London Line closed in 2006 but has since been extended and reopened as part of the London Overground network. A new, larger station has been constructed at Shoreditch High Street.

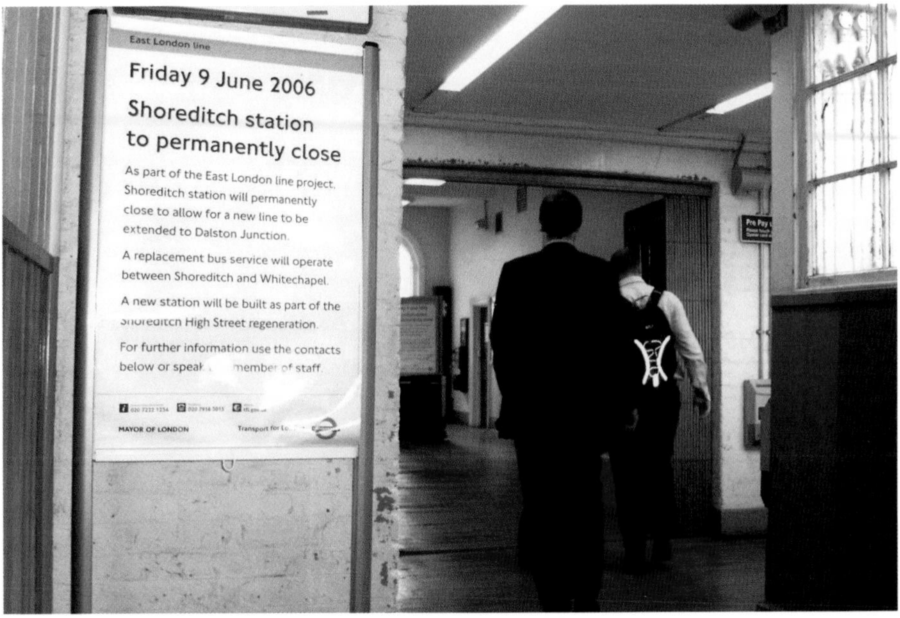

West Croydon and Crystal Palace. It also expanded the line north, making use of the disused Kingsland Viaduct, which had carried the lines into Broad Street station until it closed in 1986, providing four new stations at Shoreditch High Street, Hoxton, Haggerston and Dalston Junction. Soon afterwards the route was linked to the North London Line at Highbury & Islington.

A second phase of work was completed in 2012, providing a new branch from near Surrey Quays to connect with the existing South London Line, and an Overground connection to Clapham Junction where the West London Line begins. A new station at Surrey Canal Road/ New Bermondsey is planned but was postponed due to failure to agree a funding package.

The London Overground now links 23 of London's 33 boroughs and every day the concession holder operates more than 1,400 train services.

BELOW Canary Wharf Crossrail station has a lattice roof – here seen under construction – consisting of glue-laminated timber beams with transparent air-filled plastic pillows.

The future

New Overground trains and new services have proved popular with TfL, which reported in 2013 that passenger numbers had quadrupled during the first six years of Overground services[36] (although the extensions of the East London Line and the absorption of the former Underground route into the Overground network contribute to this).

To respond to growing demand, TfL has progressed the £320m London Overground Capacity Improvement Programme to increase capacity on the network by 25% by lengthening four-car trains to five carriages. Station platforms have been extended to accommodate the longer trains, which are due to be in service by the end of 2015.

London Overground took over the management of the services from Liverpool Street to Enfield Town, Cheshunt (via Seven Sisters) and Chingford, and those from Romford to Upminster on 31 May 2015. TfL is buying new trains for these West Anglia services although initially existing rolling stock will continue to be used after undergoing a deep clean. Services will be run by London Overground operator LOROL until November 2016, when

ABOVE A Silverlink Metro train at North Woolwich station before this section of the North London Line was shut in December 2006. Part of the route is being reused for Crossrail.

the current London Overground concession is due to end. The Liverpool Street services will then become part of the overall London Overground concession, which will be relet.

TfL had hoped to add services in South East London to the Overground network, but this was rejected by the Government in 2013 following concerns from Kent County Council that TfL might prioritise services in the capital. This highlights the issue of attempts by the Mayor and TfL to gain control of more London rail services – most metro routes do not neatly fit within the GLA boundary and therefore authorities outside London fear that if TfL takes control of a route it will give priority to stations within the capital. That could mean more stops and longer journey times for those commuting to and from the Home Counties.

The Government has agreed a funding package that will see the Gospel Oak to Barking line (GOBlin) electrified by 2019 with new trains being procured alongside those for the West Anglia routes. Provisional backing has also been granted to extend GOBlin to Barking Riverside to support development of what is said to be the largest single site in London for new housing, with the potential to accommodate a population the size of Windsor.[37]

Crossrail

Crossrail is a major new railway across London. Tunnels have been dug under central London and will connect with upgraded surface routes to increase London's rail-based transport network capacity by 10% (the largest increase since the Second World War), as well as dramatically cutting journey times across the capital.[38] For many journeys to London's West End and Docklands for which passengers would previously have needed to change on to an Underground train, they will in future be able to travel direct.

Unlike the London Underground, Crossrail tunnels are big enough to accommodate standard-gauge trains, a new fleet of which has been ordered from Bombardier. The new tunnels are scheduled to open by the end of 2018, with the full Crossrail service operating by 2020.

Crossrail trains will run through twin tunnels from/to Reading and Heathrow Airport in the west, through new underground stations at Paddington, Bond Street, Tottenham Court Road, Farringdon, Liverpool Street and Whitechapel. At Stepney Green there is a junction where the railway bifurcates, a north-east branch surfacing next to the Queen Elizabeth II Olympic Park site near Stratford, and Crossrail trains continuing on to Shenfield in Essex. Another branch runs south-east through new stations at Canary Wharf, Custom House and Woolwich, eventually surfacing in Plumstead, with trains continuing to a rebuilt Abbey Wood station.

The programme is jointly sponsored by the Department for Transport and Transport for London, but the DfT has handed TfL responsibility for delivering the scheme through a subsidiary company, Crossrail Ltd. Powers to build Crossrail were put in place by the 2008 Crossrail Act.

Funding

Crossrail infrastructure has a funding envelope of £14.8bn – although the Coalition Government said that it expected the programme to cost no more than £14.5bn. Rolling stock is extra and has an estimated capital cost of £1.3bn. Additional money has been allocated for Crossrail purposes – for example, private-sector contributions at Canary Wharf and Woolwich, public realm enhancements, and accessibility improvements to surface stations.

CROSSRAIL INFRASTRUCTURE FUNDING[39]

Funding source	£ billion
TfL direct funding	1.9
Business rate supplement, borrowing and direct contribution	4.1
Sale of surplus land and property	0.5
Community Infrastructure Levy	0.3
Developer contributions	0.3
Total TfL underwritten	7.1
DfT direct funding	4.8
City of London Corporation	0.3
Heathrow Airport	0.2
Total DfT underwritten	5.3
Network Rail	2.3
Voluntary funding from London businesses	0.1
Total funding envelope	**14.8**

In 2010 more than £1bn of project savings were identified through station and engineering improvements, which reduced the funding required from TfL and the DfT. These changes to the project put back the Crossrail completion date.

The Mayoral Community Infrastructure Levy came into effect on 1 April 2012 and is a charge payable on most commercial property developments across the capital. Different rates are payable depending on the location of the borough – i.e. how close it is to the Crossrail route. Section 106 contributions offer another way of getting property developers to contribute to the cost of Crossrail infrastructure, but these are subject to negotiation by developers and councils, so payments are more ad hoc. The Crossrail funding package envisaged £100m of the £300m coming from the major Wood Wharf development next to Canary Wharf, a contribution that has subsequently appeared less certain. In 2013 TfL indicated that it would pool CIL and Section 106 contributions in order to raise the £600m required by Crossrail.[40]

Canary Wharf Group, which owns the Canary Wharf estate, has part-funded and built Canary Wharf Crossrail station. The fit-out of Woolwich station also falls outside the Crossrail funding envelope, with TfL, Greenwich Council and Berkeley Homes contributing to the cost.

Construction

Crossrail consists of 120 route kilometres, with 21km of new twin-bore tunnels (42km) and 8km of existing tunnels. There are five tunnel portals – Royal Oak, Pudding Mill Lane, North Woolwich, Plumstead and Victoria Dock. Two major tunnelling contracts were let, with contractors starting in the west and east and breaking through at Farringdon in the spring of 2015 to join up the tunnels.

ABOVE Completing her underground journey, Crossrail tunnel boring machine Ellie broke through at the Victoria Dock portal in October 2014. *Crossrail Ltd*

Construction of Crossrail began in 2009 and at its peak more than 10,000 people were working on the programme across 40 different sites. The train tunnels have been built using eight 1,000-tonne tunnel boring machines, which dug out earth (mainly London clay) and installed concrete rings. Around 3 million tonnes of the tunnel spoil was moved by train and boat to Wallasea Island in Essex, where it has been used to create a new 1,500-acre RSPB nature reserve.

A technique called 'sprayed concrete lining' has been used extensively during Crossrail construction to create smaller tunnels, such as those required at stations. This approach makes it relatively easy to create tunnels and caverns of different shapes and sizes.

Major tunnelling work is complete with the focus moving to station fit-out, installing railway systems and delivering the new trains and depot. The schedule envisages 2017 being dominated by testing and commissioning. Central London Crossrail stations will be fitted with automatic platform screen doors (which were first used in the UK for the Jubilee Line extension).

Building new central London stations provides an opportunity to design in step-free access, making stations (including the historic Underground stations with which they interchange) fully accessible to those with reduced mobility, children or luggage. The Crossrail plans approved by Parliament did not make provision for step-free access at some of the more lightly used stations on the surface sections that will be incorporated into Crossrail. However, in 2014 the DfT and TfL agreed to provide additional money to ensure that the small number of stations not in line for improvements will get lifts by the time the full Crossrail

service is operational. This means that Crossrail will be a fully accessible railway and able to offer step-free access to trains at all 40 stations.

Siemens will install signalling for Crossrail between Portobello Junction (west of Paddington) on the Great Western Main Line, Pudding Mill Lane Junction on the Great Eastern Main Line in the east, and Abbey Wood in the south-east.

Crossrail services will run in Automatic Train Operation (ATO) mode with Automatic Train Protection (ATP) in the central operating section from Portobello Junction to Pudding Mill Lane/Abbey Wood. Due to the need to integrate the new build Crossrail central section with existing Network Rail infrastructure, there is a requirement for trains to operate with legacy signalling and safety systems when they emerge from Crossrail tunnels.

Siemens will work with Bombardier to deliver compatible on-train equipment for the communications-based train control system that Siemens is installing in tunnels. The rolling stock will also support legacy signalling systems used on Network Rail lines and the European Rail Traffic Management System level 2 signalling that Network Rail plans to install on the Great Western route. Signalling in Crossrail tunnels could be upgraded to ERTMS in due course.

Upgrading existing overground railway forms a key part of the Crossrail programme, with Network Rail responsible for delivering £2.3bn of 'on-network' works. This includes overhead line electrification, installing 179 new switch and crossing units, extending 60 platforms, and delivering two major engineering projects – an expansion of Stockley Viaduct where the Heathrow route branches off the main line, and a dive-under at Acton to ensure that Crossrail trains are not disrupted by freight movements.

LEFT Below the Centre Point tower, work to rebuild Tottenham Court Road London Underground station can be seen under way. This is a concrete box constructed to hold a new bank of escalators to the Northern Line. Metal props support the walls while the build is in progress.

On-network enhancements and track access

In September 2008 the Office of Rail and Road approved a track access option (TAO) that granted access to the national rail network for the operation of Crossrail services for 30 years. This was necessary to secure funding for Crossrail; without the track access option the DfT and TfL would have had no certainty that Crossrail trains would be able to operate on the national rail network. The track access option is set to be amended following the 2014 decision to extend Crossrail to Reading.

The long-term rights set out in the track access option can be applied to track access agreements between Network Rail and Crossrail train operators – starting with MTR, to which in 2014 TfL awarded the concession to run Crossrail services. As with any other train operating company, the Crossrail operator is required to negotiate and enter into the track access agreement with Network Rail and pay normal access charges. TfL retains a right in the concession agreement to direct the operator in these negotiations if required.

Crossrail requires a number of significant enhancements to the existing overground railway such as electrification of the route between Maidenhead and Airport Junction, major structures at Airport Junction and Acton, new twin track from Plumstead to Abbey Wood, and other major works to stations, platforms, signalling and electrification. The Crossrail sponsors agreed that these on-network works, for which there is a funding envelope of £2.3bn, would be delivered and financed by Network Rail and added to Network Rail's Regulatory Asset Base to allow the organisation to fund the costs up front.

Network Rail will in turn be remunerated from the farebox revenues generated by Crossrail operations, and TfL has committed to paying track access charges sufficient to cover NR's financing of the cost of the on-network works up to a maximum of £2.3bn. The Government has underwritten Network Rail's costs should they exceed that figure.

The mechanism for paying back Network Rail is the Crossrail Supplementary Access Charge (CSAC). TfL is liable for paying this rather than passing it on to the contracted operator. The Crossrail operator, under the terms of its track access agreement, will still be liable (in addition to the Crossrail Supplementary Access Charge payable by TfL) for fixed and variable access charges on an equivalent basis to those levied on other passenger train operators as established by the ORR at each periodic review.

Payments for the Crossrail Supplementary Access Charge are due to be staged over 50 years to reflect the average economic life of the assets. After the 30-year period of the track access option, TfL's access rights and its liability to pay the CSAC will expire. Whether or not a further TAO is agreed, with or without the liability to pay the remaining 20-year period of the charge, will be a matter of policy and regulation to be decided nearer the time.

Preparing for operations

Complex rail schemes are notorious for running late and encountering unforeseen problems and clearly building a new railway under central London does not come without risks. To mitigate against any difficulties, a phased approach to introducing Crossrail services has been agreed, which should see passenger services through the new Crossrail tunnels begin towards the end of 2018.

Once the full service is operating the plan is to run 24 trains per hour in each direction during peak hours. This allows 12 on both the south-east and north-east branches. Fourteen trains are due to start or terminate at Paddington, leaving 10 to continue west – the intention is to run four to/from Heathrow, four to/from Reading and Maidenhead, and two to/from West Drayton. An increase in train frequency to 30 trains per hour during peak hours has been mooted.

Although Crossrail services do not start until 2017, Crossrail train operator MTR began running services on 31 May 2015 when it took

RIGHT To make space for Crossrail to surface and join the Great Eastern Main Line (to Stratford and Shenfield), a section of the Docklands Light Railway (which runs alongside part of the Great Eastern) has had to be diverted. Here the new DLR viaduct takes shape with the old alignment and old Pudding Mill Lane station seen in the background.

over the operation of local trains between Liverpool Street and Shenfield – which were previously part of the Greater Anglia franchise and will be absorbed into the new cross-London Crossrail service. MTR's service initially operates under TfL's London Rail brand to avoid associating the Crossrail name with old trains, legacy service levels and stations that have yet to be improved. The 65 new Bombardier-built Class 345 'Aventra' trains are due to enter service in 2017 on Crossrail routes and the residual services into Liverpool Street, and at that point the Crossrail brand should become obvious. Each train will be 200 metres long, fitted with air-conditioning, and maintained at

PHASED CROSSRAIL ROUTE OPENING SCHEDULE

Start date	Crossrail service
May 2017	Crossrail trains run on Great Eastern main line between Liverpool Street (high level) and Shenfield
May 2018	Crossrail trains run from Paddington (high level) to Heathrow Airport
December 2018	Crossrail trains run through central section tunnels for the first time – between Paddington (low level) and Abbey Wood
May 2019	Central section service connected to Great Eastern surface section (trains switch to Liverpool Street low level and continue through London)
December 2019	Full service operates west of Paddington all the way to Reading (as well as Heathrow Airport)

a new Old Oak Common depot as well as facilities at Ilford, Plumstead and Maidenhead.

MTR's concession to run Crossrail services takes a similar form to that let by TfL to LOROL for the London Overground – i.e. TfL takes all revenue risk.

Crossrail's future role

When it comes to figuring out how to provide additional capacity on London's congested railway network, transport planners have few attractive options. In most cases opportunities for 'quick wins' have already been followed up and where possibilities for enhancements remain they are invariably complex, disruptive and expensive. So the arrival of Crossrail presents a rare situation – a new, high-quality railway with potential spare capacity and links to other rail routes. Even before it opens, the future of Crossrail is being carefully mapped out in a bid to alleviate other rail pinch-points.

The development that will probably have the biggest bearing on the future of Crossrail is High Speed 2. As part of HS2 phase one, a station is to be built at Old Oak Common in west London to provide an interchange with Crossrail (as well as London Overground services). That means that by 2026 Crossrail could have a major new station that does not currently appear on Crossrail maps. Plans to regenerate the area around the HS2 station could ultimately result in the closure and relocation of the newly opened Old Oak Common Crossrail train depot to free up space for residential and commercial development.

One of the challenges of the HS2 programme is to rebuild London Euston station, the terminus for inter-city and commuter services using the West Coast Main Line. Such a major rebuilding project is expected to reduce capacity at Euston for several years while work is under way. What can be done? How about diverting West Coast commuter services on to Crossrail via a new short connecting stretch of railway in the Old Oak Common area? Funding has been agreed for feasibility work to investigate this possibility.

ABOVE Heathrow Connect stopping services – which link London Paddington with the airport – are due to be subsumed by Crossrail services by 2020.

Future Crossrail may also have a role in freeing up capacity at London Paddington for new train services. Network Rail has suggested that Heathrow Express trains could be diverted into Crossrail tunnels, increasing Crossrail central London train frequencies and vacating platforms at Paddington.[41]

Further developments

Crossrail 2 is being teed up as the next major rail infrastructure project for London. Although Crossrail 1 has yet to open, the progress made so far appears to have persuaded decision-makers in Government that complex railway schemes are not only desirable from an economic point of view but can actually be financed and built.

The Crossrail 2 scheme, also known as the Chelsea-Hackney line, would provide a new underground railway from North East to South West London. Like Crossrail, it would be big enough for 'normal' surface trains and would link up two national rail routes on either side of London, releasing capacity at London Waterloo by diverting trains into a new tunnel under London.

TfL says that Crossrail 2 would increase London's rail capacity by a further 10% by creating a new high-frequency, high-capacity rail line offering shorter journey times between South West and North East London. The proposed line would create additional capacity, transporting up to 90,000 people in the morning peak, and would support a raft of proposed regeneration schemes across London. Current plans suggest that the new line could open by 2030 and would cost around £25bn, including the cost of new trains.[42] A funding package is expected to use similar sources to those agreed for Crossrail 1.

Crossrail 2 has strong backing from TfL, which argues that the scheme is necessary to meet demand once High Speed 2 services start running to and from Euston, and Network Rail, which has put forward Crossrail 2 as the only practical solution to meeting demand for significant additional rail capacity on the approaches to Waterloo.

24-hour trains

All-night weekend services on the London Underground Central, Jubilee, Northern, Piccadilly and Victoria lines were scheduled to launch in September 2015. The new service is expected to reduce the length of night-time journeys around London (using other modes of transport) by an average of 20 minutes. Trains run all through the night/morning on Friday/Saturday and Saturday/Sunday with at least six trains per hour through central London.

Plans have been announced to introduce 24-hour trains on the London Overground East London Line route from 2017, and on the Metropolitan, Circle, District and Hammersmith & City lines following completion of the sub-surface railway upgrade towards the end of the decade.[43] The Docklands Light Railway will also offer a 24-hour service from no later than 2021.

7 • Ticketing

Fares accounted for more than 60% of the rail industry's income in 2013-14. Without this money it seems reasonable to assume that the rail system as we know it simply would not exist. With money changing hands for each journey comes the need for a ticketing proposition that gives passengers the authorisation to travel. And while an evolution of the paper tickets that have been around for more than a century remains common currency, our desire for ever-greater purchasing convenience coupled with sometimes staggering developments in technology mean rail ticketing is in the midst of a major transformation.

Once the money is collected, somehow it has to be divvied out to the appropriate cost centres. With one train operator that might be challenging; with more than 15 businesses – some operating overlapping routes – that requires a heavy-duty system.

Fares

Each passenger train operating company sets train fares as part of its commercial strategy. But the companies' scope to alter prices is limited – many fares are regulated and others may be determined by agreements between Government and franchise holders. Off-peak leisure fares are easier for TOCs to change, while those for what are viewed as essential commuter services are less so.

In England train fare increases take effect on 1 January every year. The rise is based on the Retail Price Index (RPI) rate of inflation for the preceding July; in July 2014 this was 2.5%, with this figure then forming the basis for the January 2015 fare changes. It has been argued that the Consumer Price Index (CPI) rate of inflation would be a fairer measure to use than RPI.[44]

With successive Governments requiring passengers to pay a greater proportion of the cost of running the railways, an 'inflation + x%' mechanism has been adopted. In England the Coalition Government followed a policy of 'RPI +1%' in recent years, although the 1% was waived in 2014 (at an estimated cost of £35m a year) and Chancellor George Osborne announced in September 2014 that for January 2015 regulated fare rises would be limited to inflation (2.5%). In fact, on average, fares rose by 2.2% in January 2015.[45]

The annual increase applies to regulated fares – typically those paid on commuter services, which account for around 45% of all rail fares.[46] It is an average increase and under the flex mechanism train operators have had the freedom to increase individual fares by more than the inflationary increase so long as they reduce other fares to ensure that the increase for the overall 'basket' is no more than that permitted by Government. The flex was suspended in 2010 and 2015 and campaigners have argued that it should be abolished permanently.

For an example of how the system works in practice, if RPI is 3.2% and Government policy is to raise fares by RPI +1% and allow a flex of up to 2%, the maximum average increase for a basket of fares is 4.2% and the maximum increase for an individual fare is 6.2%

To complicate matters there are exceptions to these principles:

- Merseyrail's concession agreement with passenger transport executive Merseytravel limits regulated fares to an average increase of RPI + 0%.
- Northern Rail's agreement with the West Yorkshire Passenger Transport Executive Metro limits the amount by which an individual regulated fare can rise to the RPI plus a maximum of 8% within a basket of

ABOVE At King's Cross passengers must pass through ticket gates to access the bridge to the platforms. An increasing number of gates at national rail stations have smartcard readers.

fares that cannot rise by more than the RPI plus 3%. So the maximum average increase for the basket is 6.2% and the maximum increase for an individual fare is 11.2%. This arrangement may be discontinued in the new franchise due to start in 2016.

- In Scotland the Scottish Government sets fares, and the nationalists have chosen to implement a different policy from the UK Government. In Scotland train fares were due to rise by an average of 1.9% in January 2015 and ScotRail's peak fares by 2.5% at the same time, with off-peak fares frozen at 2013 prices. Scotland's Transport Minister Keith Brown said that from January 2016 regulated ScotRail fare increases can be no higher than RPI and off-peak regulated fare increases will be capped at 1% below RPI.[47]
- The devolved Governments in Wales and Northern Ireland set their own fares.

According to the Office of Rail and Road, the average change in rail fares between January 2013 and January 2014 was 2.7%. This represented a decrease in real terms of 0.1%, as over the same time period the RPI increased by 2.8%.[48]

Overall, fares in London and the South East grew by 2.8%, with season ticket prices increasing by 3.1%. The increase in season ticket prices was offset by lower increases on anytime and off-peak fares. In the Long Distance sector, ticket prices rose by 2.5%. The largest expenditure in the sector is on advance fares, which increased by 2.3% on January 2013. Within the Regional sector (including Scotland), prices rose by 2.4%. Anytime and Off Peak travel together account for more than 70% of expenditure in the sector, and these categories rose by 2.6% and 2.1% respectively.

Main ticket types

Buying a railway ticket can be a bewildering experience, particularly for those who are not regular rail users. In recent years efforts have been made by the rail industry to streamline the range of tickets available.

Nationally there are four types of tickets offered by train operators. Anytime tickets allow you to travel at any time of the day including during peak travel periods. You may need to travel by a specific route or travel with a particular train operator, but this will be stated on the ticket. You are allowed to break your journey. Anytime tickets are refundable, less an administration fee (up to a maximum of £10 per application), on any unused or part-used tickets should you decide not to travel.

Anytime Day Single or Day Return tickets are valid for one single or return journey on the date shown on the ticket. Anytime Single tickets are valid for one single journey and are valid for two days from the date shown on the ticket. Anytime Return tickets are valid for one return journey. The outward portion is valid for five days and the return portion is valid for one calendar month from the start date shown on the ticket. Often there is little difference between the price of the single and return ticket.

Off-Peak tickets are cheaper than Anytime tickets and are valid on trains that are less busy. You may need to travel at specific times of the day, on specific days of the week and sometimes on specific routes or with particular train operators. On some journeys cheaper Super Off-Peak tickets are available, which are valid on the least busy services.

The times when an Off-Peak or Super Off-Peak ticket can be used depend on the journey being made, and this should be made clear when buying a ticket. Travelling before 0930 is usually forbidden with an Off-Peak ticket. Some train operators have introduced restrictions for Off-Peak ticket holders in the late afternoon and early evening.

Off-Peak tickets are available as Day Single or Day Return tickets (valid for one single or return journey on the date shown on the ticket), Off-Peak Singles (valid for one single journey on the date shown on the ticket, but allowing the journey to be finished the following day if it cannot be completed in a single day) and Off-Peak Returns (the outward portion is valid for travel on the date shown on the ticket and the return portion is valid for one calendar month).

If you board a train with an Off-Peak ticket at a time when the ticket is invalid, you can be charged the difference between the fare paid and the cheapest valid fare for the service concerned. Should you decide not to travel, Off-Peak tickets are refundable, less an administration fee (up to a maximum of £10 per application) on any unused or part-used tickets.

Advance tickets offer cheaper fares, generally for longer-distance train journeys. The catch is that they must be purchased in advance. The further into the future you book, the better the deal, although, at the time of writing, domestic train tickets are not available more than 13 weeks in advance.

When booking an Advance ticket you need to choose a specific train and must then travel on that service. No break of journey is allowed except to change between trains. No refunds are payable on Advance tickets, but in most cases you can change your journey prior to departure for a £10 fee plus any difference in the fare payable. Some train operators allow tickets to be downloaded to a mobile phone or similar device or printed at home – in these cases different rules regarding refunds may apply.

Should you try and use an Advance ticket to travel on a train other than the one booked, you are liable to buy a new ticket for your journey. Although this will be the cheapest available on the day, for long-distance services the difference between this and the Advance fare can be substantial. However, if you miss the train booked through no fault of your own – for example, a connecting service is delayed – rail staff will normally advise that you can travel on the next service provided by the same train operator, or any alternative services, without having to buy a new ticket.

Season tickets allow unlimited travel between two stations for a specified period of time. They can be bought for periods of seven days or for any period from one month to one year.

For commuters and other regular travellers Season tickets usually offer the best value for travel by train even if journeys are made fewer than five days a week. An Annual Season ticket gives you 52 weeks' travel for the price of 40. Tickets are refundable, less an administration fee (up to a maximum of £10 per application), on any unused or part-used ticket that is no longer required.

When an Annual Season ticket is bought for a journey in the London and South East area the ticket is issued as a Gold Card. This offers the card-holder a range of benefits including discounts on other tickets – such as those for children or other adults travelling with the Gold Card holder.

Other ticket types

Some trains have First Class compartments as well as Standard seating. In these cases First Class Anytime and Season tickets will be available and you may also be able to buy First Class Off-Peak and Advance tickets for these trains. On some longer-distance services you can upgrade to First Class on Saturdays, Sundays and Bank Holidays on payment of an additional fare.

Railcards offer one-third off many fares. Passengers pay for the Railcard but can quickly recoup their money through discounted train journeys. Railcards are available for people aged 16-25 years or 26-plus in full-time education, for adults travelling with children aged 5-15, for people aged over 60, for people with a disability that makes travelling by train difficult, for leisure travel in the London and South East area, and for members of the Regular Armed Forces. In some regions there are local Railcards that offer discounts on local journeys.

GroupSave tickets enable three or four people travelling together to pay the same price as two adults. GroupSave discounts are available for many off-peak journeys, including those in the London and South East area and some other parts of the country. Many train companies provide discounts for larger groups (usually ten or more people) travelling together at off-peak times.

Plusbus combined rail and bus tickets are available for nearly 300 towns and cities across Britain. These tickets allow unlimited bus travel around town, at the start, the finish, or both ends of your train journey. Around a million Plusbus tickets are sold each year and ticketing is managed and funded by Journey Solutions, a not-for-profit partnership of Britain's five biggest bus and train operators (Arriva, First, Go-Ahead, National Express and Stagecoach), together with trade organisations ATOC, the Association of Local Bus Company Managers, and the Confederation of Passenger Transport.

Rover and Ranger tickets offer flexibility and value for money for those wanting unlimited travel within a specified area. Some include travel on associated bus and/or ferry services. Ranger tickets are generally valid for one day and All Line Rovers allow unlimited travel for 7 or 14 days.

Sleeper services link London Euston with Scotland, and London Paddington with South West England. Tickets can be booked at staffed stations or online.

Stagecoach offers discount 'Megatrain' fares for off-peak journeys provided by its rail franchises (South West Trains, East Midlands Trains and Virgin Trains) through its Megabus website. Passengers book online with fares starting at £1.50, depending on demand and how early the journey is booked. Megatrain links around 60 UK locations; passengers may be required to sit in a particular train coach and show a member of staff a print-out or receipt on their mobile phone as evidence of their booking.

For those travelling around Greater London, Travelcards allow unlimited travel on national rail (except Southeastern High Speed services between St Pancras International and Stratford International, Heathrow Express services or Heathrow Connect services between Hayes &

Harlington and Heathrow), London Underground, Docklands Light Railway, Croydon Tramlink and most London bus services. You can buy Travelcards valid for travel on a single day or Travelcard Season tickets. Travelcards can be issued as traditional paper, magnetic-strip tickets or on Oyster smartcards.

Penalty fares

Tackling ticketless travel is viewed by Government and the rail industry as a key way to boost the income of the railway without asking for additional money. To achieve this, electronic ticket gates are increasingly being installed at smaller stations as well as city termini where, in the past, accompanying a friend or a relative to a train to wave them off was a common sight. Platform tickets are sometimes issued to allow a person access through the ticket gates to see their companion board safely.

Although gates make it more difficult to travel without a ticket, penalty fares exist in England to deter those who would find ways around the system. Posters at stations are used to remind passengers when they are travelling within a penalty fares zone.

On long-distance trains, it is often possible for the onboard staff to check each passenger's ticket. On rural routes, trains stop more often, but as they usually have fewer coaches and carry a smaller number of passengers, onboard ticket checks are also possible. On these routes tickets are regularly issued on the train without a penalty being charged. However, as noted above, buying a fare on the day can leave a passenger significantly out of pocket.

However, on urban and suburban routes, where station stops are frequent and the trains are often busy, checking every passenger's ticket is impractical. Therefore penalty fares are used to encourage passengers to buy a ticket before they travel. If they get caught without a ticket by a revenue protection inspector they are liable to a penalty fare. Train operators occasionally prosecute fare evaders.

The penalty payable is £20 or twice the full single fare from the station where the passenger got on the train to the next station at which the train stops, whichever is the greater. If travel beyond the next station is required, the relevant fare from that station to the final destination must also be paid. Penalty fares can be issued if a passenger travels without a valid ticket, is unable to produce an appropriate railcard on a discounted ticket, travels in First Class accommodation with a Standard ticket, is aged 16 or over and travelling on a child rate ticket, or is travelling beyond the destination on the ticket.

A process exists to enable those who think they have been charged incorrectly or unfairly to make appeals through Independent Revenue Collection and Support (IRCAS) or the Independent Penalty Fares Appeals Service (IPFAS).

In February 2015 the UK Government launched a consultation on changes that could make it more difficult for train operating companies to make passengers pay penalty fares. Proposals included requiring train operators to remove the reference to criminal sanctions in letters chasing penalty fare payment. The Government said it would provide new guidance to train operators to make clear that the threat of criminal sanctions for non-payment of a penalty fare, which is a civil offence, is not appropriate. Criminal sanctions will still apply in suspected cases of deliberate fare evasion.

Appeal bodies could be obliged to relax time limits, which would mean that those appealing against penalty fares would not have to pay a fine until a final ruling has been reached. The 21-day deadline for payment would be suspended when an appeal was received by the appeals body, and only reinstated once a letter notifying the outcome had been issued.

A further change could require all appeals bodies to be independent of transport operators and owning groups. Currently, the IPFAS is owned by Go-Ahead, which owns and has stakes in several train operators.

ABOVE London Overground ticket machines at stations feature touch screen controls and allow passengers to top up Oyster cards.

In Scotland and Wales there are no penalty fare zones, but Unpaid Fares Notices are sometimes issued to passengers without a valid ticket. In Northern Ireland Translink says passengers travelling without a valid ticket and who have had an opportunity to purchase one will be issued with a penalty fare of £20 plus the full single fare for the journey made.

Departing thoughts

The rail industry regularly highlights the value-for-money fares that are available for travelling across the country. For those who can buy in advance and have flexibility as to when they travel, cheap tickets are available that offer a competitive alternative to travelling by road or air.

But for those who suddenly find that they need to make a train journey, the picture is less positive. Buying an inter-city fare on the day can easily cost more than £100. Although suggestions that turn-up-and-go tickets could be phased out to make travelling by train more like catching a flight have come to nothing, the cost of buying a ticket on the day means that short-notice rail trips are unaffordable for many.

With ticketing paying for about 60% of railway costs, ensuring that those who travel by train have the correct ticket makes sense. Penalty fares are used to deter ticketless travel, although enforcement policies vary across the UK. In general you must have a ticket if travelling in London and the South East and other major cities. On local routes, buying a ticket on board a train is usually standard practice. Some inter-city routes enforce penalty zones, but the high cost of buying a long-distance ticket on the day means that you probably would not want to turn up without a valid ticket anyway.

Where to buy tickets

Traditionally, travelling by train involves queuing up at a station ticket office to buy a ticket. Depending on where you are travelling from, this remains the option of choice if you wish to buy a ticket from a fellow human. But there are other options.

Tickets can also be bought over the telephone, paying with a debit or credit card. Alternatively, most stations now have self-service ticket machines that accept card payments and offer a wide range of ticket options. Another option is to use a rail-appointed travel agent, which can make reservations and issue tickets.

Online ticketing

Railway tickets are increasingly being bought on the internet. Tickets can be purchased from train operators' websites or through the national rail website – which redirects users to the appropriate train operating company (TOC) website for payment. TOCs sometimes use their websites to offer special discounts.

There are two major web-based retailers of train tickets – trainline.com (owned by Exponent Private Equity) and Red Spotted Hanky (owned by Atos). These companies supply the systems used by many train operators online, so there is a commercial relationship between these businesses and TOCs that prevents them acting as direct competitors. A booking fee may be payable on transactions.

Third parties are also permitted to sell tickets, although train operators have reduced the commission paid on sales from 9% to around 5%, prompting accusations from Passenger Focus that margins offered provide little incentive for new entrants to the market. Raileasy, owned by Ferries Trains Planes Ltd, has established itself as an independent web retailer over the past decade, although it is unable to sell some ticket types including railcards and season tickets. It does, however, allow customers to buy split tickets - multiple tickets for different stages in a journey which sometimes work out considerably cheaper than buying a single end-to-end ticket. Raileasy charges a commission for any split ticketing savings it identifies.

Goodbye ticket offices?

Given that railway tickets can be bought online and from increasingly sophisticated self-service machines at railway stations, do we still need station ticket offices? Reducing opening hours or closing ticket offices altogether can potentially cut rail industry overheads and, while closures may generate negative publicity, the question remains – do ticket offices offer passengers anything they cannot get elsewhere?

Transport for London has made the distinction between staffing stations and staffing ticket offices. A key part of its Fit for the Future programme is to close all London Underground station ticket offices. Stations will remain staffed while operational, but rather than being behind glass screens more staff will be available by ticket machines, ticket gates and on platforms so that they can assist and advise passengers. Staff will be equipped with the latest mobile technology, and stations that form the main entry points to London for visitors to the UK will get enhanced Visitor Information Centres where tourists will be able to get help and advice.

Fit for the Future is being implemented because the latest generation of self-service ticket machines at stations, combined with Oyster and contactless ticketing, mean fewer and fewer passengers have any need to interact with a ticket office. TfL says that this programme, due to be implemented during 2015, will save it £50m a year, which can be reinvested in improvements to the rail system. Closing ticket offices will also free up space at stations, allowing reconfiguration to improve the passenger experience or conversion to retail units – again helping TfL's finances.

Given that rail developments in London often provide a glimpse of how the rail system across the UK will change in the future, the continued existence of ticket offices across the national rail network cannot be taken for granted. One possibility is that they will become integrated with other social or commercial facilities. For example, Merseyrail

has introduced Mtogo outlets at some stations, which allow tickets to be bought from a convenience store – a concept modelled on the Netherlands' Albert Heijn retail chain.

ABOVE Woking station is served by South West Trains and offers passengers a range of ticket vending machines that accept cash and cards.

Smart ticketing

Train users in Britain have become used to the orange-top-and-tail magnetic-strip cardboard tickets, which were introduced in 1983. These can be issued by automatic machines and will open station ticket gates when inserted into the correct slot.

Magstrip tickets are likely to be with us for a while. A Department for Transport review of rail fares and ticketing, published in 2013, stated that despite new ticketing technology becoming available, it was likely to take 10-15 years to phase out the orange tickets.[49]

Nevertheless, railway ticketing is in the midst of a transformation, with the traditional paper ticket increasingly being replaced by ticket products stored on a smart card or electronic device. London is at the vanguard of this revolution following the introduction in 2003 of the Oyster card system, which reduced the cost of revenue collection by more than one-third. Transport for London now claims to run the world's most successful smartcard ticketing system.

The rise of Oyster

In the late 1990s an investment programme extended the installation of ticket gates to nearly all London Underground stations, replacing ticketing equipment dating back to the 1950s with the Oyster system. Oyster increased capacity by allowing 40 passengers a minute to pass through ticket gates compared to 15-20 with magnetic-strip tickets.

For London Underground passengers the changes meant using an Oyster card to 'touch in' and 'touch out' by holding their card over a circular reader at ticket gates. The correct fare is then deducted from the card.

Oyster was procured through a private finance initiative contract called Prestige; a 17-year contract was signed in August 1998 and Oyster launched in 2003. Following the establishment of Transport for London in 2000, Oyster was extended to the Docklands Light Railway and Croydon Tramlink. It was improved with the addition of the 'pay-as-you-go' and 'capping' propositions that now form the mainstay of the product. Price differentials were introduced between pay-as-you-go and cash fares to encourage passengers to use Oyster.

As Oyster use took off passengers increasingly wanted to be able to use Oyster on those national rail services in London that run through zones shared with the London Underground. Progress on this was slow, with train operating companies reluctant to participate due to the rights vested in their franchise contracts.

Between 2006 and 2009 TfL negotiated deals with all nine London TOCs to agree the acceptance of Oyster, which was subsequently made available on most London national rail services in January 2010. Oyster expansion on national rail has since been expanded beyond the London boroughs as far as Watford Junction, Shenfield, Grays and Gatwick Airport. TfL says that studies by the Massachusetts Institute of Technology have demonstrated that accepting pay-as-you-go has directly increased TOC revenues by 6% in London, or by more than £100m per year.

Among the benefits that have been delivered by Oyster are:

- interoperable ticketing accepted across all forms of public transport in London
- less reliance on ticket offices, with transactions down from about 7 million per period to less than 2.5 million per period despite a 30% increase in journeys.
- simplifying purchasing choices
- increasing ticket gate capacity
- eliminating ticket touting

However, there are also some drawbacks. Oyster is a proprietary system with a high cost base. Journey information is held on the card itself and this system does not lend itself well to online or mobile transactions. Refunds or corrections to passenger accounts are difficult to make as the correction needs to be reflected on the actual card.

In 2005/06 the cost of revenue collection was 14.3% of revenue. To reduce this cost TfL terminated the Prestige contract and awarded a new contract (the Future Ticketing Agreement – not to be confused with the Future Ticketing Programme) to Cubic Transportation Systems while also bringing some services in-house. Separate contracts were let for communications networks and the supply of Oyster cards. By 2012/13 the cost of collection had been reduced to 8.8% of revenue.

Under the new arrangements TfL secured ownership of the intellectual property of the Oyster system and has been able to license technology used in Oyster smartcard readers to transport systems in Sydney and Vancouver. TfL expects to be able to exploit the new technology being developed through the Future Ticketing Programme (see below) in a similar way.

In 2013 TfL began a further procurement for ticketing and revenue services under the name Project Electra. This contract covers the maintenance and availability of ticketing and fare collection equipment on 8,500 buses, 1,900 ticket gates at London Underground and London Overground stations, 1,600 ticket machines, and 1,800 stand-alone validators including those on the Docklands Light Railway and at the 250 national rail stations where card readers are located. There are also around 4,000 retail devices at Oyster Ticket Stops across London. The contract also involves supplying new ticket gates and card readers across TfL networks – including the new Crossrail stations – as required.

Given that Cubic staff and suppliers had been involved with London ticketing in one way or another for 30 years, TfL went to considerable lengths to try and persuade other bidders that the competition offered a level playing field in order to attract bids from companies other than Cubic. However, after shortlisting three firms, it named Cubic as winner of the new contract in July 2014.

This new ticketing and revenue collection services deal was due to commence in August 2015 and run for seven years with options to extend for a further three years. The contract is valued at £660m over 10 years. TfL says that it will deliver savings of £11m a year compared to the previous contract, as well as providing the flexibility to accommodate changes in ticketing and fare collection technology.

Future Ticketing

An Oyster card may have been high tech in 2003, but technology is changing fast. TfL has decided to reshape its ticketing system to support electronic devices with near field communication and contactless payment cards. This 'wave and pay' technology allows the use of a passenger's bank or credit card direct – removing the need to buy a separate product such as an Oyster card. To be able to make contactless payment, cards need to support the EMV (Europay-Mastercard-Visa) standard.

TfL's Future Ticketing Programme is not so much prompted by the technology as by the potential it offers to cut collection costs further by moving away from a proprietary system to a product issued by the wider payments industry.

The introduction of support for contactless payment for cards on TfL's network was also seen as an opportunity to find new ways for customers to pay for their travel without the need to get a ticket first. This enables TfL to reduce ticketing costs while also improving the customer experience compared to Oyster, because information is held in an intelligent back office system rather than on the card itself.

After rolling out support for contactless payment on London buses in late 2012, TfL introduced contactless payment for all rail modes (but not national rail) in September 2014 with support for season tickets following in 2015. The later phases of the Future Ticketing Programme involve creating a new Oyster platform that uses the back office processing system (rather than card-based processing), and finally decommissioning the old Oyster system.

ITSO

ITSO is the national standard for smart ticketing. An ITSO specification has been developed with the aim of ensuring that public transport operators across Britain can develop compatible smart ticketing systems. The aim is to avoid passengers needing to carry lots of different tickets or separate smart cards.

All ITSO-compliant systems rely on ITSO Security Application Modules (ISAMs), which are secure electronic data processing modules, the size of a mobile phone SIM card. These check the cardholders' permissions, authenticate and validate their electronic tickets, and store journey data for further processing.

The ISAM communicates with the back office system known as a Host Operator Processing System (HOPS) through another security device called a HOPS Security Application Module (HSAM). The overarching security application module in a system is known as the Primary HSAM or PHSAM.

ISAMs are inserted into railway ticketing gates and machines (or on bus, tram or ferry ticketing machines). They can also reside within handheld ticketing machines used by bus or train ticket inspectors.

When an operator sets up an ITSO system, the ISAMs are profiled using the ITSO Security Management System (ISMS), which is run by ITSO Ltd. This is the central part of the ITSO Security Sub System, which acts as the 'keeper of the keys', managing the provision of data access keys to the secure devices (ISAMs) in ticketing machines and barriers.

The electronic wallet within a smartcard that contains electronic tickets for ITSO-compliant schemes, similar to an 'app' on a smartphone, is known as a shell. The shell can be programmed to be read by machines to say 'yes this person has enough money on the card to pay for this ticket', or 'yes this person is a railway season ticket holder for this route'. This is programmed by individual transport operators to reflect their individual tickets and prices.

To set up an ITSO-compliant system, an organisation needs to pay to become an ITSO member. ITSO membership extends across national and local government in England, Scotland and Wales, transport operators, smart ticketing equipment and consultancy suppliers, and interested transport bodies and associations. Membership fees of several thousand pounds a year are payable (according to supplier turnover or local authority population). A range of other charges apply depending on the ITSO services required.

ITSO Ltd is a non-profit-distributing organisation that supports its members in implementing ITSO-compliant smart ticketing schemes. The organisation is run by a board that includes representatives from the Department for Transport, Transport Scotland, the Welsh Government and Transport for London. Ultimately, the DfT controls the direction taken by the organisation.

ITSO Ltd oversees the development of the ITSO specification including the implementation of upgrades to the technology. The company does not offer smartcards, ticketing machines or HOPS services. These are provided by suppliers, whose equipment is tested and certified by ITSO to ensure that it can run ITSO-compliant schemes.

ITSO rail systems

A variety of ITSO-based smart ticketing systems are supported by local bus services across Britain, the implementation of the technology driven in part by the national concessionary bus travel scheme, which allows those receiving the state pension to travel free of charge on local bus services.

ITSO products for use on the rail system are available in some areas, but roll-out remains limited and the prospect of being able to travel by train across Britain with a single piece of plastic is remote. The Department for Transport has said that magnetic-strip tickets can be withdrawn when the rail network is fully smart-equipped, but estimates that this is at least ten years away.[50]

DfT smart ticketing strategy currently backs the ITSO specification. An alternative token and back office model that would allow more sophisticated ticketing is said to require further development before it can be implemented on the rail network, but remains under consideration for future use.

In attempting to deliver smart ticketing across the national rail network the DfT has come up with a three-phase programme, the first of which is the South East Flexible Ticketing programme (SEFT). This began with a pilot on the Essex Thameside franchise but wider roll-out to around 300 stations depends on reaching commercial agreements with train operators, and the timescale for deployment remains unclear.

Subject to the success of SEFT and future funding, further targeted delivery programmes, likely to be in cities outside London with a significant rail commuter base, are planned to start in 2015-16. The third phase would see the rest of the rail network in England smart-enabled, but this remains a distant prospect.

Despite these uncertainties, ITSO-complaint smart cards are being used on the railway by train operators, although the range of ticket types supported varies. Train operators offering smartcards include Abellio Greater Anglia, C2C (C2C Smartcard), East Midlands Trains (StagecoachSmart), ScotRail (Smart Card), London Midland (Key), Southern (Key) and South West Trains (StagecoachSmart). As can be seen from this list, the smart card products offered tend to be linked to the parent company of the train operator. For passengers the different systems work in a similar way to Oyster with a requirement to touch in and touch out at the start and end of each journey.

The Department for Transport has committed to specifying smart ticketing in all

new rail franchises. Operators such as Merseyrail are beginning to support contactless payments made by debit/credit cards.

One of the biggest issues that has emerged to date during the development of railway smart ticketing has been the incompatibility between London's Oyster standard and the DfT-backed ITSO standard. This led to the DfT funding ITSO on Prestige (IoP), a project to upgrade more than 20,000 card readers at London stations and on buses so that passengers can use ITSO smart cards as well as Oyster cards.

Other smart ticket products

Just as London has developed its own smart cards, other city transport authorities have tried their own products, utilising the ITSO standard, with varying degrees of success and quirky brand names including Merseytravel's Walrus (the name has since been dropped) and Yorcard, developed by the West Yorkshire and South Yorkshire Passenger Transport Executives. At the time of writing the promised rail smart tickets had yet to materialise.

The Glasgow Subway has replaced its antiquated paper tickets with smartcards, which can be loaded with a range of tickets and offer pay-as-you-go and daily capping. The system is supplied by Ecebs with the technology branded 'Bramble'.

In 2011 PTE Nexus launched 'Pop' as part of efforts to modernise ticketing on the Tyne & Wear Metro. Support for pay-as-you-go and daily capping has recently been added.

The West Yorkshire Combined Authority is rolling out support for MCard, which is poised to be accepted at Bradford Interchange, Leeds and Huddersfield stations by the end of 2015 and is the second-most-used travel smartcard (after Oyster).

Transport for Greater Manchester's Get Me There platform is currently supported by Metrolink tram services, and TfGM says it will be supported by rail services in the conurbation from 2017. Passengers can use a contactless bank card (with payments deducted via the Get Me There back office system), an igo pass (for 11-16-year-olds), a TfGM-issued concessionary pass, or a dedicated Get Me There smartcard.

ABOVE At most busy stations ticket barriers restrict access to platforms to those holding a valid ticket or smartcard.

West Midlands Passenger Transport Executive Centro expects its Swift smartcard, currently accepted on buses, to be supported by Midland Metro and national rail services in due course.

Smart ticketing is not just about cards. Train operators, including Chiltern Railways and Virgin Trains, have experimented with mobile tickets that consist of a matrix barcode sent to a mobile phone. The m-ticket is bought using an app on the phone, then the phone (with the barcode displayed) is scanned over a special reader attached to ticket gates or held by train operator staff. Less sophisticated e-tickets are also offered by some train operators whereby passengers can buy a ticket online, then print off their own ticket, which includes a barcode.

Where does the money go?

Having a railway used by multiple commercial train operators throws up a conundrum: How do you ensure that the money paid for a ticket gets to the company running the train, regardless of whether the ticket is bought in Penzance, Edinburgh or online?

The process of sharing out the money collected from ticket sales is handled by Rail Settlement Plan (RSP), a company owned by the train operating companies (through ATOC), which oversees contracts for rail tickets, ticket issuing systems, reservations, fares, information services, timetables, revenue allocation, revenue settlement between train companies, ticket on departure schemes, and credit card automation.

Rail Settlement Plan also distributes fare, reservation and timetable information to train companies, retailers and agents; gathers sales data; and – perhaps most importantly – redistributes the revenue collected from ticket sales.

The actual computer system used for redistributing this revenue is known as LENNON, short for Latest Earnings Networked Nationally Over Night. It processes information from all UK train ticket sales whether purchased on a train, via the internet or at station ticket offices, then allocates daily revenues to each of the train operating companies within 24 hours of the ticket being purchased.

Before each timetable change a computer programme called ORCATS (Operational Research Computerised Allocation of Tickets to Services), which is also owned by RSP, is run. This analyses the timetable and for each start and finish station works out the route a passenger is likely to take between them. For a branch line this is relatively straightforward and will allow LENNON to allocate the ticket sale to the train operator that serves that branch line. For more complicated journeys along routes served by multiple operators, and which involve changing trains en route, ORCATS calculates the likelihood of the passenger using a particular train operator for each part of the route. LENNON then uses the ORCATS calculation to divide the revenue according to the miles the passenger is suspected of having spent on each operator's train.

With this kind of forecasting, where many different factors and journey permutations are possible, there is inevitably going to be some 'best guessing' involved. For example, if a train is full, a passenger may end up taking an alternative route that would not be reflected by the LENNON revenue allocation.

LENNON also provides the rail industry with data related to ticket sales and usage patterns, which allows demand to be monitored and can be used for planning purposes. It cannot count ticketless journeys – another reason why tackling fare evasion makes sense.

Approximately 1% of rail journeys are not recorded on LENNON, including operator-specific tickets and some tickets issued by Passenger Transport Executives in major cities. Although ORCATS is the default allocation method used for ticket sales, it is not mandatory and train operators can specify a non-ORCATS allocation for particular ticket types if they think that the ORCATS model will not produce a fair estimate of true passenger behaviour.[51]

8 • Safety and security

Travelling by train in the UK is safe. In 2013/14 1.59 billion passenger journeys were made in Britain (60.1 billion passenger kilometres) and 48.5 million freight train kilometres were recorded. No one was killed on a train during the year.

Even acknowledging the fact that many more people travel by car than train, the fact that train travel proved 100% safe is something the motoring industry can only dream of. Any sort of rail safety incident prompts headlines, yet daily fatalities on the roads have become almost routine.

The record

At the time of writing the last incident when a passenger died while travelling on a train was the 2007 Grayrigg derailment in Cumbria. In 2013/14 there were no passenger train derailments, the first year that this has been the case since reporting began more than 20 years ago. Four passengers died at stations after falling from the platform or coming into contact with trains while standing too close to the platform edge.

One of the reasons why train travel is safe is because of a rapid reduction in the number of signals passed at danger (known as SPADs) following the implementation of the Train Protection and Warning System (TPWS).

While the statistics show that travelling by train is safe, encountering a train en route is certainly not. At 308, the number of fatalities to members of the public in 2013/14 was the highest recorded. Eight of the fatalities were members of the public at level crossings: two were occupants of the same road vehicle, who died when their car was involved in a collision with a train, and six (including one cyclist) were pedestrian users of footpath crossings.

The remaining 300 fatalities to the public resulted from trespass or suicide. While most of the safety metrics used for rail show an improving picture, the industry has struggled to reduce trespass/suicide rates. The 2013/14 figures show an increase of 22 on 2012/13. When Control Period 4 (2009-14) is compared with CP3 (2004-2009), there has been no observable improvement in reducing trespass and suicide rates.[52]

A National Suicide Prevention Group has been formed to tackle the issue of railway suicide, comprising Samaritans, Network Rail, British Transport Police, representatives of train operating companies, the Rail Safety and Standards Board and rail unions. Samaritans branches work locally with station managers, station staff from TOCs and Network Rail, and the British Transport Police in prevention and post-incident support work.

Three members of the railway workforce, all infrastructure workers, were killed in 2013/14. Two men died in the same accident, which was a road traffic collision while on duty. The third worker was acting as lookout for a small group working south of a station when he was struck by a passenger train approaching the station.

Excluding suicides, during 2013/14 there were 36 recorded rail-related fatalities, 440 major injuries, 11,382 minor injuries and 1,238 cases of shock/trauma.

In terms of crime on the railway, figures suggest that in general Britain's rail networks are safe places to be. Statistics from the British Transport Police show that in 2012/13 crime fell for the ninth successive year – despite more people travelling by train year on year. While the number of thefts increased, this is perhaps not surprising given the array of easily saleable high-tech devices, such as smartphones and tablets, increasingly carried by passengers.

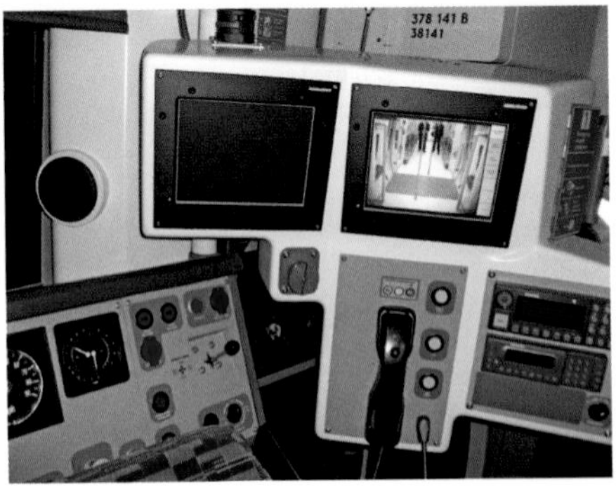

ABOVE Control rooms provide information from different railway systems to allow decisions to be taken in the interests of train performance and network safety. Often staff from train operators and Network Rail work side by side to ensure a coordinated response to any incident.

LEFT The cabs of modern rolling stock, such as this London Overground Class 378, allow train drivers to monitor internal and external CCTV cameras.

Level crossings

According to the Office of Rail and Road, level crossings account for nearly half of the catastrophic train accident risk on Britain's railways.

Unfortunately the historic development of the railway means that much of the network is littered with crossings, many of which carry volumes of road traffic that were never considered when the crossing was built.

There are approximately 8,000 level crossings in Great Britain. Around 6,500 of these are managed by Network Rail with the rest located on heritage railways, metro systems and industrial railways. Given the risk the crossings pose, Network Rail is keen to shut as many as possible. However, building new roads or tunnels to carry traffic is expensive, while closing long-established shortcuts for pedestrians across rail routes often provokes a public outcry.[53]

During Control Period 4 Network Rail managed to close almost 10% of its level crossings, and for CP5 nearly £100m has been allocated to close around 500 more – which Network Rail has indicated will achieve a 25% reduction in risk.[54] However, the organisation says that in the majority of cases the risk associated with the use of individual level crossings is insufficient to make a clear case for their closure and/or diversion. Level

ABOVE Network Rail has been funded to reopen the railway between Bicester and Bletchley. However, adding level crossings to the operational network is deemed unacceptable on safety grounds, so most of the former crossings on the East-West route are likely to be closed with alternative solutions sought (such as building a footbridge).

BELOW User-worked level crossings are convenient for farmers and walkers but present a risk to safety that has been exacerbated by increases in train frequency as more people travel by rail.

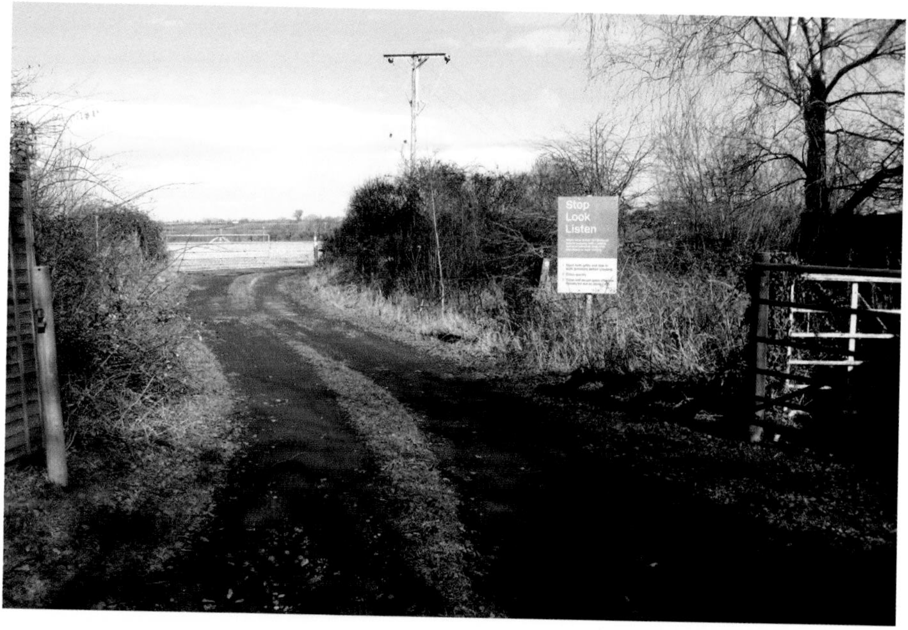

TYPES OF LEVEL CROSSINGS

Gated crossings operated by railway staff – protected by gates, on both sides of the railway, which complete the fencing of the railway when closed across the road or the railway.

Barrier crossings operated by railway staff – protected by road traffic light signals and lifting barriers on both sides of the railway. An audible warning to pedestrians is also provided.

Barrier crossings with obstacle detection – protected by road traffic light signals and lifting barriers on each side of the railway. An audible warning to pedestrians is also provided.

Automatic half barrier crossings – protected by road traffic light signals and a lifting barrier on both sides of the railway. Audible warning to pedestrians is also provided.

Automatic barrier crossings, locally monitored – appears to the road user to be similar to an automatic half barrier crossing. It is protected by road traffic light signals and a single lifting barrier on both sides of the railway.

Automatic open crossings, locally monitored – no barriers, but protected by road traffic light signals and an audible warning for pedestrians.

Open crossings – do not have barriers or road traffic light signals. Only road traffic signs are provided. Road users must give way to trains at the crossing.

User-worked crossings for vehicles – normally protected by gates, or lifting barriers on both sides of the railway. The gates, normally closed across the road and hung so as to open away from the railway, are operated by the users.

Footpath and bridleway crossings – where the railway crosses a footpath or bridleway.

Foot crossings at stations – found between platforms at stations; may be the only route between platforms or the only practicable route for people who cannot use steps.

Source: ORR

crossings look set to remain a feature of how the railway works for decades to come.

Considerable effort is being expended to make existing level crossings safer – for example, by using new technology such as audible spoken warnings and obstacle detection systems – and campaigns are being presented to members of the public to highlight the dangers of misusing the crossings. And while abolishing level crossings may be difficult, there is little enthusiasm for opening new ones. Network Rail says that provision of new level crossings would introduce additional risk and therefore would be permitted only in exceptional circumstances.[55] The ORR is also reluctant to countenance new crossings: it ruled out allowing a new crossing in Portishead that would enable a new station to be built closer to the town centre. While this approach avoids introducing new risks, it can make life difficult for those wanting to reopen former rail lines across which, since their closure, roads have been built.

ORR and HM Railway Inspectorate

Following implementation of the Railways Act 2005 the Office of Rail and Road is the independent health and safety regulator for the railway industry, including metros, light rail and heritage lines. Its remit covers the safety of the travelling public as well as workers on the railways. As the independent economic and safety regulator, the ORR can take enforcement action to ensure that those who have duties under the law are held to account for failures to safeguard health and safety.

ORR's health and safety strategy is to secure the proper control by duty holders of risks to the health and safety of employees, passengers and others who might be affected by the operation of Britain's railways. HM Railway Inspectorate (HMRI) sits within the ORR and has inspectors and policy advisers who work together to develop and deliver the strategy.

The term 'duty holders' means railway operators such as Network Rail, the freight and train operating companies and contractors who have responsibilities under health and safety law. The organisations that manage the business of the railways have the direct responsibility for health and safety, but HMRI aims to work with the rail industry to help them in identifying common problems and to agree actions and priorities.

The Railways Act 1993 brought all railway safety legislation within the framework created by the Health and Safety at Work Act 1974, as amended, and confirmed the Health and Safety Commission as the principal provider of policy advice to ministers on railway safety issues. The duties of the ORR with respect to railway safety for the most part replicate those of the Health and Safety Commission as set out in sections 11 and 50 of the 1974 Act.

A Memorandum of Understanding exists between the Health and Safety Executive and ORR in order to ensure effective coordination and cooperation between these organisations in relation to regulation of health and safety, including policy matters and the enforcement of health and safety law, on railways, tramways and other guided transport systems in Great Britain. HMRI carries out inspections and audits to check that the rail industry has management systems in place and that they are effective in controlling health and safety risks. HMRI also targets risk areas of particular concern using what are called mandatory inspection programmes.

HMRI is responsible for the investigation of breaches of criminal law and health and safety legislation on the railways, while the ORR and the Rail Accident Investigation Branch (RAIB) investigate accidents on the railways. The RAIB carries out investigations into the most serious rail accidents and incidents, without apportioning blame or liability, with a view to enabling lessons to be learned, improving safety on railways and preventing similar reoccurrences. HMRI is responsible for implementing any recommendation made by the RAIB following the completion of its investigation.

The Railway Industry Health and Safety Advisory Committee

The Railway Industry Health and Safety Advisory Committee (RIHSAC, previously RIAC) was established in 1978 by the Health and Safety Commission. It advises the ORR on railway health and safety, exchanges information, comments on proposed new regulations and guidance, and works to progress health and safety issues and other related developments within the industry. It includes representatives from a wide range of rail industry organisations and meets three times a year.

Setting standards

Established in 2003 in response to recommendations made following a public inquiry into the Ladbroke Grove accident, the Rail Safety and Standards Board (RSSB) is a not-for-profit company limited by guarantee and owned by major rail stakeholders. It manages industry-wide programmes of research, development and innovation in cooperation with the Department for Transport, Network Rail and other partners.

The RSSB's primary objective is to support its members in improving safety and performance and value for money across the industry. To achieve this it works to help rail organisations understand risk, oversees industry research and innovation programmes, and encourages industry collaboration that will lead to improvements.

Its responsibilities also include developing the content of Railway Group Standards, which define what must be done to achieve technical compatibility on the national rail network. Railway Group Standards set out technical requirements applicable to vehicles or the infrastructure as well as processes applicable to transport operators.

The best-known Railway Group Standard is the Rule Book, a mandatory safety document that comprises a set of modules and handbooks containing instructions for railway staff. This sets out the operational rules for application on the rail network that are necessary to enable the safe and timely delivery of people and goods to their destination and to provide the framework to enable safe engineering operations. The RSSB says that around 100,000 people have a printed copy of the Rule Book. Changes to the book are set out in a Periodical Operating Notice, published every three months by Network Rail, which is available to train operators.

The Rail Accident and Investigation Branch

Created to investigate railway accidents, the Rail Accident and Investigation Branch (RAIB) was formed in response to Lord Cullen's inquiry report on the 1999 Ladbroke Grove rail accident in which 31 people died.

The RAIB became operational in October 2005 as the UK's independent body for investigating accidents and incidents occurring on the railways of Great Britain and Northern Ireland, and tramways in England and Wales. Although it is part of the Department for Transport, it operates independently in a similar way to the Air and Marine Accident Investigation branches. The RAIB Chief Inspector reports directly to the Secretary of State on matters concerning accident investigation.

RAIB responsibilities and duties are set out in the Railways and Transport Safety Act 2003 and the Railways (Accident Investigation and Reporting) Regulations 2005. These also include details of the scope of the regulations and the categories of accidents that the industry must notify to the RAIB.

Together, the Act and the Regulations also implement the requirements of the European Railway Safety Directive (2004/49/EC). The RAIB has a duty to cooperate with other European rail accident investigation branches created under the European Directive; this is particularly relevant for cross-border services such as those in Ireland and the Channel Tunnel. Additionally, the RAIB has a duty to report to the European Rail Agency on accidents and incidents occurring on the railways in the United Kingdom.

Through its investigations, the RAIB's aim is to improve the safety of the railways and prevent railway accidents and incidents by determining the causes and circumstances of such events, together with any other factors that contributed to the event or made the outcome worse.

During an investigation the RAIB will look for evidence, which comes from a number of different sources including the trains, the track, the signalling system and other infrastructure items, or maintenance, design and training documents. Evidence may also be in different forms, including damaged equipment, data from monitoring equipment on trains and in the signalling system, or records relating to operations and maintenance.

RAIB inspectors have been granted powers to enter railway property, land or vehicles; seize anything relating to the accident and make records; require access to and disclosure of records and information; and require people to answer questions and provide information about anything relevant to the investigation.

When an investigation is completed, the RAIB publishes a report explaining the circumstances of the incident and makes recommendations, which are intended to reduce the likelihood and mitigate the consequences of similar events occurring in the future. Publication of investigation reports provides all parts of the railway industry and the public with the opportunity to consider the findings and learn from them.

What happens when something goes wrong?

When a railway-related accident or incident occurs the infrastructure manager, train operator or maintenance firm whose workers are involved in the incident are obliged to notify the RAIB.

The RAIB gives an example of such a situation: 'If, for example, staff of a maintenance contractor, of either rolling stock or infrastructure, during the course of their work were to find a cracked axle or broken rail, then the RAIB would regard that member of staff as

having been "involved" in an incident, and his employer, as a railway industry body, as being under a duty to notify the Branch accordingly.'[56]

If a rail industry body is informed by someone else of an incident that relates to their organisation, the duty is on that body (rather than the person who alerted them to the situation) to report the incident to the RAIB.

The notification will usually be made by telephone, followed up by completion of a written form. For serious incidents (including deaths, serious injuries, collisions and derailments) notification is required immediately, whereas less serious incidents must be reported within three working days (for example, train fires) or a month (for example, damage to rails that has resulted in a line closure or speed restriction).

For all accidents in the Channel Tunnel, wherever they happen, it has been agreed that both the RAIB and its French counterpart, BEA-TT, should be notified.

Normally the RAIB will publish a report setting out the findings of its investigation within 12 months. This will usually contain recommendations setting out what the industry bodies concerned can do to avoid a similar incident occurring in the future.

ABOVE The busy approaches to London Waterloo. Strict protocols are essential across the railway network to ensure that trains are operated safely and maintenance is carried out without risk. The ORR is the independent health and safety regulator for the industry while the RAIB investigates any accidents.

The RAIB is not a prosecuting body and the investigations into offences under the regulations will be conducted either by the safety authority (the ORR) or by the police after consultation with the Crown Prosecution Service, or in Scotland the Crown Office and Procurator Fiscal Service.

British Transport Police

British Transport Police (BTP) is the national police force for Britain's railways, providing a service to rail operators, their staff and the 6 million people a day who use the rail network. The BTP also covers the London Underground, Docklands Light Railway, the Midland Metro, Croydon Tramlink, Tyne & Wear Metro, Glasgow Subway and Emirates AirLine.

The British Transport Police Authority (BTPA) is the independent body responsible for ensuring an efficient and effective British Transport Police force. Its duties and functions are similar to those of the Scottish Police Authority or a police and crime commissioner in England and Wales – although it oversees a force responsible for policing a much larger area.

The BTPA was established on 1 July 2004 by Act of Parliament to ensure that British Transport Police is appropriately managed and funded. It has 13 members, who bring industry knowledge of passengers, policing and the railways, and oversee the work of the force and its 2,866 officers who police Great Britain's 20,000 miles of track. Following a restructure, BTP divides the country into three divisions: B – London, C – North of England, the Midlands, Wales and the South West, and D – Scotland. The split is divided into seven smaller sub-divisions and each has a superintendent who oversees the day-to-day policing on his or her patch.

As well as deciding the force's budget, the BTPA sets the strategy for policing the railways and the policing targets to achieve this each year, appoints its senior officers – including the chief constable – employs all officers and staff, and holds the force to account. The authority operates out of offices in Camden, London, and holds six meetings a year, which are open to the public.

Every three years the BTP and BTPA publish key objectives linked to a longer-term strategic plan. The current strategic plan runs from 2013 to 2019. Policing Plans are published every year.

Most funding for BTP and the BTPA comes from train operating companies, Network Rail and London Underground. Further contributions come from smaller rail networks that use BTP

BELOW British Transport Police officers are funded by train operators and help ensure that users of national rail and light rail services feel safe.
British Transport Police

ABOVE British Transport Police can be found at most major stations. This is the concourse at London Liverpool Street.

officers, and counter-terrorism funding comes from the Home Office. In 2014/15 BTP was expected to have a net budget requirement of £213m.[57] The organisation faces a number of financial challenges including meeting higher pension and Airwave radio usage costs. Between 2013 and 2015 the BTPA has agreed that £8m will be found from efficiency savings and directed to the frontline to provide 208 more police officers.

British Transport Police deal with a wide range of crimes on the railway including trespass and vandalism, pickpocketing, begging, sexual offences, anti-social behaviour and terrorism.

Cable theft

Since 2006 the price of copper – the metal inside cables widely used by the rail industry – has increased sharply, prompting a wave of attempts to steal these cables. Network Rail has estimated that cable theft can cost the industry up to £16m a year but, perhaps more significantly, passengers' journeys can be affected if signalling or other railway systems are disrupted because of damage to cables.

BTP and other organisations have put in place a package of measures designed to tackle the problem. In 2012 the Home Secretary announced an end to cash payments for scrap metal and higher penalties designed to deter cable theft. Network Rail engineers have designed cables that are easier to identify and harder to steal; the organisation said that in 2012-13 cable theft more than halved compared with the previous year.[58]

During the ten years since the BTPA's inception, crime on the railway has fallen each year in succession, and there are 75% fewer robberies on the rail system than in 2004.[59]

9 • People

That people are at the heart of how the railway works is not so much a cliché as an indisputable fact. The UK rail industry employs more than 190,000 people, from train drivers and station staff to those responsible for managing and maintaining the network's 20,000 miles of track. Once you add in all the people involved in enhancement projects and the services on which the railway depends, the number of people making a contribution is likely to be even larger.

In this chapter the aim is to give an indication of what a railway career in the 21st century looks like. More precisely, it aims to demystify the notion of 'working in rail' and to showcase the variety of career options. Many are linked to managing the complex organisational structures that are required to make the railway work. Others are connected to the railway's increasing dependence on technology. And yes, there are train drivers too.

One aspect of the people factor that cannot go ignored is the skills shortage facing Britain's railway. This chapter suggests reasons for this and considers some of the major initiatives that have and are being put in place to respond to this challenge. Finally, it looks at the trade unions, which are hugely influential in shaping the railway workplace and also have considerable clout in steering policy and investment decisions.

Career options

For people with the right skills, there are plenty of options. Between 2013 and 2020 an estimated £25bn will be invested in Britain's railways, and by 2019 10,000 new recruits will be needed – 40% to make up for people retiring and 60% to accommodate the growth in jobs arising from planned future investment.[60]

The Routes into Rail website, developed by the National Skills Academy for Railway Engineering (NSARE) with support from industry stakeholders, suggests that courses in the following subject areas will equip students for a railway career: Civil Engineering, Mechanical Engineering, Electronics and Electrical Engineering, Economics, Computer Science, Environmental Science, Mathematics and Statistics, Materials Science, Human Factors and Ergonomics, Design Engineering, Logistics, Data Science, Finance Electronics and Electrical Engineering, Physics, Materials Science, Robotics and Autonomous Systems, Social Science, Architecture, Psychology, Chemical Engineering, Transport Studies, and Risk and Safety Management.

Apprenticeships

Network Rail offers a wide range of apprenticeships providing a chance to earn while learning. Types of apprenticeships include:

- **Track** – This apprenticeship involves learning how to inspect track with specialist equipment to prioritise repair and maintenance work, responding to unexpected faults to reduce the risk on the line, or planning the materials, manpower and equipment for work on site in order to manage the delivery of work safely. This could lead to a job as a supervisor leading a team on the track, becoming a technical specialist, section manager or project engineer.
- **Overhead line electrification** – Inspection, maintenance and repair of the 10,000 miles of overhead power line can only take place when trains are not running, so careful planning is essential. Working at height is routine and specialist tools are used to measure, adjust, repair and modify cables and wires. An apprenticeship provides the opportunity to progress to a specialist or

ABOVE Cab simulators are used to train drivers, ensure route knowledge, and make sure that staff are familiar with any safety issues.

BELOW The railway relies on experienced and suitably qualified drivers to operate services, meet performance targets and keep the system safe for everyone.

supervisory position in maintenance, repair or planning.

- **Signalling** – This covers a wide range of equipment and technology, from mechanical to computer-based systems and safety and performance enhancement schemes. Every day rail workers check, test, clean and fix thousands of signals throughout the country. This is done by taking and recording electrical and mechanical values of equipment. Signalling engineering is also all about delivering new and improved infrastructure, which involves design, delivery, installation and testing. The first step for those interested in this area is to become a signalling technician, a junior designer or a tester. Developing technical expertise can lead to a career as a signalling or project engineer.
- **Telecoms** – An apprenticeship in this area involves working with a trackside team on a wide range of systems to develop a broad practical knowledge of telecoms. There is an opportunity to specialise in one of the following areas:
  - Transmission: the transmission of data and voice quickly and effectively.
  - Cables: the backbone of railway telecommunication infrastructures.
  - Telephone exchange: communications between signal boxes and the trackside.
  - Radio: the exchange of instructions between train drivers and signalling, using both analogue and digital systems.
  - Customer information systems: including station display boards, CCTV, public address and emergency evacuation.
- **Electrification and plant** – During a three-year apprenticeship skills are developed in contact systems, distribution and lineside plant (such as back-up generators and electrical point heaters). As an electrification and plant engineer one can go on to be involved in inspections and repairs or installations and maintenance, working on anything from cabling to high-voltage protection systems or signal boxes.

Transport for London offers a range of apprenticeship programmes in areas including commercial procurement, human resources, information management, software engineering, testing, and London Underground operations.

In addition to the ongoing requirements of the rail industry for apprentices, major projects have secured funding partly by promising to deliver a skills and jobs legacy. For example, Crossrail had a target of creating 400 apprenticeships during the construction of the new railway, a figure that has been surpassed with at least 450 apprentices having worked on the project. Crossrail apprentices have been trained in a range of skills from construction to accountancy, quantity surveying to business administration.

Graduate positions

Network Rail offers two main routes for graduates, which can lead to a variety of different career paths.

For those who want to work outside, on site, the engineering option is likely to be the most appropriate course. Graduate trainees might end up using high-end technology, such as ultrasonic testing equipment, or contributing to new innovations, like battery-powered trains (see Chapter 11). Within engineering there are three specific schemes: civil engineering, electrical and electronic engineering, and mechanical engineering.

Alternatively, the business management strand may appeal to others – particularly candidates who are self-motivated, and comfortable with change. In business management Network Rail offers a number of different schemes: finance, general management, property, strategic planning, project management, supply chain, and business technology.

For those not starting their career in rail straight from university or college the company's engineering conversion programme may provide the right opportunity. Network Rail says that for many of its roles a specific background is not important although, given the specialist nature of many rail industry systems, there is a need to help engineers from outside the rail industry adapt. The nine-month engineering conversion programme aims to do just that, and offers a postgraduate diploma upon completion.

Transport for London also offers a range of graduate opportunities. It recruits for disciplines including architecture, business analysis, civil engineering, commercial procurement, commercial and quantity surveying, electrical engineering, finance, information management, marketing and communications, rail management, mechanical engineering, project management, software engineering, and transport planning.

From time to time positions also become available in Government. The DfT needs project and programme managers, policy advisers, digital communication specialists, engineers, economists, transport modellers, statisticians, researchers, accountants, and lawyers.

Tackling skills shortages

As investment in Britain's railways has been ratcheted up in recent years, the need to actively plan for training tomorrow's workforce has increased. Major tunnelling and high-speed rail projects mean that skills that in the past the railway has been able to do without are now very much in demand. Acknowledgment that during the post-privatisation era training staff was perhaps not the industry's priority has also pushed the skills issue towards the top of the agenda. If this was not reason enough for Government involvement, the political benefits that flow from creating jobs and getting young people into vocational education seem to have cemented the case.

Tunnelling and Underground Construction Academy

A £13m Tunnelling and Underground Construction Academy (TUCA) at Aldersbrook Sidings on the border of Newham and Redbridge in east London welcomed its first students in 2011.

BELOW The Tunnelling and Underground Construction Academy in east London includes a mock-up of a railway tunnel and an example of a locomotive used to transport workers between a tunnel portal and the tunnelling face.

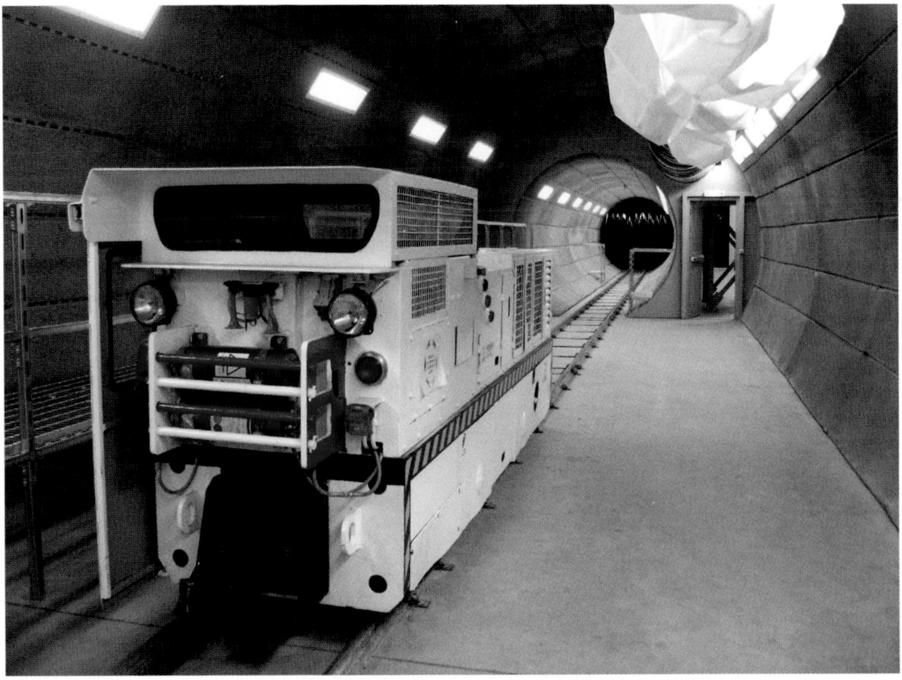

TRAINING OFFERED AT TUCA

- Pre-employment training to help local people access construction jobs
- Tunnel Safety Card (a mandatory requirement for Crossrail)
- NVQ Level 2 Tunnel Operations (a mandatory requirement for Crossrail)
- NVQ Level 3 Supervisory Management
- Working at heights and in confined spaces
- Construction Plant Competence Scheme loco driver training
- Construction Skills Health and Safety Test
- Sprayed concrete applications
- Laboratory Technician training in materials testing
- Apprenticeships in a range of tunnelling and construction related occupations

Source: Crossrail Ltd

The facility was developed to support Crossrail, providing a centre where those people required to build Crossrail tunnels could go and learn their craft. However, TUCA is expected to go on to train the workers needed by other rail tunnelling projects such as the London Underground Northern Line extension to Battersea and High Speed 2.

Training courses offered include the Tunnel Safety Card, a pre-requisite for anyone who wants to work below ground on Crossrail, and Construction Skills Certification Scheme health and safety card training. Other courses focus on pre-cast concrete manufacture and tunnel operations training.

Vocational training areas have been equipped with tunnelling plant and machinery, allowing trainees to try their hand at spray concrete lining and experience life within a simulated tunnel environment. Up to 150 students can attend courses offered by the facility at any one time. The National Construction College is contracted to deliver skills and training at the academy.

Crossrail Ltd expects TUCA to provide training for at least 3,500 people over the lifetime of the Crossrail project. The only other tunnelling training facility in Europe is located in Switzerland, and TUCA is the only centre in Europe dedicated to teaching soft-ground tunnelling techniques.

Up to £7.5m will be invested in TUCA as part of the Crossrail programme, while £5m has been provided by the Department for Business, Innovation and Skills via the Skills Funding Agency. The building was designed by Capita Symonds and constructed by Volker Fitzpatrick. Sponsorship has been provided by suppliers, including BASF.

National College for High Speed Rail

The Government has set out plans to create a new higher education college that will work with a network of employers, other educational institutions and providers to equip people to work on the High Speed 2 programme. An estimated 400,000 jobs will be underpinned by HS2 with around 2,000 apprentice places promised during the entire 15-year construction period.

Scheduled to open in 2017 when construction of HS2 phase one is supposed to begin, the college will provide the specialist training and qualifications needed for high-speed rail and other future infrastructure projects across the UK. The intention is to offer the necessary technical training to make HS2 a success and ensure that it can be built by British workers with expertise in rail engineering, environmental skills and construction.

As well as rail engineering, the college's core offer is expected to include skills in new technologies associated with engineering design, construction and management, including building information modelling (BIM). The hope is that it will meet the wider economic need for an increased supply of engineers, delivering engineering courses that are not explicitly focused on the rail industry and having a purpose beyond the timeframes of HS2.

In 2014 the Government announced that two sites had been selected for the new college. Birmingham city centre – the location of HS2 Ltd's construction headquarters – will host the main campus and the college will also have a site at Doncaster's Lakeside Campus.

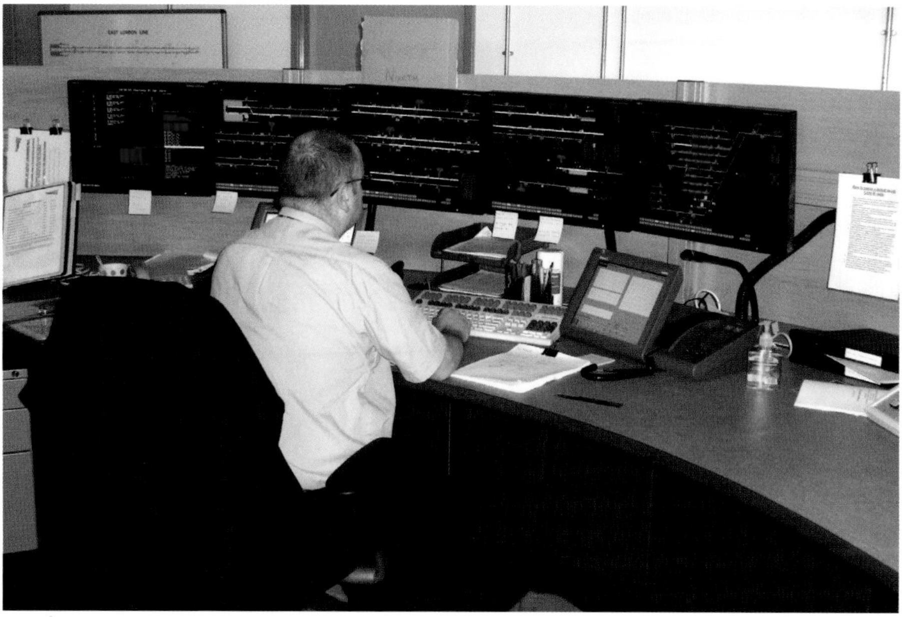

ABOVE **Signalling staff have an overview of traffic across part of a route, communicate with drivers, and path services to minimise delays to passengers.**

National Training Academy for Rail

Opened in autumn 2015, the National Training Academy for Rail (NTAR) has been developed by the National Skills Academy for Railway Engineering in collaboration with Siemens, which is putting up half the cost.

The new academy will specialise in traction and rolling stock skills and be located at the site of Siemens' existing train depot and UK service headquarters in Kings Heath, Northampton.

Around 13,500 people work in specialist traction and rolling stock roles across the UK, and NTAR will focus on addressing the future skills shortage in this part of the UK rail sector, forecast to be around 4,500 people over the next five years.

The Northampton training centre will act as a national hub with regional spokes located at other train care facilities around the country. The 50/50 funding agreement will release half of the academy's training capacity to the wider UK industry with the remainder used by Siemens' own employees in the rail sector. Up to 170 students will attend NTAR at any one time using facilities that include an overhead crane, embedded tracks, AC and DC power supplies and an underground train access pit.

In addition to encouraging more entry-level talent, as both apprentices and graduates, existing rail industry employees will be offered opportunities to upskill in response to advancements in the rail industry such as 'fly-by-wire' train controls and the European Rail Traffic Management System.

The National Skills Academy for Railway Engineering (NSARE) is an organisation rather than a place. It was established in November 2010 by then Business Secretary Vince Cable. The not-for-profit company, limited by guarantee, is responsible for galvanising the rail industry's efforts to tackle current and future engineering skills needs. Since 2013 it has been financially independent from Government and it has more than 330 member organisations who pay £250 or £1,000 a year (depending on size) for membership.

Worker representation

Trade unions play a significant role in Britain's rail industry. By standing up for their members' pay and conditions they force employers – particularly Network Rail, London Underground and train operators – to think carefully about the way they handle staffing issues and remunerate workers. The salaries of train drivers are indicative of the unions' bargaining power.

As well as representing workers' individual needs, the rail unions add a powerful collective voice to calls for investment in the railway, which benefits the industry as a whole. Perhaps unsurprisingly they are less keen on changes to working practices, which may be sold by Government as a condition of investment. One example of this is the move towards Driver Only Operation (where train doors are controlled by the driver rather than a guard, reducing the number of skilled staff required per train), a development opposed by the unions.

The National Union of Rail, Maritime and Transport Workers (RMT) describes itself as Britain's largest specialist transport trade union and claims to have more than 80,000 members from the main-line and underground railways, shipping and offshore, buses and road freight. The union's primary objective is to at least protect, if not better, members' pay and conditions. It does this by negotiating with more than 150 companies in the rail and transport sectors.

For 2015 the standard membership rate was £241 a year. For that members get workplace representation, legal cover, access to a credit union and a range of membership benefits including accident and retirement benefits.

The RMT's influence extends across the rail sector but is particularly noticeable on London Underground, where strikes typically occur every few months following RMT ballots over issues such as the dismissal of a member of staff, safety concerns and modernisation of work practices. The union is opposing Transport for London's Future Stations programme, which includes the closure of station ticket offices across the network.

Although the RMT is clearly a powerful force for staff to have on their side, concerns have been raised that the union is able to disrupt too easily, and despite a limited mandate from members, what for many people is an essential service. The Mayor of London and the Conservative Prime Minister have called for strike votes to be declared void unless a certain threshold of members takes part in the ballot. Unions countered that if such rules were brought in for a General Election most MPs would never be elected to office.

The Mayor has repeatedly pledged to make Underground strikes illegal and lobbied Government to put Underground workers on a similar footing to the police, which would mean, as providers of an essential service, that they would not be allowed to walk out on strike. Following the election of a Conservative Government in May 2015, the Queen's Speech promised to place a Trade Unions Bill before parliament. If passed, this would introduce a 50% voting threshold for union ballot turnouts and retain the requirement for there to be a simple majority of votes backing any proposed strike. In addition, for members of public services including transport to walk out, there would be a new requirement for at least 40% of those entitled to vote to vote in favour of industrial action.

The second biggest trade union in the rail sector is ASLEF (the Associated Society of Locomotive Engineers and Firemen), which predominantly represents train drivers and has more than 18,500 members belonging to 180 branches across the UK. The union is led by an executive committee, elected by members within each district, which in turn elects a president from among its members. Other unions that can claim to have members working on the railway include the Transport Salaried Staffs' Association (TSSA) and Unite, Britain's largest trade union.

ABOVE Contractors such as Balfour Beatty rely on engineers and construction professionals to deliver major railway projects. This is the worksite for the new Crossrail station at Woolwich.

10 • Supply side

Behind the day-to-day operation of trains is a vast industry that does everything from maintaining the track on which each service runs to supplying the sandwiches available from the snack trolley.

Suppliers can be considered from two perspectives. One is how the industry is organised to actually make the railway work – the contractual structures and commercial agreements that enable Britain's railway network to function. The second is the benefits the industry provides to society as a whole in creating jobs, paying tax and stimulating the economy.

Overview

Railway maintenance and enhancement schemes are delivered by main contractors, usually appointed by Network Rail, who may subcontract some elements of the work depending on the terms of their contract.

The number of these top-level, 'tier one' suppliers appears to be dwindling as the industry consolidates and takeovers are agreed. In some areas, including train manufacture and leasing, a small number of firms dominate and therefore exert significant influence. As will be explored in Chapter 11, Network Rail's work

RIGHT At New Cross Gate, London Overground has a depot for Class 378 'Capitalstar' electric multiple units.

BELOW Railway maintenance equipment is becoming increasingly advanced. Here workers watch a demonstration of a mobile track vehicle that can weld rails.

Table 7: Network Rail top suppliers[61]

Supplier name	Specialism
Amalgamated Construction (AMCO)	Infrastructure
Amey	Infrastructure, structural inspection services
Atkins	Signalling, infrastructure, consultancy services
Babcock Rail	Track, infrastructure
Balfour Beatty (BB Civil Engineering and BB Rail)	Track, infrastructure
BAM Nuttall	Infrastructure
C. Spencer	Infrastructure
Carillion	Infrastructure
Colas Rail	Track, infrastructure
Costain	Infrastructure
DB Schenker	Rail logistics
EDF Energy	Electricity supply
Geoffrey Osborne	Infrastructure
Siemens	Signalling, infrastructure
J. Murphy	Infrastructure
Signalling Solutions[62]	Signalling/infrastructure contracting
Tata Steel	Rail supply
VolkerFitzpatrick	Infrastructure

GETTING GRIP

Network Rail uses an eight-step Governance for Railway Investment Projects (GRIP) approach to manage and control projects that enhance or renew the national rail network. This has been developed to minimise the risks associated with delivering schemes by drawing on best practice advocated by the Office of Government Commerce, the Association of Project Management and the Chartered Institute of Building. The eight steps are:

1. Output definition
2. Feasibility
3. Option selection
4. Single option development
5. Detailed design
6. Construction test and commission
7. Scheme hand back
8. Project close out

The rail industry often refers to the award of a GRIP contract. For example, a GRIP 5-8 award would refer to the main contract to build/deliver an enhancement scheme.

programme is constrained by the limited number of signalling specialists.

Working with the big firms, and often crucial to their success, is an army of small specialist firms that make up the railway supply chain. The Derby & Derbyshire Rail Forum claims to represent the largest cluster of rail companies in the world – more than 100 businesses across the East Midlands, employing more than 25,000 people and contributing £2.6bn to the local economy. However, companies supplying the rail industry can be found all over the British isles.

This has been highlighted by several major contract wins. The Government decision to order a fleet of Thameslink trains to be built by Siemens in Germany proved a turning point. Critics of the deal – including trade unions and suppliers – argued that the decision threatened the viability of the UK's last remaining train factory (Bombardier's plant in Derby) as well as missing an opportunity to create jobs and economic growth at home.

Since then the Government, buying organisations such as Network Rail and Transport for London, and major suppliers have taken pains to emphasise the economic benefits of any contract they award, including the number of jobs that will be created. Siemens (with Thameslink) and Hitachi (with the Intercity Express Programme) have highlighted the number of subcontracts they have placed with UK-based suppliers. These days it is not enough to get the best deal for the railway – it must also be seen to benefit the UK economy.

Identifying opportunities

How do suppliers win contracts from the rail industry? To have a hope of winning a contract companies will usually submit expressions of interest. These will then be evaluated by the purchasing authority, which will weed out firms that do not comply with its requirements. Remaining bidders will then be issued with invitations to tender, which will be judged and a shortlist drawn up. Further rounds of sifting may occur, depending on the complexity of the contract, after which time a preferred bidder is announced. When all requirements have been met, the contract will be signed and, if a major one, will be subject to a mandatory standstill period under EU rules, allowing the decision to be challenged if there is any suggestion of irregularity. Assuming that there are no complications, the contract will be confirmed.

The organisation letting a contract is often referred to as the client. The way a client manages and organises the procurement process is important because it will often determine the success or failure of a project.

Under the traditional contracting model the client will let a main contract to a large contractor. This 'tier one' company then subcontracts those elements of the package where it needs to bring in external skills or other resources to which it does not have access in-house. 'Tier two' contracts may then be subcontracted further, creating a supply chain with several levels.

Early contractor involvement

Early contractor involvement (ECI) is widely viewed as a sensible approach to procurement for complex schemes. Rather than the client waiting until it has a final design before letting a contract, the contractor will be appointed at an earlier stage in the project cycle and involved in finalising the design. This makes use of the contractor's experience and reduces the likelihood of a client developing a scheme that proves flawed when construction is due to get under way – a situation that would be likely to delay the scheme. ECI will involve an integrated contractor and designer team and may be structured as an incentivised two-stage contract with a break point between the first (developing a design, construction planning and agreeing a works price) and the second (detailed design and build).

London Underground Ltd is backing a form of ECI that it calls 'innovative contractor engagement' (ICE). This is designed to address the situation whereby several companies may come and work with the client during initial development but once a contract is awarded those firms not selected for the contract batten down the hatches and any expertise outside the winning team is lost. With ICE, first used by London Underground for the Deep Tube Programme/New Tube for London, there is an attempt to put a value on intellectual property across the shortlisted bids, allowing the client to benefit from the best ideas and pay for innovative approaches it deems of particular merit.

Under ICE London Underground agrees to pay shortlisted bidders a proportion of their bid costs in recognition of their contribution to the development of the scheme, and because preparing bids for this sort of complex project is expensive. It is able to buy certain elements of unsuccessful bids if it thinks these will benefit the project.

LU capital programmes director David Waboso explains the thinking behind the development of ICE: 'Procurement has always swung around this conundrum – How can I stop myself from giving the job to the cheapest possible bid because the cheapest capital build cost is rarely the best overall long-term solution.'[63]

In search of better contract models

Some clients, notably London Underground with its station stabilisation programme, have tried a different approach that sees it engage specialist trades – what would normally be regarded as 'tier two' or more suppliers – directly. Not only does this reduce the layers of mark-up for profit in the supply chain, but it also allows the client to have greater control of the work being done. The downside is that the client has to manage this rather than passing the responsibility over to a main contractor. Although Crossrail relies on its main contractors subcontracting to create a supply chain with several levels, 'tier one' contractors are not allowed to award a subcontract without the approval of the client. In this way Crossrail Ltd exerts control over the top tiers of the supply chain.

In the rail industry frameworks are regularly used. Companies bid for a place on the framework and, if successful, they have access to contracts awarded under the framework but are not guaranteed work. The process can make sense if there are a lot of similar contracts to let by avoiding the need to run multiple procurement competitions. Network Rail uses lots of frameworks (such as the Multi Asset Framework Agreement – MAFA) with frameworks used on big rail construction projects such as Crossrail (including design and enabling work frameworks).

For large projects the client often signs up a delivery partner. This involves letting a contract that will provide access to specialist staff and resources that will be available throughout the course of the project. Using a delivery partner introduces an extra layer of cost – bringing in experts does not come cheap – but if this ensures that the project is delivered on time and to budget it may be viewed as money well spent, particularly for complex undertakings. There are a limited number of companies in a position to act as a delivery partner for rail schemes – Bechtel and CH2M Hill are two such firms. Delivery partners are being used for the Crossrail and High Speed 2 programmes.

ABOVE There are no UK-based companies that make tunnel boring machines, so Crossrail has used TBMs manufactured in Germany. *Crossrail Ltd*

BELOW During construction of Crossrail two temporary factories were established to manufacture concrete segments to line the new tunnels.

ABOVE Underground railway structures are often constructed with diaphragm walls. This involves excavating a trench, which is kept intact using a muddy-looking bentonite fluid, then filling the trench with reinforced concrete to make an underground wall.

Alliances

In recent years Network Rail has championed the establishment of alliances for major projects, moving away from the traditional client/contractor relationship in favour of an integrated team where staff from Network Rail and its suppliers work alongside each other.

The exact form an alliance takes varies but defining features can include:

- Early contractor involvement and mechanisms to ensure that suppliers benefit from identifying ways to deliver a project more efficiently
- Attempting to encourage mutual trust by giving suppliers greater responsibility and avoiding 'man-marking' where the client employs members of staff to check that the supplier's staff have done the job they were appointed to do.
- Streamlining finance – for example, by ensuring prompt payment and full reimbursement for any expenses incurred by a contractor while working as part of an alliance team
- Following the eight-step BS11000 standard for collaborative business relationships.

Projects using alliances include the rebuilding of London Bridge station as part of the Thameslink Programme and the Edinburgh to Glasgow Improvement Programme. In 2013 Network Rail announced what it described as the rail industry's first 'pure construction alliance' to deliver the Stafford Area Improvement Programme with Atkins, Laing O'Rourke and VolkerRail. Based on an approach used in Australia, this promised one unified agreement where all parties shared the benefits and the risks of the project, moving away from the traditional 'hub and spoke'-style of contracting.

With alliances and delivery partners it may not be obvious to an outsider who works for which company, but this is all part of the ethos of creating a single team that co-locates and where staff focus on the overall project rather than maintaining a 'silo' mentality. Collaborative working can be beneficial in many ways, but it is worth remembering that however embedded suppliers are in a client's activity, their involvement is ultimately motivated by the need to turn a profit.

Marketplaces

Major contracts by public-sector organisations to supply the railways or deliver rail-related works have to be advertised in the Official Journal of the European Union. Published every working day since the Treaty of Nice came into force on 1 February 2003, contracts can be viewed in more than 20 different languages. Although described as a journal, the hard-copy version ceased publication in 1997 and contracts are now accessed online via Tenders Direct.

When an organisation wants to advertise a contract it will publish what is widely referred to as an OJEU notice. This gives details of the services being procured, the requirements, and the timescale for submitting an expression of interest. Once the contract has been awarded, the contracting organisation is obliged to publish another notice setting out which company (or companies) has been awarded the contract.

The level of detail in these notices varies considerably, but can provide an insight into projects being undertaken by the rail industry. Sometimes additional notices are published, such as prior information notices, which alert the marketplace to an upcoming contract before the procurement begins. This can make sense for a complex procurement, such as buying a new fleet of trains, when there may be a requirement to sound out suppliers or give companies time to prepare for what is likely to be a complex bid.

Contracts over a certain value must be advertised in the Official Journal of the European Union, and thresholds are updated regularly. The threshold for works packages was just over £4.3m as of January 2014, although some supply contracts worth significantly less must also be advertised. Purchasing authorities can use the myTenders website to publish OJEU and lower-value tenders.

OJEU notices can provide an insight into rail market activity, but it is possible to avoid the need to publish details of an upcoming contract. Specialist marketplaces such as Link-up will publish an overarching contract notice that can embrace hundreds of supply categories. Individual contracts can then be procured confidentially within this marketplace while having satisfied the requirement to advertise in the OJEU. An example of this was Eurostar's 2010 announcement that it would be buying a new fleet of trains from Siemens, news that took most within the rail industry by surprise.

Link-up – recently restructured and renamed the Railway Industry Supplier Qualification Scheme – is run by Achilles Information, a company founded in Norway in 1990. It provides a marketplace and pre-qualification system widely used by the rail industry. Suppliers pay a subscription of between £365 and £1,285[64] to access contract notices placed by more than 110 buyers including Network Rail and the Rail Safety and Standards Board. The aim is to standardise the information required for bids and streamline the process for buyers and sellers.

Link-up is governed by a RISQS (Rail Industry Supplier Qualification Scheme) Board, compromising cross-industry representation, and the RISQS Board members contribute to the development of the service.

A range of other online marketplaces exist. The Coalition Government supported open data initiatives that helped small and medium-size enterprises find and bid for contracts relating to rail and other infrastructure sectors.

One that has gained recognition in recent years is CompeteFor, a free service that enables businesses to bid for contract opportunities linked to major public and private

ABOVE Alstom maintains many of the trains used on inter-city routes. At this facility in Liverpool the company is refurbishing wheelsets, also known as bogies.

sector buying organisations. Use of CompeteFor by Crossrail has made this a useful place to identify contracts, particularly smaller opportunities that would not warrant an OJEU. CompeteFor is operated by BiP Solutions.

Rolling stock

The days of British Rail building its own trains are long gone, and today train and tram building is dominated by four foreign-owned companies – Alstom (France), Bombardier (Canada), Hitachi (Japan) and Siemens (Germany). A fifth, CAF of Spain, has made limited inroads into the UK, supplying trains for Northern Ireland and new carriages for the Caledonian Sleeper.

Although these companies have a variety of traincare centres around the country that can undertake maintenance and refurbishment activity, only one volume train building facility survives – Bombardier's Litchurch Lane factory in Derby. In June 2011 the announcement that Siemens had been selected to build (abroad) the new fleet of more than 1,100 Thameslink train carriages, one of the biggest rolling stock orders of recent times, was followed by Bombardier announcing hundreds of job cuts and warning that it could end train building at Derby altogether.

The episode prompted much soul-searching, questioning the acceptability of building trains overseas for use in Britain. Among the more vocal contributors to the debate, trade unions have strongly opposed jobs going abroad, and MPs in areas such as Derby have unsurprisingly weighed into the debate warning about the implications for local businesses and communities.

Although the Thameslink order with Siemens has since been signed, rolling stock procurement processes have been tweaked to ensure consideration is given to where the train will be built, and home-grown manufacturing is back in fashion. Ministers and others with influence have focused on

ABOVE Bombardier has a train-building facility at Litchurch Lane in Derby and has delivered recent orders for London Underground. The company also won the contract to build the new train fleet required by Crossrail.

ensuring that Bombardier's production lines are kept busy. The announcement in February 2014 that Bombardier is to build the new fleet of Crossrail trains appears to have shored up the viability of Litchurch Lane for the next few years at least.

Meanwhile, in a significant development for the UK rail sector, Hitachi committed to open a train-building centre in Newton Aycliffe, County Durham, in 2015. This will produce the new Intercity Express Programme trains to replace aged 125s and 225s on the Great Western and East Coast main lines. With panels for the new train due to be manufactured in Japan before being shipped to Britain, caution is perhaps needed in describing this as a factory. Nevertheless it represents a significant commitment by the Japanese conglomerate to the UK, one that is comparable to Nissan's decision to open a car-building centre in Sunderland. The new train fleet ordered by Transport Scotland for the Edinburgh to Glasgow Improvement Programme is also to be built at Newton Aycliffe.

Welcome as this may be on many fronts, Hitachi's arrival is not without controversy. Japan's rail industry remains largely off limits to British companies that might fancy doing business in the Far East. But more importantly, the impact of the Thameslink order on Bombardier seemed to suggest that the ongoing requirement for new UK trains is not sufficient to keep one UK train-building centre in business, let alone two.

Hitachi counters that it is using Britain as a base to go after business across Europe, reinforced by its decision to shift its European headquarters to Britain. But until it manages to break into continental markets, where there is often more inertia to foreign suppliers than over here, Hitachi is a threat to Bombardier's Derby operation. New product launches have underlined the Japanese company's commitment to winning new business in Britain to keep Newton Aycliffe production lines occupied. And in a further development, Alstom – which shut down its train-building centre in Birmingham in 2003 – has signalled that it might be prepared to resume train manufacturing in Britain.[65]

ABOVE Hitachi has opened a new train-building centre in the North East of England as part of efforts to grow its business in Europe. This is a mock-up of the AT200 commuter design that the company will supply to ScotRail.

BELOW The Class 395 'Javelin' order was Hitachi's breakthrough into the UK train market. Since then the Japanese company has secured further contracts to supply Intercity Express and Edinburgh to Glasgow programmes.

ABOVE The Thameslink Programme has prompted one of the UK's biggest train orders. This is a body shell for a Class 700 'Desiro City' manufactured by Siemens. *Siemens*

Does it really matter where trains are built? Siemens has made sure the media are aware that components for the new Thameslink 'Desiro City' fleet will be supplied by UK-based firms from Tyneside to Somerset. And while the trains will be assembled abroad, Siemens will manufacture components, including cable harnesses, drivers' instruments and control desks in the North East. Indeed, when it comes to sourcing specialist equipment, different train manufacturers often turn to the same small suppliers.

Perhaps more important to ensure that the manufacture of trains and their components supports jobs and prosperity in Britain is the need to maintain a reasonably steady supply of orders. While privatisation has led to many large fleet replacement orders, this has been dependent on the franchising schedule and in turn presented suppliers with feast or famine – orders wait on Government decisions, which once made result in a glut of business. Following privatisation, no train order was placed for nearly three years, with a similar dry period between 2008 and the end of 2011.

The leasing companies

During the privatisation of Britain's railways the state-owned trains were sold off to rolling stock leasing companies. Today most of the trains that run on the national rail network are owned by three RoSCos. These companies lease the rolling stock to the train operating companies, which then deploy it on their services. There are three main RoSCOs – Porterbrook, Angel and Eversholt.

Porterbrook has been sold on three times since the firm took on a third of British Rail's rolling stock during rail privatisation in 1994. Following a management and employee buyout in January 1996, the company was sold to Stagecoach in August of the same year. In April 2000 it was bought by Abbey National Treasury Services, then in December 2008 was purchased by a consortium of investors – Antin Infrastructure, Deutsche Bank, Lloyds TSB and OP Trust Markets Group (a Canadian company that also owns rail equipment). Lloyds TSB exited the consortium in October 2010.

In 2014 Porterbrook was bought by Canada-based Alberta Investment Management Corporation, Allianz Capital Partners, France's EDF Invest and Hastings Funds Management, which has its headquarters in Australia.

In August 2008 a consortium of investors acquired Angel Trains from the Royal Bank of Scotland Group. The consortium includes Arcus Infrastructure Partners, AMP Capital Investors and International Public Partnerships; Public Sector Pension Investment Board.

Eversholt Rail is owned by Eversholt Investment Group, a consortium consisting of investment funds managed by 3i Infrastructure plc, Morgan Stanley Infrastructure Partners and STAR Capital Partners.

In the past concerns have been raised that RoSCos may be charging train operators disproportionately high leasing costs for old British Rail-bought trains where the investment costs have already been recouped. Attempts by Government to explore this issue have resulted in the Competition Commission (now succeeded by the Competition and Markets Authority) acknowledging that RoSCos have had weakened incentives to compete on lease rentals, but attributing this to the structure of the rail franchising system (for which Government is ultimately responsible) rather than anti-competitive behaviour by leasing companies.[66] The Coalition Government chose not to pursue the issue.

Who orders new trains?

One of the uncertainties of Britain's privatised railway surrounds the question of who is responsible for ordering new rolling stock. Privatisation was accompanied by the ordering of new train fleets by new train operators, significantly reducing the average age of rolling stock and resulting in some very noticeable changes of trains – for example, the introduction of Virgin's Class 390 'Pendolino' fleet on the West Coast Main Line.

With the concept of private-sector innovation being at the heart of the new railway model, this approach might have continued but for a range of factors. First, there has been a recognition in the industry that new operators anxious to showcase a new brand do not necessarily order rolling stock that meets the railway's complex needs – for example, technical capability, flexibility for deployment on alternative routes, long-term cost and passenger comfort. Second, it is difficult for an operator or leasing company to make a long-term decision to buy new trains without knowing Government railway policy for years ahead. Linked to this, no private company is going to commit to buy rolling stock costing many millions of pounds without a cast-iron guarantee that it will get a return on its investment. As franchise lengths have shortened, franchisees have been unable to justify spending on new trains.

That leaves the Government to take the lead. Yet ministers have repeatedly told Parliament that it is for train operators and RoSCos to decide how many trains the railway needs and make the necessary arrangements – an approach that is set out in a DfT Command Paper published in 2012. High-profile exceptions have clearly been made – the Intercity Express Programme and Thameslink Class 700 fleet have been centrally led and justified on the basis that their scale, complexity and duration is such that it would be impossible for a franchisee to manage and finance such an investment.

Back at franchise level the expectation is that it is for the operator and its RoSCo partners to determine rolling stock need – yet here too the Government has intervened. When invitations to tender for new Northern and TransPennine franchises were issued in 2015 the Government insisted that bidders put forward plans to buy new trains that will replace the aged, and widely scorned, 'Pacer' fleet, rather than leaving it to market forces or considering alternative approaches that could represent better value for money.

The situation can perhaps best be summed up by this written parliamentary answer given by Baroness Kramer in March 2014: 'It is not generally the Department's policy to specify the provision of specific rolling stock in franchises. However, there may be exceptions made to protect Government investment or to aid the smooth running of the programme.'[67]

11 • Rail revolution

The railway is part of our shared history. Not only were most of the lines across the UK that we still use today built well over a century ago, but the railway has a place in our collective identity. It is an enduring symbol of British life which we take for granted and is part of our social fabric.

But there is a revolution under way. While the railway may be a product of a forgotten industrial age and will to some seem an anachronism, what was once viewed as a transport mode of yesteryear is being reinvented for the 21st century.

The digital railway

Much of this is the result of developments in technology. Network Rail chiefs now talk about the digital railway, an umbrella term that can refer to all sorts of systems including cutting-edge signalling and train control technologies. Network Rail needs technology like this (which can allow more trains to run on existing infrastructure) to accommodate the surge in demand for train travel: passenger kilometres increased 50% between 2004 and 2014 and are forecast to rise by a further 50% by the mid-2030s. Even if the money could be found, building new lines fast enough to meet demand is simply not possible. The digital railway is therefore held up as the best way to solve the problem of needing to significantly increase capacity.

Much is being pinned on the digital railway. Luckily, many of the technologies the railway needs have matured, and clever ideas that had to be abandoned a decade ago are now ready, or nearly ready, to be deployed across the network. Still, for all the innovations delivered

BELOW The move towards a digital railway includes consolidating signalling operations and introducing traffic management systems that can work out the best way to path myriad services in the event of disruption to the normal timetable.

Network Rail's ambitions are truly staggering and, at the time of writing, none of the proposed train control systems have yet been implemented on a main line in the UK. Therefore the question arises – will things work as planned? More importantly, is it wise to base so many long-term plans on systems that, for all their potential, are not yet in service on workhorse routes?

It's not just about the logistics of running trains – the digital railway is also about providing information services to passengers. Where once a train running late might have been seen as something the passenger must tolerate, today's travellers want to know what is going on and are quick to vent their frustration on social media if train providers do not meet expectations. During times of disruption people expect to be told what's happening on station and train information screens and via social networks.

Passengers also expect technology on tap as an adjunct to their train travel experience. Just as it is generally taken for granted that we will be able to buy a cup of coffee and visit the lavatory during a long train journey, today we also expect wireless internet access. Increasingly the expectation is that it should be free – or at least built into our ticket price.

ABOVE As more and more people choose to cycle to and from stations, additional facilities for bikes are required. Network Rail has introduced double-deck parking racks at London stations where space is at a premium.

The rail revolution is not just about technology. When the London Underground Victoria line was built in the 1970s no one seems to have cared that wheelchair users would be unable to make use of this new railway. Today step-free access is expected. Delivering that across an aged station estate is, not surprisingly, taking time, but Crossrail is setting the standard by offering 100% accessibility.

Accessibility

By 2020 all trains in Britain in passenger service should be accessible to people in wheelchairs or with other disabilities.

Regulation 45 of the Railways (Interoperability) Regulations 2011 makes it unlawful for a passenger rail vehicle to be used in

ABOVE Developments in technology mean that new rolling stock will be fitted with real-time journey information. This is a prototype display on a mock-up of Hitachi's AT200.

service on the trans-European rail system in the UK after 31 December 2019 unless it complies with the current or future versions of the Technical Specification for Interoperability – Persons with Reduced Mobility (PRM TSI) and/or defined domestic accessibility standards such as the Rail Vehicle Accessibility (Non-Interoperable Rail system) Regulations 2010 (RVAR).

Having said that, there is provision for derogations and dispensations from the TSI to be made. The main means of allowing fleets to operate past 2019 without fully complying with the accessibility regulations is for the Department for Transport to grant a dispensation under Regulation 46 of the Railways (Interoperability) Regulations 2011.

Rolling stock leasing companies are under pressure to carry out significant work to ensure that legacy fleets meet the 2020 deadline. Sometimes these can be met with minor works such as installing new handrails or PA systems. In other cases work such as replacing doors or toilet units can be expensive and have a significant bearing on the economics of a fleet.

According to the DfT's 2013 report on rail vehicle accessibility exemption orders[68], more than 5,800 heavy rail vehicles (47%) and nearly 1,500 non-heavy rail vehicles (30%) have been built to the standards set out in RVAR or PRM TSI. The latter figure is dominated by London Underground trains, many of which were built before RVAR came into force.

All older heavy and light rail vehicles receive accessibility improvements as and when they are refurbished, and the Equality Act 2010 requires the Secretary of State to make regulations to ensure that all passenger rail vehicles are accessible by no later than 1 January 2020. The DfT is working with the Disabled Persons Transport Advisory Committee and the rail industry to ensure that non-compliant vehicles are modified by 2020.

The DfT's 2013 report noted that, when the accessibility improvements made to 600 older vehicles are added to the new-build compliant units, Britain has more than 7,850 fully accessible rail vehicles, representing 46% of the entire fleet.

ABOVE European efforts to standardise railway systems are gradually removing barriers to international operations and allowing trains, such as this Eurostar e320 Class 374, to carry less equipment by reducing the requirement to support many different domestic standards. *Eurostar*

BELOW Walkthrough carriages give passengers a sense of security by providing clear views and making it more difficult to become isolated in part of a train.

Despite the various legislative instruments, it remains to be seen exactly how compliant the UK will be by 2020. The situation may be affected by decisions to withdraw older fleets of trains and timescales for procurement that will determine when non-compliant rolling stock can be phased out of service.

The DfT says that while an accessible rail fleet will be achieved by 1 January 2020, it is likely that a small number of trains will not fully comply with the PRM TSI or RVAR regulations by that time. It adds that it is inevitable that some exemptions will remain necessary, although work is under way to keep these to a minimum.[69]

Stations

The Equality Act 2010 states that transport must be accessible to all, regardless of any disability. Therefore any major station enhancement scheme that gets the go-ahead will now include provision for step-free access to and from platforms alongside any other work planned.

Work to make a station fully accessible generally involves providing lifts, ramps or a combination of the two so that passengers with limited mobility, small children or luggage do not have to use escalators or stairs to move between the street and the platform. Often this is achieved by building a new footbridge with lift columns linking the platforms.

Access for All is a programme of Department for Transport grants established in 2006 and designed to provide step-free access at stations that were built before much consideration was given to those for whom stairs present a problem. The DfT chooses which stations should receive funding. In Scotland, ministers recommended stations to the Secretary of State for Transport. Network Rail manages implementation of the schemes.

STEPS TOWARDS MAKING TfL's NETWORK STEP-FREE

Lifts or ramps will be built to provide step-free access at several other TfL stations in the next few years:

2015: Bank (Waterloo & City line), Greenford, Kensal Rise, New Cross Gate, South Tottenham
2016: Bromley-by-Bow, Tottenham Court Road, Tower Hill, Vauxhall, West Hampstead (London Overground), Whitechapel
2017: Bond Street
2018: Ealing Broadway, Victoria, Finsbury Park
2019: Peckham Rye, Queen's Park, Blackhorse Road
2021: Bank (Northern line), Elephant & Castle (Northern line)

New stations built as part of the Croxley Rail Link, Northern Line extension and Crossrail will also have step-free access.

London Underground

Transport for London faces a particularly tough challenge to provide step-free access at historic Underground stations, some of which date back to 1863. Complex, expensive underground engineering solutions are often called for and no date has been set for achieving a fully accessible Underground network.

In 2014 there were 260 London Underground-owned stations, with 66 providing step-free access. Forty-four of the 83 London Overground stations were step-free – changes to the network mean that these figures will change over the next few years. All Docklands Light Railway stations offer step-free access.

Step-free access projects do not always create level access between the platform and the train, but new trains procured by TfL are designed to minimise the step and gap between platform and train. At some stations platform humps have been installed – raised areas on the platform from which wheelchair users can easily board trains.

Signalling

The global railway signalling market is a highly specialised one, dominated by five large companies – Thales, Bombardier, Alstom, Siemens (which acquired Invensys Rail in 2013)

ABOVE Railway systems today – the overhead wires and coloured-light signalling seen on many inter-city routes.

BELOW Away from the track, railway signalling relies on high-tech interlocking systems. This is a control room at Reading.

ABOVE Conventional coloured aspect signalling is widely used across the railway. As lines are upgraded to ERTMS Level 2 and beyond, these lights-on-sticks will no longer be required.

and Hitachi (which acquired Ansaldo in 2015). Although these suppliers have a range of products in use around the world, the deployment of new signalling products in the UK often requires extensive research and development before it is ready for use in day-to-day service. Thales's SelTrac system, now deployed on the London Underground Northern and Jubilee lines, is an example of this.

With Britain constrained by railway infrastructure dating back to the 19th century, new signalling technology provides an opportunity for operating more trains along routes that would be prohibitively expensive and inconvenient to rebuild to provide the capacity required by modern travel patterns. On the national rail network the choice of technology is being influenced by European directives designed to make different railways interoperable. Meanwhile London Underground has turned to bleeding-edge technology to compensate for the limitations of tunnels that no longer meet modern needs. For both, bringing the latest signalling technology into use has proved slow, complex and anything but straightforward.

Signalling evolution

Signalling on the national rail network varies considerably and reflects the history of the railway. Semaphore signals have largely been phased out, but can still be seen in a few locations. Most lines today used coloured light signals that show green when a 'block' between two signals is clear of another train or obstruction so that the train driver knows it is safe to proceed and enter that block. The more blocks into which a route is divided, the more trains can safely operate on that line.

Track circuits are used to detect the presence of a train. A weak current is passed through the two rails and the presence of the metal train wheels and axles causes a short circuit that can then be reflected on a display in a signal control centre. However, track circuits can be unreliable and are increasingly being replaced with axle counters that count the number of axles passing a beacon embedded in the track and compare this number with the data recorded by the previous axle counter.

Interlocking is the name given to the signalling system that controls whether or not it is safe to proceed. Mechanical interlockings are increasingly being replaced with computer-based trackside equipment that uses track circuits/axle counters to detect a train, then sets signals, points, level crossings and other equipment accordingly as well as conveying these details to the relevant signal control centre.

Network Rail and its suppliers have started to use modular signalling. The idea is that equipment can be manufactured and tested off site, then transported to the railway and plugged in with minimal further testing or other work required. The aim is to reduce the cost of resignalling and to speed up commissioning, minimising disruption to passengers and the compensation payable to train operators.

Train protection systems

Automatic train protection systems, which work in conjunction with signals, have been installed in an effort to reduce instances of signals passed at danger (SPADs), which can have and have had catastrophic consequences. Following the Harrow & Wealdstone tragedy in 1952, when 122 people died as a result of a train going through a red signal, the Automatic Warning System (AWS) was installed across the rail network. The system uses a pair of magnets to provide a visual and audible signal in the train cab when approaching a signal set at danger. The driver must acknowledge this by pressing a button, or the train brakes are automatically applied. As long as the alert is acknowledged, the driver may continue to drive the train at any speed.

In the early 2000s the Train Protection Warning System (TPWS) was installed across the national rail network. This automatically applies the brakes of a train if it approaches a red signal or buffer stops too quickly, overriding the actions of the driver. The system, which is recognisable by grids (used to measure a train's speed) fitted between the two rails, is designed for use at speeds up to 75mph, although an enhanced TPWS+ provides protection up to 100mph.

On the Great Western Main Line and routes operated by Chiltern Railways trains use an automatic train protection system which goes by the same name, ATP. Installed by British Rail in the 1990s, the technology provides additional safety information to displays in the driver's cab, and gained recognition as a protection system for inter-city routes following the 1997 Southall accident in which the train that caused the accident had the ATP system switched off. It is now mandatory for High Speed Trains on the Great Western route to operate with ATP operational, but calls to roll out the technology nationwide were rejected as impractical for a range of reasons including cost and the fact that the technology had been superseded.

Today the application of train protection systems to UK railways is linked to the requirements for European interoperability, and this directs track and train providers to the European Rail Traffic Management System, which, among other benefits, provides a protection system for use on slow and fast railway lines.

On single railway lines tokens are often used to avoid head-on collisions. The token – either in physical or electronic form – is issued by the signaller to the train driver and prevents additional trains accessing the line until the token has been returned. Interlocking is designed to prevent more than one token being issued.

Tilt Authorisation and Speed Supervision (TASS) has been introduced on the West Coast Main Line to prevent tilting trains (Class 390 'Pendolinos' and Class 221 'Super Voyagers') from tilting where it is not safe for them to do so. Balises (electronic beacons or transponders) fixed between rails transmit a signal to an antenna under the train telling it whether it may tilt. If the train is going too fast along a section where it is not authorised to tilt, the brakes will automatically be applied.

Control centres

Power signal boxes were widely implemented in the 1950s and 1960s, replacing manually operated signalling levers with control centres that are responsible for larger geographic areas of track, the status of which is reflected on one or more large displays. More recently Integrated Electronic Control Centres (IECC) have replaced these displays with computer screens monitored by operators responsible for specific sections of route. Scalable IECCs can easily be expanded with new control desks added as required.

Network Rail has embarked on a programme of consolidating signalling control at a handful of large state-of-the-art facilities. Getting rid of the traditional cabins operated by a lone signaller is nothing new – the number of signal boxes has fallen from more than 5,000 in 1960[70] to around 800. However, Network Rail's plan is to eventually reduce control to 12 Rail Operating Centres (ROCs). These will be multi-purpose facilities staffed by signallers and other Network Rail staff as well as train operating companies, simplifying lines of communication – of particular use in the event of any disruption to services. Network Rail says modern equipment and a reduction in the number of signalling sites has the potential to reduce railway operating costs by £250m a year.[71]

This will not happen overnight. Network Rail sees consolidation of signalling as a 20-30-year programme. The locations chosen for Rail Operating Centres are Basingstoke, Cardiff, Derby, Didcot, Edinburgh, Glasgow, Gillingham, Manchester, Romford, Rugby, Three Bridges and York.

Alongside the ROC programme, Network Rail plans to deploy sophisticated traffic management systems that reduce the number of manual interventions required when controlling the railway and will provide greater operational flexibility. With daily timetables consisting of thousands of services that have myriad implications for other trains at different points along their route, traffic management systems will be able to quickly work out the implications of making a change – such as pathing a train along a diversionary route – which would otherwise rely on guesswork.

The traffic management programme remains at an early stage. In 2014 Network Rail announced that it had selected Thales to deploy traffic management technology at the Cardiff and Romford Rail Operating Centres. In 2015 Hitachi was appointed to provide a traffic management system for the Thameslink Programme to ensure 24 trains an hour in each direction can run between St Pancras and Blackfriars.

WHAT IS TRAFFIC MANAGEMENT?

Traffic management - part of Network Rail's much vaunted digital railway - is a combination of computer software and hardware that provides assistance to signallers and controllers to help improve the efficiency and reliability of a railway. It looks at where all the trains are in an area and then predicts where they will be in the future so the signaller can make informed decisions to ensure that trains arrive in the right place at the right time.

The system also offers a simulation function - often called plan/re-plan - to allow signallers to test their hypotheses. For example, "if I hold train A at Station X, what will the effects on trains B and C be?"

In normal service, the traffic management software 'talks' to the actual signalling system and can run it automatically, with the signaller overseeing it, much like a human pilot would do with an automatic pilot in an aircraft. That way instead of spending his or her time pulling levers, pushing buttons and dealing with the mechanics of moving trains around, the signaller can focus on the strategic running of the railway.

Moving block

Computers have led to the development of more intelligent automatic train control systems that are responsible for running an entire railway operation. These ATC systems offer a combination of automatic train operation and automatic train supervision, which enables more efficient and reliable operation of services. Explanations of the different system levels can be found in Chapter 6.

By transferring from a system that uses a fixed block between signals to 'moving blocks' – i.e. maintaining a set distance between a train and the one following rather than a specific stretch of track – it is possible to run more trains – thereby increasing line capacity and the ability to recover from any interruption to services.

Historically, these ATC systems have evolved over time and are bespoke to each signalling supplier. As such each system architecture is different, with more or less trackside infrastructure versus centralised infrastructure; there are no standard interfaces; each has its own inherent operating rules; and each requires some degree of adaptation for every implementation.[72]

Communications-based train control (CBTC) is the generic name given to systems that tend to be used for metros in urban areas and are characterised by a continuous bi-directional communications link between trains and the signalling control room. With CBTC there is no need for any physical vehicle detection systems such as track circuits or axle counters, which reduces the overall wayside equipment required, and eliminates any additional maintenance costs. CBTC systems also provide an automatic train protection function.

CBTC systems are used by the Docklands Light Railway and London Underground's Victoria, Jubilee and Northern lines, after overcoming extensive technical difficulties bringing the new signalling equipment into service. London Underground is planning to install CBTC on the sub-surface lines (Circle, Metropolitan, District and Hammersmith & City) by 2022; the complexity of this enterprise is highlighted by the fact that London Underground has had to abandon two contracts for this new signalling and control system. In December 2013 LU scrapped its contract for Bombardier's Cityflow 650 system after it became clear that there was no prospect of the supplier being able to deliver the outputs required on time or on budget.[73] Thales has been appointed to deliver the new contract, and in March 2015 LU revealed that it expected completion of the resignalling scheme to be delivered four years later than planned (and previously agreed with Government).

Moving block on national rail lines in Britain remains an aspiration. Development of the European Rail Traffic Management System envisages support for this under Level 3 (see the next section), but the technology is still in development. Remarkably, plans were drawn up in 1994 to resignal the West Coast Main Line using moving block signalling[74], only to be dropped when it became apparent that the appropriate technology did not yet exist.

European Rail Traffic Management System

The European Rail Traffic Management System (ERTMS) is a next-generation signalling and train control system that is to be deployed on UK railways but remains in development. It consists of two main parts – European Train Control System (ETCS), the equipment fitted on board trains, and GSM-R, the mobile radio standard used on the railways, which provides a link between ETCS-equipped trains and a control centre.

ERTMS offers a number of advantages over conventional signalling systems. It has been designed to be interoperable so that, in theory, any train in Europe would be able to run in the UK and vice versa. In practice suppliers have interpreted ERTMS specifications in different ways, which has resulted in a great deal of work being required to ensure that the various components are compatible with each other.

A tantalising prospect for Network Rail, train operators and Government is the potential of ERTMS to reduce costs and increase route capacity. Trackside signals are not required under the more advanced ERTMS set-ups, eliminating the cost of maintenance and replacement as well as the risk of equipment failure or vandalism. And by taking out the standard trackside signal 'blocks' and replacing them with dynamic 'moving blocks' between trains there is the potential to run

ABOVE Trains fitted with ETCS are granted movement authority appropriate to their location. If a driver tries to exceed the permitted speed for a route section an alarm will sound and the system will intervene to cut off acceleration.

more services without investing in new railway lines and other expensive new infrastructure.

The implementation of ERTMS and ETCS is applied in different 'levels'. ERTMS Level 1 is provided as an add-on, or overlay, to a route already equipped with conventional lineside signals and train detectors. Communication between track and train is provided by track balises that are usually located between the rails next to lineside signals and are connected to the train control centre. A 'movement authority' is communicated from the balises to the ETCS equipment on board a train, which then automatically calculates the maximum speed of the train and the next braking point. This movement authority is displayed to the driver as a band outside the speedometer dial on a screen in the cab. The speed of the train is continuously supervised by the ETCS onboard equipment and if the driver exceeds the movement authority limit alarms will sound/display and the train will brake.

The main benefits offered by ERTMS Level 1 are interoperability been countries and safety, since the train will automatically brake if the driver exceeds the maximum speed allowed under the movement authority.

ERTMS Level 2 does not require lineside signals. Movement authority is communicated directly between control centre and train by using GSM-R. Balises are only used to transmit 'fixed messages' such as location, gradient and speed limit. A continuous stream of GSM-R data informs the driver of line-specific data and the presence of any trains ahead, allowing the train to reach its maximum speed while still maintaining a safe braking distance factor. The driver receives the information from the onboard display rather than trackside signals. As with Level 1, if the driver attempts to go too fast, the computer intervenes.

ETCS Level 2 still requires interlockings for the safe setting of routes and junction control. Between these and the control centre screens is a Radio Block Centre, which interprets the requirements for the train path and translates this into a movement authority that is sent to the train. As well as stripping out the costs associated with lineside signals, ERTMS Level 2 also presents the possibility for substantial line capacity increases by enabling higher operational speeds and reduced headways.

ERTMS Level 3 remains at an early stage of development and allows for the introduction of moving blocks. Rather than using track circuits, axle counters or other track-based detection equipment, continuous position data is supplied by GSM-R from the train direct to the control centre. As the train continuously monitors its own position there is no need for the fixed blocks of Levels 1 and 2 – the train itself will be considered as a moving block.

Different uses of ERTMS have been given different names. ERTMS Regional is an implementation of Level 3 designed for relatively low-use lines, and does not use moving block. Level 0 is sometimes used to describe a basic system that controls the maximum speed of a train but does not provide a movement authority.

In the UK the intention is to install ERTMS Level 2. To date there is just one route in the UK that uses ERTMS – the Cambrian line in Wales. This was selected as a pilot project because it is a lightly used, mainly single-track, route. The new system was installed by Ansaldo STS (since taken over by Hitachi) and – after a series of delays – went live along the full route in 2011.

Despite being one of Britain's lesser trafficked railways, the Cambrian ERTMS project was one of the first Level 2 systems to be retrofitted to an existing line rather than being installed as part of a new line or major upgrade project. ETCS equipment had to be fitted to existing trains, including 24 Class 158 diesel units. Again, installing new ETCS kit on old trains proved something of a learning experience and threw up unforeseen difficulties such as sunshine through cab windows providing a glare effect that made it impossible for drivers to see information on the ETCS screens.

GSM-R explained

GSM-R stands for Global System for Mobile – Railways, and has become the established communications standard for track-to-train voice communications in the UK.

The system now covers most of the national rail network, replacing older systems such as Cab Secure Radio and the National Radio Network. Despite widespread roll-out having only been achieved recently, the technology is relatively old-fashioned and compares to the 2G GSM standard for public use that has been superseded by 3G (with 4G increasingly available). Replacement technologies are being considered by railway organisations, but various barriers to implementation – and the investment made in GSM-R – mean that major change before 2021 is unlikely. There are two key suppliers of GSM-R infrastructure – Kapsch and Siemens.

GSM-R was conceived to serve as a reliable voice communication system. However, since the standard was adopted new demands have emerged for text and data transmission. The move towards ERTMS has also brought with it fresh demands by relying on GSM-R to provide the link between control centre and on-train ETCS equipment that ultimately provides movement authority. Unfortunately GSM-R does not offer sufficient capacity to maintain multiple continuous open connections between trains and ERTMS controllers in busy areas such as terminus stations and junctions.

One solution being investigated is to use the General Packet Radio Service (GPRS) standard, which works within GSM and sends data in small packets (defined units of data) to reduce the burden on the system. This could provide the communications capacity needed by ERTMS but, despite being a well-used consumer standard, must be proven to work robustly and safely in railway operation.

Further deployment

The experience of installing ERTMS on the Cambrian line and from continental Europe has led to a cautious approach to further UK implementation and the creation of a dedicated test route. But after various delays the commitment to rolling out ERTMS in Britain has been reaffirmed by Network Rail. By 2020 ERTMS is due to be operational on the Great Western Main Line between Paddington and Bristol and the Thameslink core through central London. Installations on sections of the East Coast Main Line and Northern City Line (Moorgate to Drayton Park) are also scheduled for completion by 2020.

While Crossrail has opted not to provide ERTMS through the central operating section from route opening, it will be used as part of the Thameslink Programme, which is due for completion by the end of 2018. To achieve the challenging 24 trains per hour in each direction through the central core, automatic train operation is required whereby computers take over from drivers on a short section of the route. Therefore the ETCS package fitted to trains will require an ATO overlay, a pioneering set-up that will put the UK at the forefront of ERTMS deployment. Siemens, which is supplying the new fleet of Thameslink trains, is responsible for delivering the ERTMS system.

Hertford Loop

As Network Rail prepares to roll out ERTMS along some of the UK's busiest main lines and commuter routes, it has established a test track on the Hertford Loop to the north-east of London. Off-peak only one train an hour travels in each direction along this route, so a 5-mile stretch of one of the double tracks has been commandeered for testing purposes. This is known as the ERTMS National Integration Facility (ENIF).

Network Rail has appointed four teams to an ETCS framework. These companies (Alstom, Bombardier/Carillion, Siemens and Hitachi) are competing for the long-term business of rolling out ERTMS. Each supplier has its own proprietary interlocking and Radio Block Centre technologies. In turn each is allowed to use the ENIF to prove the compatibility of its equipment with those of the others. Siemens and the Thameslink team have access to the facility to test the pioneering systems due to be installed along the Thameslink core.

Tests are controlled from the ENIF control centre at Hitchin. A Class 313 test train has been fitted out with ETCS train equipment and the four suppliers have installed the necessary railway equipment, including the track-mounted balises that confirm details of a train's position to the signalling control system.

The work at Hertford and subsequent testing at Old Dalby will inform the roll-out of ERTMS across the national rail network and the installation of ETCS on trains. The experience of the Cambrian line pilot means that, where possible, it will be fitted as standard to new trains rather than retro-fitted. However, with existing trains expected to remain in service for years to come, some retro-fitting will be required not only for passenger rolling stock but also freight trains, Network Rail's fleet of engineering vehicles, charter and heritage operations. There are no plans to roll out ERTMS in Northern Ireland in the foreseeable future.

Skills crunch

Amid technological changes and the transformation of signalling, one problem persists: experienced signalling contractors and engineers are in short supply. In 2013 Network Rail let framework contracts for signalling renewals divided into eight regions and selected a primary and back-up contractor for each. These 16 appointments were split between Siemens, Signalling Solutions and Atkins.

Since then the contractors have repeatedly missed committed dates for signalling commissioning. Why? In Control Period 5 the Government has funded a record volume of signalling work, with which the supply chain appears unable to cope – in part because of a skills shortage that has been linked to a decision by signalling contractors to stop recruiting trainees when Railtrack collapsed in 2001.[75]

In most industries a client in this situation would seek out other companies with the

ABOVE **Third rail electrification is used south of the River Thames by Southeastern, Southern and South West Trains services. The system is generally regarded as less efficient and capable than overhead line electrification, but the cost of replacement has proved prohibitive.**

people and capability to complete the job. Unfortunately for Network Rail, there appear to be no firms that are in a position to take on such a large and technically complex workload. So, despite signalling projects being funded and ready to go, making them happen on the ground presents a significant challenge.

Electrification

Signalling is not the only area where skills shortages are a cause for concern. The railway has embarked on a major programme of electrifying lines and is having to recreate resources for the job after wiring up rail routes fell out of favour with Government for the best part of three decades.

In 2013-14 electrified railway accounted for 5,268km of route length, 33.4% of the total national network. Although electrification requires gantries to support overhead lines, which many people may find unsightly and which introduce another asset to maintain, the case for electrification is strong. Electric trains do not have to carry fuel or engines and can therefore include more seats than diesel trains of the same length. They also accelerate more quickly, reducing journey times as well as carrying more passengers.

Network Rail claims electric trains emit 20-35% less carbon per passenger than a diesel train. With zero emissions at the point of use, they improve air quality in pollution hotspots such as city centres and main-line stations. Electric trains are quieter than diesels and are virtually silent when waiting at stations.

Further advantages come from the fact that electric trains are cheaper to operate, require less maintenance and have lower energy costs than their diesel counterparts. As electric multiple units are lighter than diesel trains, they cause less wear on the track, in turn helping to reduce maintenance costs and increase the reliability of infrastructure.

By using carbon-neutral fuel (through purchasing electricity from suppliers who use nuclear or renewable generation), the railway can also enhance its environmental credential and offer a sustainable alternative to most forms of road transport.

This range of benefits has been used to build a business case for the electrification of well-trafficked lines, and the Coalition Government in Westminster as well as the Scottish Government committed to what has turned into a rolling

ABOVE A major electrification programme is under way and will see wires go up above many routes, including this section of the Great Western through historic Sydney Gardens in Bath.

BELOW At Reading new masts have been installed ready for electrification of the Great Western route, but the wires have yet to go up. This is the unusually quiet scene at Easter 2015 during engineering works.

programme of electrifying lines, with around 800 route miles scheduled to turn electric. This includes adding wires to the Great Western Main Line as well as routes between Edinburgh and Glasgow and several schemes across the North West of England.

Again, getting funding signed off has proved to be surprisingly easy compared to completing the work. Network Rail and its contractors have had to buy new equipment, train staff and redevelop forgotten working practices. Electrification is transforming many rail routes but it is happening much more slowly than planned while costing a lot more money. In June 2015 Transport Secretary Patrick McLoughlin announced that electrification of the Midland Main Line and North TransPennine routes would be "paused" following significant cost increases and to allow Network Rail to focus on the Great Western electrification programme.

Again, getting funding signed off has proved to be surprisingly easy compared to completing the work. Network Rail and its contractors have had to buy new equipment, train staff and redevelop forgotten working practices. Electrification is transforming many rail routes but it is happening much more slowly than planned while costing a lot more money.

Overhead wires are seen as superior to the third rail system used south of the River Thames on south-eastern, southern and south-western rail routes because the wires allow trains to reach higher speeds. Trains that pick up power from a third rail beside the track are generally run no faster than 90mph and there is also the possibility of a layer of snow or severe ice leaving the train-mounted shoe gear unable to pick up a current.

A case for the conversion of third rail routes to overhead electrification has been made by senior figures within the rail industry and the Coalition Government agreed to the conversion of a section of route through Basingstoke, which as well as forming part of the Electric Spine scheme linking Southampton and the Midlands would also act as a test case for third rail conversion.

Batteries included

Could battery-powered trains become a regular sight on the national rail network? A team of engineers at Bombardier think they could and have fitted batteries to a train used in East Anglia as part of an experiment designed to see if electric trains can serve routes where there are no wires or third rail.

Engineers are investigating the feasibility of an Independently Powered Electric Multiple Unit (IPEMU), which would offer an alternative to diesel rolling stock on parts of the network that have not been electrified. The IPEMU concept is attractive because it would provide flexibility, allowing trains to operate on electrified routes before continuing along track without wires. This could be useful as lines are gradually electrified, and would allow electric multiple units to operate on branch lines where there is unlikely to be a sufficient economic case to justify erecting overhead wires. IPEMU batteries would be recharged at station termini.

Funding for the initiative has been allocated by Network Rail, the Rail Safety and Standards Board and the Department for Transport through the Future Railway programme. A pilot scheme saw Bombardier adapt a Class 379 unit to accommodate two different types of batteries: lithium (iron magnesium) phosphate, and hot sodium nickel salt.

Following tests off-network at the Old Dalby track near Melton Mowbray, the battery-powered train – the first to run on the national rail network in more than half a century – was used in weekday timetable service for five weeks between Harwich International and Manningtree stations in early 2015.

By demonstrating the potential of the IPEMU the partners in the scheme hope to encourage investment in the concept. Any future IPEMU would most likely be designed as a new train and not an adapted unit in order to minimise energy consumption.

As part of the Intercity Express Programme the new Hitachi Class 800 and 801 train sets will be fitted with batteries to provide back-up power. This will allow them to travel short

ABOVE Up-to-date passenger information is expected by railway users. Increasingly social media is being used to provide on-the-go updates, complementing stations displays such as these screens at King's Cross.

distances at low speed if there is no overhead power supply or the diesel engine (on the hybrid trains) fails.

Sharing information

As technology has developed, the rail industry has built and gradually refined systems that use computers and the internet to provide information to passengers. Up-to-date information on the running of train services has become something that is expected as part of the modern railway. However, in times of disruption providing the right information can be difficult, but when absent social media allows passengers to make their frustration very public.

As the internet has evolved and the use of mobile technology has taken off, the railway is shifting from a position where it is the source and gatekeeper of all information to one where it is willing to share its data with others. This means web developers and other technology specialists can use their knowledge to build innovative systems and apps that potentially provide information sources more closely matched to passengers' expectations.

National Rail Enquiries is owned by train operating companies and the NRE website serves as the origin of official train information on the internet. However, the data used by NRE is linked to a range of sources and piped to other industry systems. Increasingly this data is also available to third parties, which can develop other information tools and products for rail users.

Darwin

'Darwin' is the National Rail Enquiries information service paid for by train operators; it analyses raw data from rail industry sources to predict the arrival times of trains. Up-to-date train information on arrivals and departures is available for all stations in the national rail network. The intellectual property in Darwin is owned by Train Information Services (TIS) Ltd – the company owned by franchised TOCs that provides NRE services.

Information is delivered to the public through live departure boards and the internet. The service also provides information to other systems via a number of interfaces. Some of the key systems Darwin brings together include:

- TSDB – the UK timetable service database
- TRUST – the central train reporting system
- The train operators' own messaging systems
- Individual station customer information systems

In May 2014 the Rail Delivery Group announced that public-sector organisations and small commercial or private users would be able to access the National Rail Enquiries Darwin system for free. Previously organisations and developers that used the service had been charged and required a licence. The RDG says that changing the system will make it easier for people and organisations, including public-sector bodies, to use live train-running information to develop apps and other online tools.

Under the new arrangements only the biggest commercial or private users, whose services are used more than 5 million times in a four-week period, will have to pay. (In May 2014 only one client fell into this category, although if other commercial developers' services grow to be used more than 5 million times in a four-week period, they will begin to incur charges). Free access is now granted to public bodies, including Transport for London, passenger transport executives and local authorities, regardless of how many requests for information their customers make.

Data feeds for developers

The opening up of access to Darwin is part of a move towards sharing certain information. There appears to be growing recognition that it is reasonable for publicly owned organisations to offer data feeds that allow web and software developers to come up with new applications that may be of benefit to rail users.

Data feeds offered by Network Rail include:

- SCHEDULE – daily extracts and updates of train schedules from the Integrated Train Planning System
- MOVEMENT – train positioning and movement event data
- TD – train positioning data at signalling berth level
- TSR (Temporary Speed Restrictions) – details of temporary reductions in permissible speed across the rail network
- VSTP (Very Short Term Plan) – train schedules created via the VSTP process that are not available via the SCHEDULE feed
- RTPPM (Real-Time Public Performance Measure) – performance of trains against the timetable, measured as the percentage of trains arriving at their destination on time
- SMART – train describer berth offset data used for train reporting
- Corpus – location reference data
- BPLAN – train planning data, including locations and sectional running times

Transport for London also offers a range of data feeds including:

- Journey planner
- London Underground departure boards, line status and station status
- Station locations and facilities
- London Underground passenger counts data
- Oyster card journey information

Internet access all areas

In many ways the experience of train travel in Britain is similar to that of passengers decades, even a century, ago. But one thing the travellers of yesteryear would have had no concept of is the idea of being able to access messages, games, news and other information on the move.

Early attempts to provide wireless internet access, or wi-fi, on board trains were patchy. A few train operators signed up technology firms to provide onboard networks, and passengers would pay a few pounds for access, possibly being allowed free access if they had purchased a First Class ticket, with the quality of reception varying considerably. Those deciding not to pay, or without the option, would have to rely on intermittent signals from their mobile phone network provider.

The railway is now moving towards a model where passengers expect wi-fi not only to be available at stations and on board trains, but that the service should be provided at no additional cost to them. Just as passengers expect to have a seat on a train (not that this will always be the case), wi-fi is increasingly being viewed as part of the standard railway offer rather than a nice-to-have add on.

For the national rail system Network Rail is making use of the trackside fixed telecommunications network (FTN) that it has built to support GSM-R and that will form the backbone of efforts to create a digital railway. The fibre-optic and copper cabling that makes up the FTN can be linked to masts that then communicate with trains to provide internet access for trains. Equipment is being fitted to trains that magnifies the 4G signals emitted by masts alongside the railway. Network Rail has committed to making the new technology available for public use on 30% of Britain's rail network – routes that account for 70% of all passenger journeys – by 2019.[76]

In July 2014 the DfT announced that it would spend a £53.1m fine imposed on Network Rail for missing performance targets to fit trains with new wi-fi equipment that would link up with the GSM-R system. It said that this will enable passengers to access mobile broadband connections, equivalent to speeds and bandwidth available at stations and off the railway at least 10 times better than existing services. Hull Trains became the first train operator to offer passengers 4G-enabled wi-fi on the move in October 2014.

In early 2015 the Government said that all train operators bidding for new franchises and direct award agreements will have to make provision for free wireless internet access on trains. Where no new franchise agreement was due to be signed in the next two years, £47.8m would be released by the DfT (from the Network Rail fine) to ensure that wi-fi is available on selected services from 2017. Arriva Trains Wales, Chiltern Railways, GoVia Thameslink Railway and Southeastern were to receive handouts under this initiative. The remaining £5.3m from the Network Rail fine was allocated to the Scottish Government in line with the proportion of the penalty paid by NR for late train running in Scotland. Later in the year the DfT said that free wi-fi internet access will be available on all Northern and TransPennine trains by 2020 at the latest.

City networks

Transport for London has partnered with Virgin Media to offer wi-fi at more than 150 London Underground stations. The service was introduced in 2012 and passengers can access the internet from anywhere in the station including ticket halls, corridors and platforms. Customers of Virgin Media, EE, Vodafone, O2 and Three can access the service at no extra cost – others can buy a Virgin Media Wi-fi Pass (2015 prices: £2 a day or £15 a month).

On the London Overground, Transport for London has agreed a deal with BSkyB-owned The Cloud to offer wi-fi at more than 56 Overground stations. Wi-fi access is available in most ticket halls, corridors and platforms and free for the first hour of use.

In 2015 Manchester's Metrolink network became the first light rail system in England to offer wi-fi on board all trams. £1.7m was spent to provide internet access on all 96 trams in the fleet as part of a city scheme that included on-street coverage and providing wi-fi in more than 200 public buildings. In Scotland Edinburgh's trams offer passengers free wi-fi. A 3G/4G mobile data signal is received by the on-tram router, which then broadcasts a wi-fi signal within the vehicle.

Innovation everywhere

The transformation of Britain's railway continues on multiple fronts. The potential of technology and the importance of innovation have been recognised in recent years with the creation of committees and industry bodies going by names that seem anything but exciting, but which have the remit to deliver major changes to the way the rail industry works.

Among them is Future Railway, a body set up by the rail industry to accelerate research, development and innovation to deliver the Rail Technical Strategy, a Government document drawn up to help suppliers by presenting a unified view of where the industry is expected to direct its technical development over the coming decades. It also supposedly helps operators, infrastructure managers and industry planners understand how technical developments could support them in delivering a higher-capacity, better-performing and more cost-effective railway.

Future Railway's work is led by the Technical Strategy Leadership Group, which includes representatives of the DfT, ORR, Network Rail, RoSCos, train operators, Transport Scotland and the Rail Safety and Standards Board.

Specialist trains

Among the innovations already delivered, Network Rail is increasingly relying on special factory trains that can install new rails and clean and replenish ballast. Ballast is the bed of stones on which the rails and sleepers rest, and when maintained correctly it ensures a safe, smooth and comfortable train ride.

Network Rail has five high-output ballast cleaners. In March 2015 the company completed the insourcing of more than 500 Amey/Colas staff who had previously operated the high-output kit. This marked the largest people transfer into Network Rail since maintenance activities were brought in-house in 2005.

Network Rail also has a measurement train, a converted High Speed Train equipped with scanners, lasers and digital video cameras that can instantaneously measure and report on the condition of the track and other components while travelling at up to 125mph. It is able to count every sleeper it travels over as well as individual rail clips, and can also check the 25kV overhead cabling system that powers electric trains.

By providing up-to-date reports on the condition of rails and other assets, Network Rail is able to tailor its maintenance regime and fix potential problems before they affect the performance of passenger and freight services.

Asset management

One of the challenges set Network Rail by the Office of Rail and Road is to gain a better understanding of its assets. As one of the country's largest infrastructure owners, this is no small undertaking, but clearly Network Rail will be able to operate more effectively if it has up-to-date information on the condition of rails, structures, equipment and all the other myriad assets for which it is responsible.

The £300m-plus ORBIS programme has been developed to improve the way Network Rail acquires, stores and uses asset information. Part of this involves ensuring that staff in offices and at the trackside have appropriate access to the data and information they need to do their jobs, as well as to enable them to provide data on work undertaken, which will then update the system. This asset management database can also be enhanced using information collected by the measurement train.

Network Rail is working to deliver ORBIS during Control Period 5. The ultimate goal of this complex endeavour is to ensure that the organisation has reliable information about the condition of assets, which can then be used to plan and deliver effective maintenance, predicting track failures and other problems before they occur. By implementing this approach it should be possible to improve the reliability of the network and reduce disruption to train operators and their customers.

Building Information Modelling

Building Information Modelling, or BIM, is a process that brings together and shares digitally information used by designers, architects, engineers and builders. Used extensively in the aerospace and automotive industries, BIM is now being applied in some parts of the rail industry, notably Crossrail, and others are likely to come on board after the Government announced that all suppliers that wish to bid for public works contracts worth more than £50m must use BIM tools and techniques from 2016.

The modelling part of BIM will be recognisable to many people in the form of CADCAM and three-dimensional modelling computer software. But BIM provides several major advantages over stand-alone CAD software: it manages not only graphics but also information. This allows drawings, reports, schedules and more to be generated automatically, and helps all those involved in the project to make better-informed decisions. A tiny change to a design could have major implications across the programme if not communicated effectively.

But BIM goes beyond clever approaches to design and construction – it examines what happens to the buildings and other structures created after construction is complete. A typical railway project is carefully planned and executed, but once a new line or station opens the job is done. BIM allows consideration of how the new infrastructure will operate and be maintained even before construction gets under way.

This is all about using the information that is copiously collected during development of a project to allow the end result to function more efficiently. BIM becomes a platform for asset management, helping a future system manager with the planning of maintenance regimes and day-to-day management. Digital systems such as radar and train-based monitoring equipment can be used to keep the asset files up to date, and in time could replace the tedious process of filling out endless paperwork to maintain records.

Trans-European Trunked Radio

London Underground makes use of a radio communication system based on the Trans-European Trunked Radio (TETRA) standard. TETRA uses a lower frequency than GSM and has a longer range, meaning that fewer transmitters are required to cover a defined area.

In 2009 London Underground signed up to a private finance initiative known as Connect – a 20-year deal to supply a system capable of carrying voice and data, radio and video across the London Underground network. Connect gives LU enhanced radio services delivered through a new TETRA digital radio system to provide integrated mobile communications to trains, stations and depots across the Underground. Thales is responsible for maintaining the system.

Connect is also used by Airwave, another TETRA system that was implemented in 125 below-ground stations in 2007 following a report on the 2005 London bombings, which noted that during the emergency police were unable to communicate with colleagues above and below ground and across forces.

Airwave basically ensures that emergency services can communicate with each other underground. As a result of its implementation members of the British Transport Police no longer have to carry two radios and, for the first time, a radio system can be used underground by both Metropolitan Police and City of London Police officers. Airwave is operated by Airwave Solutions, a company owned by the Macquarie European Infrastructure investment fund.

12 • Light rail

The UK has nine of what the Department for Transport would describe as modern light rail systems. These have varying characteristics – from sharing track with conventional trains to operating as stand-alone tram systems.

Opened in May 2014, Edinburgh is the newest light rail system in the UK, although since then other networks have opened new lines. Department for Transport figures for 2013-14 (prior to the Edinburgh opening) show that across the eight light rail systems in England there were 227 million passenger journeys in 2013/14, a 2% increase on the previous year. London accounted for nearly 60% of these journeys as a result of Croydon Tramlink and the Docklands Light Railway, the latter being by far the most used light rail system in the UK.

Light rail and tram revenue increased by 6% in real terms to £290m in 2013/14 compared to 2012/13.

Blackpool Tramway

Old postcards and film footage show that tramways were once a familiar sight in many UK towns and cities. Blackpool is the only one of these historic, municipal systems to have survived into the 21st century.

In 2012 a £104m upgrade of the system was completed with a comprehensive maintenance programme saving the aged track from disintegration and delivering a fleet of 16 Bombardier Flexity trams together with a modern depot. The new trams now operate alongside some of the heritage trams that preceded them, including double-decker vehicles.

Trams run along an 11-mile (17.7km) stretch of coastline between Starr Gate and Fleetwood Ferry and are operated by council-owned Blackpool Transport. A short extension is planned from the Promenade at North Pier to Blackpool North railway station, where it will be integrated with the Talbot Gateway Central Business District retail and office development.

Table 8: Overview of UK light rail systems

	Opened	Route kilometres	Passenger journeys 2013/14 (millions)	Vehicles available for service	Stations/ stops
Blackpool Tramway*	1885	18	4	26	37
Croydon Tramlink	2000	28	31	30	39
Docklands Light Railway	1987	38	102	149	45
Edinburgh Trams	2014	14	N/A	27	15
Manchester Metrolink*	1992	78	29	81	77
Midland Metro*	1999	20	5	16	22
Nottingham Express Transit*	2004	14	8	15	23
Sheffield Supertram*	1994	29	13	25	48
Tyne & Wear Metro	1980	78	36	90	60

* Expansion of system under way or committed to at time of writing
Source: DfT/ONS (except Edinburgh)

ABOVE **Croydon's Tramlink system is owned by Transport for London and is being extended in response to development of a new shopping centre.**

Croydon Tramlink

South London's 28km, three-line Tramlink network opened in 2000, bringing together sections of neglected heavy rail lines, such as the Wimbledon to West Croydon route, with an on-street loop through Croydon town centre and an all-new alignment to the satellite development of New Addington. In the first year of operation 18.5 million passengers were transported, that figure rising to more than 31 million by 2013/14.

A private finance initiative (PFI) was used to raise funds for building the network and included rights to operate trams for 99 years. However, in 2008 Transport for London bought out the PFI concession, Tramtrack Croydon Ltd, which it accused of failing to invest in maintaining and developing the system to meet passenger demand.

Proposed new lines have so far failed to materialise, but TfL has bought ten new trams (increasing the fleet size to 34) and double-tracked part of the single-line section of the Wimbledon branch. A second tram platform has been built at Wimbledon, these works allowing 12 trams per hour to run in each direction along the route – a 50% increase in capacity.

Services are operated by Tram Operations Ltd, a subsidiary of First Group, which is contracted by TfL to run trams until 2030. TfL specifies tram frequencies and retains responsibility for fares and revenue.

Using developer receipts from the new Westfield shopping centre in Croydon, TfL intends to build a second tram loop in Croydon town centre.

Docklands Light Railway

The Docklands Light Railway is the largest light rail system in the UK by passenger numbers and number of vehicles. Opened in 1987, with 11 trains serving 15 stations, it carried 6.7 million passengers during its first year. By 2013/14 it had 45 stations, 38 route kilometres and transported more than 101 million passengers a year.

The system is synonymous with the redevelopment of London's Docklands, the reason for its creation in the first place. As businesses have moved to the area and new offices have been constructed, the system has been extended and rebuilt to accommodate growing passenger numbers. For example, South Quay station is into its fourth incarnation – although one of the rebuilding projects was prompted by damage caused by an IRA bomb in 1996. In 2014 Pudding Mill Lane station, rebuilt as part of a DLR diversion needed to deliver the Crossrail programme, became the network's largest station.

DLR played a major role during the London 2012 Olympic Games when 6.9 million journeys were made – up by more than 100% on normal levels. More than 500,000 journeys on a single day were made for the first time on Friday 3 August 2012.

Transport for London manages the DLR. Its Docklands Light Railways Ltd subsidiary owns most of the infrastructure and trains, although 24 of the vehicles are owned by the Royal Bank of Scotland under a finance lease signed in April 2005. The infrastructure on the Lewisham branch remains private-sector-owned under a PFI concession whereby a consortium was responsible for the design and construction of the infrastructure and its subsequent maintenance and renewal until 2021.

In July 2014 a 70/30 joint venture of Keolis and Amey was selected to operate and maintain the DLR until 2021 with an option for extension to 2023. The contract has a value of more than £700m – a figure that represents the sum of nominal fees payable over the life of the franchise, including the extension period. It does not include any performance payments or deductions related to service enhancements.

Keolis/Amey took over from Serco, which had operated the DLR since 1997. The new contract also saw changes to maintenance arrangements, with Amey becoming responsible for the Stratford International, Woolwich Arsenal and City Airport sections, which had previously been the subject of separate maintenance arrangements outside the DLR franchise, a legacy of other PFIs that had been taken over by TfL. Maintenance of the Lewisham branch continues to be handled by the Lewisham PFI concession.

The DLR is one of the highest-performing rail networks in the country, with train punctuality regularly above 99%, even though punctuality is calculated to the nearest 3 minutes, rather than 5 minutes – the measurement used on the national rail network.

Transport for London is in the process of buying a new fleet of trains for the DLR as it seeks to boost service frequencies and provide the capacity to accommodate the growing number of people using the system.

Edinburgh Trams

Edinburgh's new tram line opened to the public at the end of May 2014 and runs from Edinburgh Airport to York Place in the city centre. Trams are operated by Edinburgh Trams, part of Transport for Edinburgh, the city council-owned company that also runs Lothian Buses. A tram depot has been built at Gogar to the west of Edinburgh.

To say that development proved difficult would be understating the case somewhat. Edinburgh was to have had a tram network but as costs escalated ambitions were scaled back and the opening of what is now a single line was repeatedly delayed. Edinburgh has 27 CAF-supplied trams, ideal for the proposed network but far more than is required for the single 14km route built to date.

Siemens and Bilfinger Berger constructed the new route after signing a contract in 2008. Other companies were tasked with relocating on-street utilities, which proved a major challenge with initial estimates of the work required proving wildly optimistic. City of Edinburgh Council's former delivery agency Transport Initiatives Edinburgh clashed with the main contractors and work on the tram scheme was halted in 2010 as relations soured.

A settlement was eventually agreed in 2011 to deliver the tram line for £776m, significantly more than the previous £545m

ABOVE **In Edinburgh trams operate between the Airport and York Place in the city centre.**

funding envelope. The Scottish Government has provided £500m after honouring a commitment to the tram scheme made by the previous administration, leaving the council to put in place long-term borrowing arrangements to plug the funding shortfall. A public inquiry is to investigate the reasons for the project's problematic development.

Manchester Metrolink

Manchester Metrolink is the largest light rail system in the UK by route miles, and recorded 29.2 million passenger journeys in 2013-14.[77] Seven lines radiate from Manchester city centre and provide services across Greater Manchester. The system makes use of former heavy rail lines complemented by on-street running and new alignments. Transport for Greater Manchester owns the network and RATP is set to operate trams until at least 2017 when a new contract to run the system is expected to begin.

The initial line, between Manchester Victoria and Bury, opened in 1992, becoming the UK's first modern street-running rail system and the second tram line (given that the Blackpool tramway was the only original municipal tram system that had survived).

Since then a series of expansion schemes, including a programme of new lines originally known as the 'Big Bang', have been delivered to provide routes to Eccles, Rochdale, Ashton-under-Lyne, Altrincham and East Didsbury. The opening of a new line to Manchester Airport in November 2014 brought the size of the Metrolink network to 92.5km (57.5 miles), serving 92 stops.

The system is poised to expand further. Construction of the Second City Crossing, which, as it name implies, will provide a second route through Manchester city centre to increase system capacity, is scheduled for completion in 2017. Funding has also been agreed for a new line to Trafford Park, branching off the existing Eccles line, which is slated to open by 2020.

Metrolink has replaced its original fleet of T68 aquamarine, black and grey trams with Bombardier M5000 Flexity vehicles with a yellow and grey livery. A series of incremental orders, including trams bought for the Trafford line, takes the total fleet size to 104 vehicles. Sometimes the trams are joined together to provide double-length formations to accommodate peak demand.

Midland Metro

Midland Metro is the West Midlands tram system linking Birmingham with Wolverhampton via West Bromwich, Bilston and Wednesbury. It operates seven days a week with trams every 8 minutes in each direction during the day and every 15 minutes during the evenings and Sundays. In 2014 the line had 23 stops, four of which act as park and ride facilities.

The 12.7-mile (20.1km) system opened in 1999, the route following the alignment of the former Great Western Railway main line, closed in 1972, between Birmingham Snow Hill and Wolverhampton.

In 2015 a new stretch of line opened, extending the Metro from Snow Hill station to Birmingham's main station, New Street, in the heart of the city centre. New stops have also been built at St Chad's and Upper Bull Street. Funding has also been announced for further extensions to Centenary Square, then on to Five Ways/Hagley Road, and to Birmingham Eastside, linking with the proposed High Speed 2 station. Development of a short extension at the Wolverhampton end is also under way.

The first of 20 vehicles in a £40m fleet of new Midland Metro trams went into service in September 2014. The new Urbos 3 trams, built by Spanish manufacturer CAF, are a third bigger than the 16 existing Ansaldo Trasporti models, carrying 210 passengers compared to

BELOW Midland Metro under construction: Stephenson Street is now the route for an extension, opened in 2015, to Birmingham New Street. The station – pictured to the left of the photo – has recently been upgraded, a project that involved cladding the exterior with reflective steel panels.

ABOVE As part of the expansion of the Nottingham Express Transit, a fleet of Alstom Citadis trams has been introduced into service. *Taylor Woodrow/Alstom joint venture*

BELOW Vinci Construction's Taylor Woodrow division has laid track for two new Nottingham Express Transit routes. *Taylor Woodrow/Alstom joint venture*

156. The new trams are expected to increase overall capacity by 40%, easing the overcrowding that can sometimes occur at peak times.

Line 1 (the only line until planned extensions are delivered) now carries more than 5 million passengers a year. National Express Midland Metro operates the system on behalf of the West Midlands Passenger Transport Executive, Centro.

ABOVE Named after Nottingham's twin town in Germany, the Karlsruhe Friendship Bridge was built to carry the extended tram route over the railway. *Taylor Woodrow/Alstom joint venture*

Nottingham Express Transit

Opened in 2004 as a single route (from Nottingham railway station, south of the city centre, north past Nottingham Trent University to Hucknall), Nottingham Express Transit more than doubled in size in 2015, gaining a second and a third route. These run south and south-west from the city centre to Chilwell and Clifton.

The £570m 17.5km expansion of the system is being paid for through a private finance initiative signed in December 2011 with the Tramlink consortium (nothing to do with Croydon) consisting of Alstom, Keolis, Trent Barton-owner Wellglade and Vinci Construction, with financial backing from Meridiam Infrastructure and Infravia Fund. In a first for the UK, Nottingham City Council is using receipts from a workplace parking levy to provide the one-third of the project cost to which it has committed (the Department for Transport will provide the remainder). The workplace parking levy is paid by employers in the city that have 11 or more car parking spaces for employees' vehicles.

A hybrid fleet of Bombardier Incentro and Alstom Citadis trams serve the system and are operated by Tramlink.

Sheffield Supertram

Completed in 1995, Sheffield Supertram consists of three light rail routes covering 29km, with half of the system on-street and running alongside other traffic. The tram network has 48 stops and links six park and ride sites with the city centre, universities, cathedral and sport arenas.

Built in 1992, the 25 Supertrams have three articulated sections with eight powered axles and can travel at up to 50mph and comfortably carry 250 passengers. On-board conductors sell tickets to passengers.

The Supertram network is owned by South Yorkshire Passenger Transport Executive, which implements policy set by the South Yorkshire Combined Authority. The trams are operated by Stagecoach.

Development of the network is linked to the tram-train initiative (see below), which will allow trams to continue on to heavy rail infrastructure via a new junction at Meadowhall. Vossloh has been awarded a contract to provide seven new trams to support this initiative.

Tyne & Wear Metro

At least until tram-trains start running, Metro is the sole UK example of light rail and national rail services sharing track: Metro services operate over Network Rail lines east of Pelaw and share track and Sunderland station with national rail services to the far side of Sunderland (13km). From there to the terminus at South Hylton (a further 5km) the infrastructure is owned by Network Rail but only used by Metro trains.

Opened in 1980 and subsequently extended, the Metro network now has 48 route miles (77.2km) and 60 station stops. Services are provided by 45 electric two-carriage trains built between 1975 and 1981 and widely referred to as Metrocars.

The network is currently undergoing a £350m 11-year modernisation of tracks, stations, power and other support equipment intended to secure the system's future. Refurbishment of 86 Tyne & Wear Metrocars and the introduction of smart ticketing is included in this programme, which is variously referred to as 'Metro: all change' and 'Metro reinvigoration'.

Nexus, the Tyne & Wear Passenger Transport Executive, which implements policy set by the North East Combined Authority, oversees Metro services and is responsible for delivering the investment programme. However, as part of the funding deal agreed with Government a concession was let to outsource the running of trains and stations. Deutsche Bahn won this contract, which is due to run until 2019.

Nexus continues to own the Metro and sets fares. It pays DB Regio Tyne & Wear agreed amounts over the length of the contract, included in which is a bonus and penalty element based on performance, particularly in relation to train operations, service quality and revenue protection.

Further investment is under discussion with Government, including replacement of the rolling stock and possible installation of automatic signalling, with a view to implementation from 2020.

Tram-train

The tram-train concept – where lightweight tram vehicles can operate on both heavy and light rail lines – has been latched on to by successive transport ministers keen to deliver the benefits of rail at a fraction of the cost of new heavy rail lines. Used in continental Europe, tram-trains require less fuel than conventional trains and have faster acceleration and deceleration rates – offering passengers shorter journey times. They are also lighter, which may reduce wear and tear on tracks, in turn reducing the need for disruptive maintenance work.

A pilot scheme is under way in South Yorkshire, which will connect the Sheffield Supertram light rail system to the national rail system near Rotherham. Dual-voltage trams will become the first trams in the UK to run on both heavy rail and tram networks.

While this is a novel scheme and requires Network Rail to deliver new points and platforms, development has been slow. In its current form the project was announced in 2009 but the new service linking Rotherham Parkgate and Sheffield city centre is not expected to launch before 2017. The first two years of operation will then be used to trial the tram-train concept so that the UK railway

TRAM-TRAIN VERSUS TRAM – WHAT'S THE DIFFERENCE?

- Higher vehicle crashworthiness allows for the higher average speed operations of tram-trains and other trains, and resists slow-speed collisions with heavier trains
- Enhancements to signalling systems minimise the risk of a collision between trains and tram-trains. This involves installing the train protection and warning system (TPWS) at all signals, whereas TPWS is currently only installed at junctions and sites with high levels of SPAD (signal passed at danger) incidents
- Road Traffic Act-compliant headlights and direction indicators are needed for on-street operation and to meet rail main-line lighting requirements for visibility
- Tram-trains require additional main-line signalling and communications equipment such as TPWS and the Global System for Mobile Communication – Railway (GSM-R)
- There is more seating than a tram for longer-distance journeys
- The wheel profile needs to be suitable for both tramway and standard main-line track

Source: DfT press release 17 May 2012, 'Revolutionary new Tram-Trains to be piloted in South Yorkshire'

industry can understand and assess the technical issues involved.

Tram-trains are regularly suggested as an option for meeting current and future transport requirements, but future projects hinge on the outcome of the Sheffield Supertram trial. If it proves successful other tram-train initiatives could follow, with Transport for Greater Manchester enthusiastic about the potential of this mode. A tram-train link to Glasgow Airport has also been mooted.

The future

In the UK a dichotomy exists in that light rail appears to be widely recognised as a means of achieving a step-change in the standard of local public transport provision, yet new systems are not being built. Once the merits of light rail have been agreed on, and necessary decisions on finance and construction have been taken, it seems that making light rail a reality in the UK is just too expensive and too difficult.

Deputy Prime Minister John Prescott's pledge in 2000 to deliver 25 light rail systems certainly has not come to pass, and today there remain many obstacles facing would-be tram promoters. The recently opened Edinburgh line shows just how much can go wrong and the consequences for reputations, careers and council taxpayers. However, it has also proved how quickly the problems of development can be forgotten as passenger numbers exceed forecasts.

In England the last new light rail system to be built, in Nottingham, opened more than a decade ago yet, despite its success, has not been imitated.

Considerable attention has been lavished on the reasons for light rail's difficulties and has highlighted issues such as the lack of technical standardisation. Yet despite the formation of an all-party light rail group and UKTram – comprising the Passenger Transport Executive Group, Confederation of Passenger Transport, Light Rail Transit Forum and London Tramlink – no new UK light rail systems have come forward.

Tram-train has emerged as a new approach that could allow the rail industry to cut costs and provide links to under-served destinations with a minimum of new infrastructure. Yet the promised revolution has been undermined by the time it has taken to get even a trial of a system already used across the English Channel up and running in the UK.

On a more positive note, light rail seems certain to get a shot in the arm from High Speed 2. Plans to provide integrated transport links to HS2 stations mean that extensions to the Midland Metro and the Nottingham Express Transit Chilwell branch to Toton appear highly likely in due course.

13 • High-speed rail

'High-speed rail' is a term that can easily cause confusion. It is regularly used to reference the modern railway, hence its appearance in announcements of new train fleets. Yet in Britain we call the inter-city workhorses introduced on main lines in the 1970s and 1980s and with a top speed of 125mph High Speed Trains. While these were revolutionary in their time, modern they no longer are.

Internationally, the 'high-speed rail' label has a more specific purpose. The European Union uses High Speed to refer to rail lines or trains offering speeds of at least 250km/h (155mph)[78]. In the UK we currently have one such route – High Speed 1 – while plans for HS2 would create a high-speed rail network. There is also a proposal for HS3, although the outline plan for using a combination of new and upgraded infrastructure probably will not offer speeds that live up to the EU definition.

High Speed 1

The Channel Tunnel Rail Link – connecting the Channel Tunnel to St Pancras – opened on 6 November 2007, having been rebranded as High Speed 1 the previous year.

High Speed 1 was built in two sections over a nine-year period. The result was more than 109km of new high-speed railway including the world's longest-span concrete high-speed rail bridge and 47km of tunnels.

HS1 Ltd's railway infrastructure has physical connections with Eurotunnel, the DBS freight

BELOW Eurostar transferred its operations from London Waterloo to St Pancras following completion of High Speed 1. This left the Waterloo International platforms vacant for several years.

ABOVE Since 2007 St Pancras International has been the London terminus for trains to and from France and Belgium.

depot at Dollands Moor and the Network Rail 'classic' railway at Ashford, Ebbsfleet, Ripple Lane and domestic lines north of London.

Prior to HS1 opening, Eurostar trains used classic lines to get between London and the Channel Tunnel, switching on to dedicated tracks when the first Channel Tunnel Rail Link section was completed in 2003, and in 2007, when the full route was ready. Five international platforms were added at Waterloo station ready for Eurostar services to start in 1994. But when the dedicated HS1 route opened, Eurostar decided it only needed one London terminus and transferred operations to St Pancras. This left Waterloo International vacant – apparently a surprise to policy-makers.

Given that the station was designed as a secure facility, like an airport, it required significant adaptation to be suitable for domestic trains – including making it possible for passengers to move on and off the platforms at the same time and creating links to the main concourse of Waterloo national rail station and the Underground station. The first of the five platforms was ready for use by regular domestic trains by 2014. The remaining platforms are due to be converted by the end of Control Period 5 (2019).

As well as St Pancras International, High Speed 1 also serves Ebbsfleet, Stratford and Ashford International stations. Despite being called Stratford International, the east London station is not served by international train services.

London & Continental Railways

In 1996 London & Continental Railways (LCR) was awarded the contract to build and operate the high-speed Channel Tunnel Rail Link (HS1) and to own and operate the UK arm of the Eurostar International train service. LCR delivered the new railway including the transformation of St Pancras into an international station and new stations at Stratford and Ebbsfleet.

The company was nationalised by the Government in 2009 and is now wholly owned by the Department for Transport. Prior to the acquisition shareholders included Arup, Bechtel, EDF, Halcrow, National Express Group, SNCF, Systra and UBS. LCR's debt was already underwritten by the Government.

The financial restructuring was designed to separate London & Continental's High Speed 1 and Eurostar subsidiaries from their past construction liabilities, enabling HS1 to charge a commercial rate for access to the route and paving the way for a concession to be let. The deal also facilitated the restructuring of Eurostar, allowing a complex ownership model split between three countries to be converted into a more conventional set-up where the shares were split to give SNCF 55%, SNCB 5% and LCR 40%. LCR's share was later transferred to HM Treasury.

In 2010 London & Continental Railways sold HS1 with its 30-year concession for the track and stations to a consortium of two Canadian pension funds, comprising Borealis Infrastructure and the Ontario Teachers' Pension Plan, for £2.1bn. Thus, as owner of HS1 Ltd, the consortium holds the concession from Government to operate, manage and maintain the high-speed railway infrastructure until December 2040, when a new concession can be let.

In 2014 the UK Government launched a process to sell the Treasury's 40% stake in Eurostar, a move condemned by trade unions. In March 2015 came the announcement of an agreement to sell the UK's entire holding in Eurostar International Limited for £757.1m. A consortium comprising Caisse de depot et placement du Quebec and Hermes Infrastructure would acquire the 40% holding for £585.1m, while Eurostar, on completion of the sale, would redeem the UK Government's preference share, providing a further £172m for the Exchequer.

LCR reinvented

Having divested HS1, London & Continental Railways' primary focus is in the area of property development and land regeneration. LCR is a joint venture partner in two major regeneration programmes at King's Cross, in partnership with Argent and DHL, and The International Quarter, Stratford City, in partnership with Lend Lease. The King's Cross and Stratford schemes together represent more than 100 acres of development on strategically important brownfield land and on completion will deliver two new office districts and up to 2,350 homes.

On 30 September 2013 LCR took over properties held and managed by BRB (Residuary) Ltd (BRBR) prior to it being wound up. BRBR was created in 2001 to manage the majority of the remaining properties, rights and liabilities of the British Railways Board – the British Rail leftovers that did not fit into the organisations constituting the recently privatised railway. But as part of a drive to reduce the number of quasi-autonomous non-governmental organisations (or quangos), the Coalition Government decided that BRBR was an anomaly and shared its responsibilities out between a range of organisations.

London & Continental Railways was one of the beneficiaries. Among the assets that were passed on were the disused Waterloo International site and the disused Eurostar North Pole depot in west London – part of which is being brought back into use for the Intercity Express Programme. LCR has also been providing property advice to HS2 Ltd in respect of the regeneration opportunities at each of the proposed stations.

Operating HS1

HS1 Ltd holds a concession (until 2040) to operate, maintain and renew the 109km high-speed rail line between London St Pancras and the Channel Tunnel. This is the UK's only high-speed rail line serving four stations (St Pancras, Stratford, Ebbsfleet and Ashford) along the route.

The primary business of HS1 Ltd is to provide high-speed rail access to domestic and international passenger and freight train services. HS1 Ltd's revenue comes from access charges that are paid by train operators to use its track and stations. It also receives income, which is not regulated, through its retail facilities and car parking at stations. Unlike Network Rail, HS1 Ltd does not receive any Government grant.

A concession agreement sets out the terms of the agreement between HS1 Ltd and the Government, which owns the HS1 railway infrastructure. This includes the charging framework, minimum operational standards, including proper asset stewardship, protections against termination, and protection from material adverse changes.

Many of the functions that HS1 Ltd must perform as infrastructure manager (such as track operation and maintenance, signalling and timetabling) are contracted out to Network Rail (High Speed), a wholly owned subsidiary of Network Rail Infrastructure Ltd. The relationship between HS1 Ltd and Network Rail (High Speed) is governed by an operator agreement. This is a commercial arrangement between the parties that is not subject to any regulatory approval or scrutiny.

Network Rail (High Speed) is HS1 Ltd's contractor for maintaining and operating the railway infrastructure and three stations, St Pancras International, Stratford International and Ebbsfleet International. This deal is expected to run until at least 2025.[79]

In November 2013 HS1 Ltd awarded outsourcing company Mitie a contract to operate Ashford International station for the next five years. Mitie manages and operates the international station with responsibilities including station management, maintenance, cleaning and security.

Regulating HS1

The Office of Rail and Road is responsible for regulating HS1 Ltd and the HS1 network with the concession agreement providing the primary means for achieving this. The ORR's role includes the monitoring of operational performance (and the ability to implement enforcement procedures in the case of failure to comply), the monitoring of asset stewardship obligations (which must be delivered as if HS1 Ltd was responsible for the stewardship of the infrastructure for a period of 40 years from the date such activities are planned or carried out), and the carrying out of a five-yearly periodic review of access charges – as well as any interim reviews if required.

In addition to those set out in the concession agreement, the ORR has responsibilities concerning the regulation of HS1 Ltd under The Railways Infrastructure (Access and Management) Regulations 2005. These functions include a pre-approval role for new and amended framework agreements, ensuring that charges for use of the infrastructure comply with the requirements of the regulations, and ensuring that HS1 Ltd is provided with incentives to reduce the costs of provision of infrastructure and access charges.

HS1 periodic reviews

The concession agreement also sets out the purpose of the process for conducting periodic reviews – similar to the five-year reviews used to determine Network Rail spending.

The 2014 Periodic Review of HS1 Ltd (PR14) was the first periodic review of HS1 Ltd. PR14 has set some of the elements of HS1 Ltd's access charges, the outputs that HS1 Ltd will deliver, and the efficient cost for delivering these outputs, during what for the high-speed railway is labelled Control Period 2. PR14 has also established the regulatory framework for CP2. This includes the financial framework within which HS1 Ltd will operate and the incentives that will apply to it and train operators in order to encourage them to outperform targets set out in the determination. CP2 runs from 1 April 2015 to 31 March 2020.

In advance of each Control Period, HS1 Ltd must produce a Five Year Asset Management Statement (5YAMS). This document is the principal input into a periodic review of HS1 Ltd in accordance with a timescale set out in the concession agreement. As part of the periodic review process, the ORR is required to approve the 5YAMS or tell HS1 Ltd why it is unable to approve it. The 5YAMS for CP2 was approved by the regulator in May 2014, concluding the 2014 Periodic Review process.

PR14 has also approved new track access charges set by HS1 Ltd. These are £48.14 per train minute for international passenger services (12% lower than the equivalent CP1 charge) and £36.32 per train minute for domestic passenger services (13% lower than the equivalent CP1 charge).[80] These charges are subject to provisions relating to a GSM-R upgrade, which is due to be completed in 2015, and changes of +/-4% in traffic volumes.

To France and beyond

The Channel Tunnel was officially opened on 6 May 1994. It actually consists of three 50km rail tunnels – one for each direction with a smaller service tunnel in between, which is connected to the main tunnels at regular intervals. It cost around £9bn to build – double the estimated cost.

The two rail tunnels are 7.6m in diameter and 30m apart. Each rail tunnel has a single track, overhead line equipment (catenary) and two walkways (one for maintenance purposes and the other for use in the event of an emergency evacuation, and on the side nearest to the service tunnel). The walkways are also designed to keep a train upright and in a straight line of travel in the unlikely event of a derailment.

The service tunnel is 4.8 metres in diameter and sits between the two rail tunnels 15 metres away from each of them. In normal operations shuttles use the south tunnel in the France-UK direction, and the north tunnel when travelling from the UK to France. Two undersea crossovers provide flexibility of operation as trains can pass from one tunnel to the other during night maintenance periods to isolate a section of tunnel.

A vehicle was specifically designed for travel in the service tunnel. It is multi-functional and used for maintenance operations and in case of emergency with the aim of reaching the scene of an incident as quickly as possible.

The track in each rail tunnel has two continuously welded rails laid on pre-cast concrete supports embedded in the concrete trackbed. Fixed equipment in the tunnels comes under four categories: electricity and catenary, rail track and signalling, mechanical systems, and control and communications. Cooling pipes, fire mains, signalling equipment and cables are fixed to the sides of the tunnels and are fed by cooling plants at Samphire Hoe in the UK and Sangatte in France.

The entire Channel Tunnel rail infrastructure is controlled from the RCC (Rail Control Centre). There are two centres, one at each terminal, and each can take turns to assume control of the system. The RCC manages all rail traffic (trains and shuttles) in the tunnels and at the terminals. The system is in two parts, the Rail Traffic Management (RTM), which controls the rail traffic system, and the Engineering Management System (EMS), which controls the fixed equipment such as ventilation, lighting and power for the catenary.

Signalling in the Channel Tunnel is known as TVM 430: it functions by means of data transmission from track to train and is almost identical to the system used on the high-speed TGV Nord-Europe.

In recent years mobile phone coverage has been provided within the tunnels, and 32 miles of cabling has been installed to allow electricity to be transferred between the UK and France under the Eleclink scheme.

Eurotunnel

Eurotunnel was the company created by the French and UK Governments to finance and operate the Channel Tunnel, which, under the Treaty of Canterbury, was to be built and operated with no taxpayer subsidy. But with the tunnel operating at a loss from the day it opened, Eurotunnel's debts increased year on year and became unmanageable. A major financial restructuring in 2007 brought costs under control and in 2011 Eurotunnel began to make a profit.

Today Eurotunnel Group, listed on the London and Paris stock exchanges, is responsible for the operation of the Channel Tunnel – also known as the cross-Channel Fixed Link – in which two Eurotunnel Group companies are concessionaires until 2086. This involves managing and maintaining the infrastructure as well as supervising access to the tunnel – companies such as Eurostar and freight operators pay Eurotunnel for the right to run trains through it.

To develop railway traffic between the United Kingdom and continental Europe, Eurotunnel has set up ETICA (Eurotunnel Incentive for Capacity Additions), a system of financial support for railway operators launching new rail freight services through the Channel Tunnel.

Eurotunnel is also a train operator. It provides 'Le Shuttle' trains between Folkestone in Britain and Calais/Coquelles in France, whereby road vehicles 'piggy back' on trains through the Channel Tunnel. Unlike Eurostar services, Le Shuttle trains remain within the Eurotunnel system by means of rail loops at each terminal.

A typical journey takes 35 minutes, the terminals are connected to motorways and up to four trains depart each hour at peak times. Terminals have shops and toilet facilities. Cars are conveyed in double-deck enclosed wagons with passengers permitted to leave their vehicles and walk along the train during transit. Lorries are transported on semi-open wagons with a separate passenger carriage at the front of the train for the drivers.

Eurotunnel also runs freight trains through its Europorte companies, which include GB Railfreight, and has become the third largest rail freight operator (for hauling trains) in the UK and France.

Tunnel regulation

Economic and safety regulation for the Channel Tunnel has been the responsibility of the Channel Tunnel Intergovernmental Commission (IGC), a joint UK and French organisation.

However, there are plans to change this: in December 2014 the Department for Transport launched a consultation on draft legislation to transfer economic regulation of the Channel Tunnel from the IGC to the Office of Rail and Road and its French counterpart, ARAF. With the tunnel regulator responsible for the tunnel access charges, the DfT says transferring responsibilities would establish a streamlined and unified charging framework, consistent with the one that ORR has for High Speed 1. The change could also lead to tunnel access charges being reduced following complaints by the European Commission that the existing tariffs are too high and deter potential train operators.[81]

ORR and ARAF would have to agree their approach to regulation within the Channel Tunnel; if this could not be achieved there could potentially be different regulatory regimes at the British and French ends of the tunnel.[82]

The legal apparatus for managing the Channel Tunnel requires the regulator to work with the Intergovernmental Commission (representing the interests of the British and French Governments), the Channel Tunnel Safety Authority and the Joint Security and Economic committees.

High-speed train operators

Eurostar is a passenger train operator that since 1994 has run services between London and Paris, London and Brussels, and intermediate and seasonal destinations. The company has approximately 1,600 employees and is headquartered in London near St Pancras International station. In 2014 Eurostar ran up to 18 daily return services to Paris and up to 10 daily return services to Brussels.

Eurostar has a fleet of 27 'Trans Manche Super Trains' - also known as e300s - which operate between the UK and the continent. Recently refurbished, these train sets are 400 metres long and comprise 18 passenger carriages. There are 750 seats on each train, which can travel at a maximum speed of 300km/h (186mph). Trains in the fleet have

been used on the East Coast Main Line and SNCF's domestic rail network.

In October 2010 Eurostar announced a major investment programme to modernise its rolling stock, including the purchase of new trains from Siemens and the overhaul and redesign of its remaining fleet from 2014. Seventeen new Siemens e320 trains have been ordered to operate across the UK, French, Belgian and Dutch high-speed rail networks, with the potential to acquire additional sets. The new rolling stock is expected to have significantly lower operating and maintenance costs than the original Alstom-built fleet.

The e320 trains will have a capacity of around 900 passengers (20% more than the older rolling stock), which will allow Eurostar to capture currently unmet demand at peak times such as on Fridays.

On 1 May 2015 Eurostar launched a new all-year-round direct train service from London St Pancras International to Lyon, Avignon and Marseille in the south of France. Passengers travelling from France back to the UK can board their train without the need to arrive 30 minutes before departure as check-in, security and immigration checks take place at Lille Europe, where passengers have to disembark from the train before continuing their journey to Ashford and London. By the end of 2016 Eurostar is expected to launch a new direct service to Amsterdam calling at stations in Antwerp, Rotterdam and Schiphol.

ABOVE Southeastern high-speed services operate at up to 140mph between St Pancras and towns and cities in Kent.

Southeastern

Train operator Southeastern runs the UK's first high-speed domestic train service, with trains travelling at up to 140mph (225km/h) – slower than the Eurostar maximum of 186mph. Other domestic trains are limited to 125mph, although 'Pendolino' and 'Super Express' trains on the West Coast, East Coast and Great Western routes are capable of running at 140mph if infrastructure is upgraded.

The Southeastern high-speed service began in 2009 and links the domestic high-speed platforms at St Pancras International with other

High Speed 1 stations, with trains then continuing on 'classic' lines to destinations including Dover, Folkestone and Ramsgate. Hitachi Class 395 units are used for this service and are often referred to as 'Javelins', the name coined for the high-speed shuttle service they provided between St Pancras and Stratford International stations during the London Olympic and Paralympic Games in 2012.

Travelling on these trains it is possible to get from Ashford to central London in less than 38 minutes, and commuter journey times from the Kent coast into London have been significantly reduced. Passengers have been charged higher fares than for slower routes to help pay for the new trains.

Freight

When the Channel Tunnel Rail Link was built it was designed with connections to the classic rail network and depots that would allow freight trains to run on the new infrastructure. Passing loops were built to allow passenger services to overtake freight trains. HS1 Ltd says it is 'in a state of readiness for freight operating companies to operate high-speed services on the network.'[83]

Freight train company DB Schenker has operated freight services using HS1 including refrigerated containers of perishable foodstuffs and automotive components from Valencia, Spain, to Barking and Dagenham in east London, and twice-weekly services to and from Poland.[84]

HS1 Ltd says that, due to size dimensions of the freight, it is something that can only be carried in the UK on the high-speed network, offering the shipper a seamless European rail service. The company is keen to expand this market.

Deutsche Bahn

In 2010 Germany's state-owned train operator Deutsche Bahn brought an ICE 3 high-speed train to St Pancras International. At an event attended by the UK rail minister, the organisation's chairman Dr Rudiger Grube announced plans to introduce new cross-Channel train services. Eurostar would no longer be the only train operator running international services to and from the UK.

BELOW Eurostar has bought a new fleet of Siemens 'Velaro' Class 374 trains to enable the cross-Channel operator to introduce new routes between London and the continent. *Eurostar*

ABOVE The first visit of a Deutsche Bahn ICE train to St Pancras International in 2010 attracted plenty of attention, but the promised services between London and Germany have been repeatedly postponed.

BELOW Deutsche Bahn's proposed international services would use High Speed 1 and could compete with Eurostar.

Regular ICE services were planned to start in 2013 and would incorporate three return train journeys between Frankfurt and London via Cologne, Brussels and Lille. These would include connections from Amsterdam via Rotterdam to London. A journey from Cologne to London should take less than 4 hours, and from Frankfurt to London just over 5 hours.

Five years after the launch event there are no signs of Deutsche Bahn passenger services appearing on the departure and arrival boards at St Pancras any time soon. Bringing ICE trains to Britain has clearly ended up being more complex than envisaged; proving that its train formations comply with all relevant safety regulations within the Channel Tunnel has proved a technical and legal minefield for Siemens. There have been issues with signalling and control systems across Europe to resolve, as well as questions of how to conduct passport checks and how to pay for the necessary facilities at stations. A pressing need to address issues within its domestic operation has also seen new Siemens 'Velaro' train sets prioritised for the home market, putting back the launch of services to the UK.

Nevertheless, the launch of international Deutsche Bahn trains to the UK from Germany is only a matter of time. Eurostar is unlikely to remain the only international passenger train operator using High Speed 1 for much longer.

High Speed 2

High Speed 2 is an ambitious programme to build a new north-south railway with trains operating at up to 225mph. The plan is for a Y-shaped network that would run from London to Birmingham, where separate branches would continue to Manchester and Leeds.

Supporters of the scheme argue that it is vital to provide the additional rail capacity Britain needs, with many routes, including the West Coast Main Line, predicted to be operating at maximum capacity by the early 2020s. The upgrade of the West Coast route, officially completed in 2008 at a cost of £9bn but only after years of controversy, disruption and descoping, is held up as an example of why it makes sense to build a new line rather than improve those we already have. Providing a new railway would free up space on existing routes for additional freight and passenger services and could allow a major recast of timetables and the introduction of new services. There are various supporting claims that it will help rebalance the UK economy and create new jobs.

Support for HS2 tends to be strongest in and around the northern cities, which expect to benefit from better connections with London. But there is well-organised opposition in some areas, particularly around the Chilterns, one of 46 designated areas of outstanding natural beauty in England. Opponents argue that HS2 is unaffordable and the money would be better spent upgrading existing routes. They claim faster trains are not required, with HS2 underestimating the ability to work on board a train during a journey. Many councils in north London and the South East have campaigned against the project. There are also concerns from cities such as Coventry and Leicester on current inter-city routes, which fear that they could lose direct services if their fast links to London are replaced by HS2. So far cross-party support has ensured that HS2 development progresses despite the opposition.

The project is being overseen by HS2 Ltd, a non-departmental public body wholly owned by the Department for Transport and tasked with managing the delivery of a new national high-speed rail network.

How to build it

HS2 has been developed in two distinct phases. Phase one would run from a rebuilt London Euston station to the West Midlands via a new interchange with Crossrail and other rail services at Old Oak Common in west London. An interchange station would be built near Birmingham Airport and a spur off the main route would run to a new Curzon Street station in Birmingham city centre.

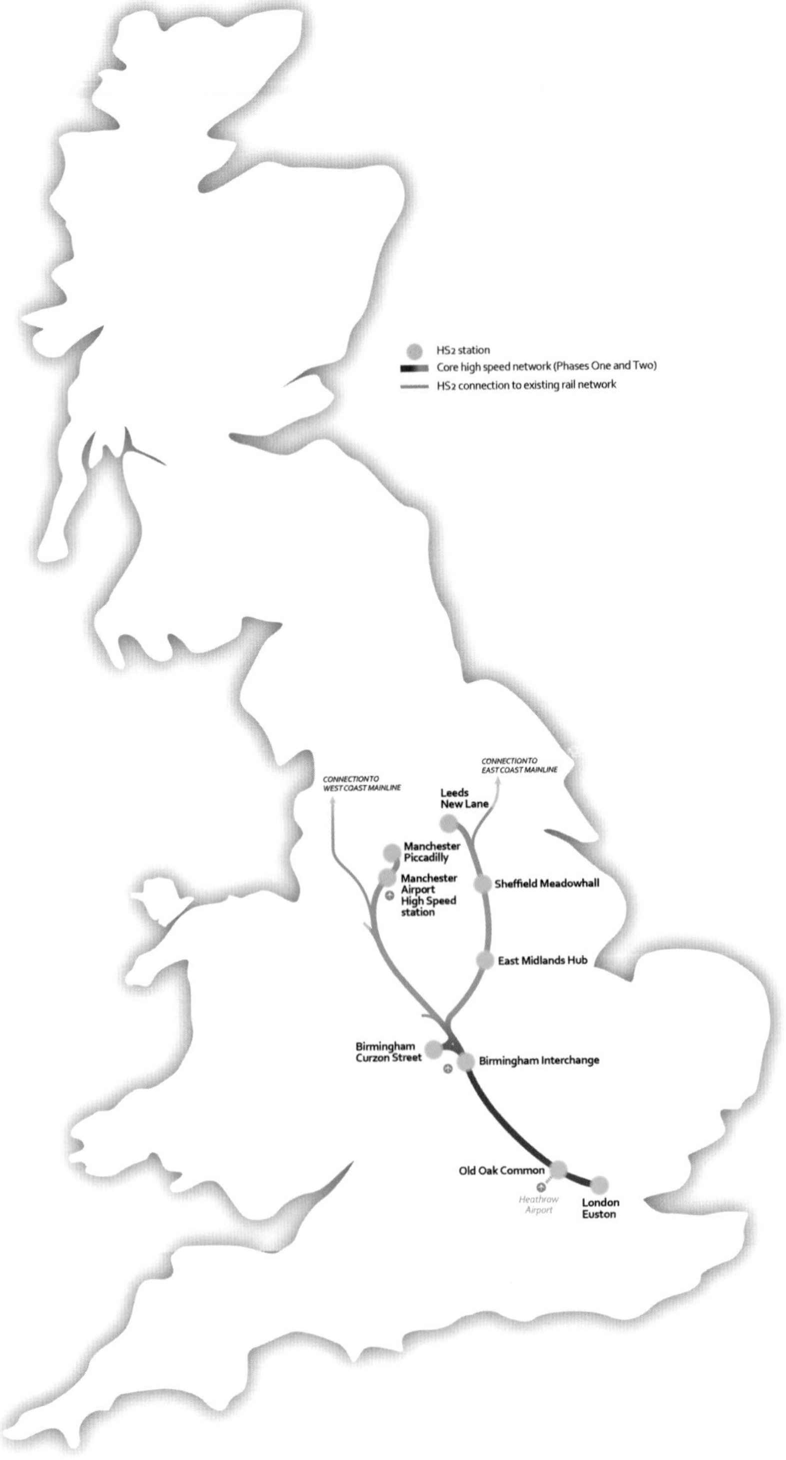
HS2 station
Core high speed network (Phases One and Two)
HS2 connection to existing rail network
CONNECTION TO WEST COAST MAINLINE
CONNECTION TO EAST COAST MAINLINE
Leeds New Lane
Manchester Piccadilly
Manchester Airport High Speed station
Sheffield Meadowhall
East Midlands Hub
Birmingham Curzon Street
Birmingham Interchange
Old Oak Common
Heathrow Airport
London Euston

ABOVE Euston will be the southern terminus for High Speed 2, requiring a complex and disruptive rebuilding of the existing station.

LEFT High Speed 2 is a programme to build a new railway between London and the West Midlands. A second phase would provide separate routes onwards to Manchester and Leeds. *HS2 Ltd*

This first phase would be around 140 miles long with more than half the route in cuttings or tunnels. In the Chilterns more than 11 miles of the route is to be in tunnel, green tunnel or cutting, with just over 1½ miles on the surface.

Phase two includes a north-west branch to Manchester city centre via Manchester Airport, where a station may or may not be built. There would be connections to the West Coast Main Line, and the Government is considering a new high-speed station at Crewe, which could act as a major interchange. This western branch would be around 95 miles long.

The eastern branch – approximately 116 miles – heads for Leeds via new stations in the East Midlands, serving Nottingham and Derby, and Sheffield, where a station is likely to be built on the outskirts of the city, at Meadowhall, where it could also serve satellite towns. A connection would be provided to the East Coast Main Line.

During development there have been various alterations to plans. A spur to Heathrow Airport is no longer part of the programme, and plans for a link to High Speed 1 have also been dropped after being deemed poor value for money. But the Government has committed to look at other options that could, in the long term, result in a tunnel link being proposed.

Two fleets of trains are likely to be procured – one to run just on the new infrastructure and a second that would be able to continue on to 'classic' rail routes, allowing services to continue (at conventional speeds) to Liverpool, North Wales, Newcastle and Scotland. HS2 is expected to run up to 14 trains per hour in each direction for phase one, rising to 18 for phase two. Trains will be up to 200 metres long, or 400 metres when operated as a pair. There will be up to 1,100 seats per train.

To secure powers to construct the new line separate hybrid bills (similar to the legislative process for Crossrail) are planned. The first of these has been approved by MPs at Westminster and is, at the time of writing, going through a lengthy committee stage, which allows those affected by the phase one route to submit petitions arguing for changes to the bill. The Government had hoped to secure Royal Assent – the formal passing of a bill into law – before the 2015 General Election, but proved unable to meet this target.

Assuming that the legislation is enacted shortly after the election, construction of phase one could get under way in 2017 with the aim of opening the railway in 2026. Phase two is projected to open in 2033 with a new station at Crewe possible by 2027.

How much will it cost?

The current budget allows around £50bn for the new infrastructure and trains, including a substantial figure for contingency, which HS2 Ltd says it expects to reduce. The target price for delivering phase one of HS2 is £17.16bn at 2011 prices.

Table 9: HS2 funding

	Funding allocated (£ billion)
Phase one	21.4 (including 5.7 contingency)
Phase two	21.2 (including 8.7 contingency)
Rolling stock	7.5 (including 1.7 contingency)
Total	**50.1 (including 16.1 contingency)**

Source: HS2 Ltd website[85]

High Speed 3

High Speed 3 is an emerging programme to improve rail links between cities in the North of England in order to create what senior members of Government have described as a 'northern powerhouse' – a network of cities with excellent transport connections. This is seen as a way of counterbalancing the economic success of London and South East England amid recognition of a growing divide between the capital and the rest of Britain.

The HS3 name is deceptive because, unlike HS1 and HS2, the plan is not to construct an all-new railway but to progressively upgrade existing infrastructure, perhaps with some new sections of route, focusing first on halving journey times between Leeds and Manchester. In the long term there is an aspiration to upgrade routes from Liverpool to Hull and Newcastle to Sheffield. Because this will not be a new railway, train speeds are likely to be limited to the 125mph of the existing 'classic' network – although there is a suggestion that 140mph may be possible on some new or upgraded stretches of track.

Development of better rail (and road) links has been championed by HS2 Ltd chairman Sir David Higgins, and secured the backing of Prime Minister David Cameron in October 2014. In March 2015 the Government and Transport for the North – a new transport agency representing authorities across the North of England as well as the Department for Transport, Network Rail, Highways England and HS2 Ltd – published a Northern Transport Strategy – a long-term plan to connect the cities of the North with high-quality rail routes. This 'TransNorth' network would link Liverpool, Manchester, Leeds, Sheffield, Newcastle and Hull.

The idea is to draw up enhancements that can be considered for funding and delivery during Control Period 6 (2019-24), and that would complement High Speed 2. Transport for the North is to co-ordinate development of the plans.

What is not clear is how the High Speed 3/ TransNorth programme will be paid for. If the vision, as put forward to date, is to be delivered, billions of pounds will need to be identified before components of the scheme can be made a reality.

Notes

Chapter 1

[1] ORR, 2013-14 Annual Statistical Release – Rail Infrastructure, Assets and Environment. More stations have opened since.
[2] ORR, Passenger rail usage statistical release 2013-14, Q4
[3] https://www.gov.uk/government/uploads/system/uploads/attachment_data/file/363718/rail-trends-factsheet-2014.pdf
[4] DfT, National Travel Survey
[5] Rail Safety and Standards Board
[6] http://www.translink.co.uk/Services/NI-Railways/About-us/
[7] http://www.parliament.uk/business/committees/committees-a-z/commons-select/transport-committee/role/influencing-government-policy/

Chapter 2

[8] DfT, Annual Report 2012-13
[9] ORR, Periodic Review 2013: Final Determination, page 39
[10] ORR, Periodic Review 2013: On-rail competition: Consultation on options for change in open access
[11] Heritage Railway Association, press release, 16 July 2013
[12] Railwatch, December 2014, page 14
[13] The Sovereign Grant and Sovereign Grant Reserve Annual Report and Accounts 2013-14

Chapter 3

[14] Network Rail, Value of Freight, July 2010
[15] http://orr.gov.uk/news-and-media/press-releases/2013/rail-freight-charges-to-better-reflect-costs-and-give-industry-clarity-to-plan-for-the-future-orr

Chapter 4

[16] ORR, GB rail industry financial information 2012-13, April 2014
[17] ORR, 2013-14 Annual Statistical Release – Rail Finance, 21 August 2014
[18] http://orr.gov.uk/what-and-how-we-regulate/regulation-of-network-rail/how-we-regulate-network-rail/control-period-5-cp5/cp5-delivery-plan
[19] Network Rail, Annual Report and Accounts 2013/14
[20] Network Rail, Annual Report and Accounts 2013/14, page 40
[21] The Chiltern Railways (Bicester to Oxford Improvements) Order – Graham Cross proof of evidence
[22] Network Rail, Annual Report and Accounts 2013/14, page 40
[23] House of Commons Transport Committee: Local transport expenditure: Who decides? 13 May 2014, page 18
[24] European Commission http://ec.europa.eu/regional_policy/projects/stories/details_new.cfm?pay=UK&the=60&sto=1559&lan=7&region=ALL&obj=ALL&per=2&defL=EN
[25] Transport Briefing, news 8152, 15 December 2011
[26] https://www.gov.uk/government/uploads/system/uploads/attachment_data/file/205112/pf2_infrastructure_new_approach_to_public_private_parnerships_051212.pdf
[27] Transport Briefing, news 7984, 30 September 2011
[28] http://www.pas.gov.uk/web/pas-test-site/3-community-infrastructure-levy-cil/-/journal_content/56/332612/4090701/ARTICLE
[29] TfL, Finance and Policy Committee meeting, 27 November 2013

Chapter 5

[30] Rail North, Developing the Rail North Partnership, 24 January 2014
[31] Letter from Roger Lawrence to Patrick McLoughlin, 19 March 2014
[32] https://www.gov.uk/government/policies/expanding-and-improving-the-rail-network/supporting-pages/community-rail

[33] DfT, Simon Hankin letter to community rail consultees, 25 July 2014

Chapter 6

[34] Transport Briefing, news 7945, 14 September 2011
[35] Draft London Infrastructure Plan 2050: Transport Supporting Paper, July 2014
[36] TfL, Director of London Overground Mike Stubbs, TfL Press release, 9 December 2013
[37] HM Treasury, George Osborne's Budget, 19 March 2014
[38] http://www.crossrail.co.uk/benefits/
[39] National Audit Office, Crossrail, 24 January 2014
[40] TfL, Finance and Policy Committee meeting, 27 November 2013
[41] Network Rail, Draft route utilisation strategy for London and the South East, December 2010
[42] Pricewaterhouse Cooper, Crossrail 2 Funding and Financing Study, November 2014
[43] https://www.gov.uk/government/news/travel-boost-for-londoners-as-chancellor-and-mayor-confirm-expansion-of-night-time-services-new-wifi-for-the-tube

Chapter 7

[44] Campaign for Better Transport, rail fares briefing, January 2015
[45] House of Commons Library, Railways: fares
[46] Ibid
[47] Transport Scotland, press release, 19 August 2014
[48] ORR, 2013-14 Annual Statistical Release, Rail Finance, 21 August 2014
[49] Transport Briefing, news 9685, 10 October 2013
[50] DfT rail fares and ticketing review 2013
[51] Parliamentary answer, Transport Minister Stephen Hammond, 16 June 2014; http://www.parliament.uk/business/publications/written-questions-answers-statements/written-question/Commons/2014-06-10/200151/

Chapter 8

[52] RSSB Annual Safety Performance Report 2013/14
[53] Network Rail: Our Approach to Managing Level Crossing Safety
[54] ORR: PR13 Final Determination, p96
[55] Network Rail: Our Approach to Managing Level Crossing Safety
[56] RAIB, Guidance on the Railways (Accident Investigation and Reporting) Regulations, 2005
[57] BTPA, Strategic Plan 2013-19, page 15
[58] Transport Briefing, news 9232, 15 April 2013
[59] Chief Constable of BTP, Paul Crowther, press release, 1 July 2014

Chapter 9

[60] NSARE: Forecasting the Skills Challenge 2013

Chapter 10

[61] Based on top 20 suppliers 2012-13 from Network Rail transparency data http://www.networkrail.co.uk/transparency/datasets/#T
[62] Signalling Solutions was a joint venture between Alstom and Balfour Beatty until May 2015 when Alstom acquired its partner's 50% share, becoming sole owner of the company
[63] David Waboso, Modern Railways, August 2013
[64] http://www.achilles.com/files/communitypdfs/Link-up/Supplier_brochure/achilleslinkupsupplierbrochure.pdf]
[65] Roger Ford, Informed Sources, Modern Railways, July 2014
[66] Rolling Stock Leasing market investigation, Competition Commission, 7 April 2009
[67] http://www.publications.parliament.uk/pa/ld201314/ldhansrd/text/140306w0001.htm

Chapter 11

[68] DfT, Annual Report Rail Vehicle Accessibility Regulations Exemption Orders 1 January 2013-31, December 2013
[69] https://www.gov.uk/government/policies/

making-transport-more-accessible-to-all/supporting-pages/accessible-transport-for-all
[70] John Glover, The Principles of Railway Operation, page 44
[71] Network Rail, press release – Britain's rail revolution quickens pace as first contracts for new 'traffic management' technology are awarded, 29 May 2014
[72] KPMG: London Underground - ATC Lessons Learned Review, page 7
[73] TfL, Finance and Policy Committee, Sub-Surface Upgrade Programme Automatic Train Control Contract – Lessons Learnt, 17 July 2014
[74] West Coast Main Line Modernisation Feasibility Study, December 1994
[75] Roger Ford, Informed Sources, Modern Railways, March 2015
[76] Transport Briefing, news 9660, 2 October 2013

Chapter 12

[77] DfT light rail and tram statistics 2013-14

Chapter 13

[78] http://www.uic.org/spip.php?article971
[79] http://www.highspeed1.com/news/hs1-ltd-and-network-rail-agree-new-deal
[80] http://orr.gov.uk/__data/assets/pdf_file/0006/12102/hs1-periodic-review-2014-approval.pdf
[81] https://www.gov.uk/government/uploads/system/uploads/attachment_data/file/386245/channel-tunnel-consultation-document.pdf, page 4
[82] https://www.gov.uk/government/uploads/system/uploads/attachment_data/file/386245/channel-tunnel-consultation-document.pdf, page 23
[83] http://highspeed1.co.uk/rail/freight-rail-services
[84] http://highspeed1.co.uk/news/2014/january/hs1-ltd-db-schenker-rail-additional-freight-services-high-speed-1
[85] http://www.hs2.org.uk/about-hs2/facts-figures/route-trains-cost

Index